Moderate Conservatism

Moderate Conservatism

Reclaiming the Center

JOHN KEKES

OXFORD
UNIVERSITY PRESS

Oxford University Press is a department of the University of Oxford. It furthers the University's objective of excellence in research, scholarship, and education by publishing worldwide. Oxford is a registered trade mark of Oxford University Press in the UK and certain other countries.

Published in the United States of America by Oxford University Press
198 Madison Avenue, New York, NY 10016, United States of America.

© Oxford University Press 2023

All rights reserved. No part of this publication may be reproduced, stored in a retrieval system, or transmitted, in any form or by any means, without the prior permission in writing of Oxford University Press, or as expressly permitted by law, by license, or under terms agreed with the appropriate reproduction rights organization. Inquiries concerning reproduction outside the scope of the above should be sent to the Rights Department, Oxford University Press, at the address above.

You must not circulate this work in any other form
and you must impose this same condition on any acquirer.

Library of Congress Cataloging-in-Publication Data
Names: Kekes, John, author.
Title: Moderate conservatism : reclaiming the center / John Kekes.
Description: New York, NY : Oxford University Press, 2023. |
Includes bibliographical references and index.
Identifiers: LCCN 2022027379 (print) | LCCN 2022027380 (ebook) |
ISBN 9780197668061 (hardback) | ISBN 9780197668078 |
ISBN 9780197668085 (epub) | ISBN 9780197668092
Subjects: LCSH: Conservatism—United States. | Right and left
(Political science)—United States. | Political culture—United States.
Classification: LCC JC573.2.U6 K44 2023 (print) | LCC JC573.2.U6 (ebook) |
DDC 320.520973—dc23/eng/20220811
LC record available at https://lccn.loc.gov/2022027379
LC ebook record available at https://lccn.loc.gov/2022027380

DOI: 10.1093/oso/9780197668061.001.0001

1 3 5 7 9 8 6 4 2

Printed by Integrated Books International, United States of America

Contents

Acknowledgments vii

1. Introduction 1

2. From Simplicities to Complexities 9
    The Aim of Moderate Conservatism 9
    Conventional Lives 11
    Common Decencies 15
    Shared Modes of Evaluation 21
    Sources of Complexities 27

3. Perennial Problems 34
    Overview 34
    Contingencies 39
    Conflicts 48
    Compromises 56

4. The Problem and the Response 63
    The Problem 63
    Complex Evaluations 68
    Personal Attitudes and Our Political System 75
    Negative Capability 82
    Toward Reasonable Actions 87

5. The Rule of Law 90
    The Approach 90
    Procedural or Substantive? 96
    Doubts about Priorities 101
    The Moderately Substantive Requirement 105
    Moderate Conservatism and the Rule of Law 109

6. Justice — 114
- Justice as Desert — 114
- Why Should We Get What We Deserve? — 120
- Terms of Cooperation — 124
- The Test of Time — 129
- Justice as Desert: For and Against — 135

7. Legal and Political Equality — 142
- The Aim — 142
- Contextuality — 147
- Conditionality — 154
- Practicality — 161
- Justification — 168

8. Liberty — 173
- The Concept and Its Complexities — 173
- Negative Liberty — 177
- Reasons against Negative Liberty — 182
- Positive Liberty as Autonomy — 188
- The Exclusivist Mistake — 191
- The Secular Faith and Its Problems — 195
- Limited Liberty — 199

9. Private Property — 204
- The Reason for It — 204
- Its Importance — 209
- Interest-Based Justification — 212
- Entitlement-Based Justification — 214
- Utility-Based Justification — 217
- Complex Justification — 221

10. Last Words — 230

References — 235
Index — 241

Acknowledgments

The account of moderate conservatism developed and defended in this book has been deeply influenced by the political thought of Aristotle, Montaigne, Hume, Burke, Madison, and Oakeshott. I am indebted to them for the depth, humanism, and moderation of their political thought. They understood that political conditions are always particular, context-dependent, changing, and that thoughtful people often disagree with each other about how best to respond to them. These thinkers were political realists, not idealists. They had no illusions about human nature, nor about what politics could contribute to the betterment of lives in a society. Moderate conservatives share their political realism and the relevance of their approach to the political conditions of American society.

I am especially grateful to two anonymous referees of the manuscript. They understood exactly what I was trying to do and their comments and sympathetic criticisms helped me to do it better than I would have without their help. The referees have been selected and the manuscript has been transformed into a book by Lucy Randall, who has now been the editor of three of my books published by the American branch of Oxford University Press. She has been all that an author could wish that an editor should be. I thank her once again for all that and for being forthright, efficient, and understanding. I am also grateful to Lauralee Yeary and Chelsea Hogue for so helpfully handling the arrangements involved in making the manuscript into a book.

Portions of the manuscript have been read and commented on by Ann Hartle and Kenneth B. McIntyre. I am grateful to them for taking time from their own work to help me do mine.

Another of my debts is to Liberty Fund. In the course of 30+ years it has made it possible for me to meet with and exchange ideas with many people in the context of formal and informal conversations during conferences arranged by that wonderful foundation. Many of the ideas that have eventually made their way into this book have been developed, changed, and improved in those civilized conversations. And this has happened in marked contrast with the destructive politicization that has corrupted higher education and pervaded academic contexts.

My greatest debt is to Jean Kekes, my wife and friend. Throughout the many years of our life together, in the course of many conversations, in many contexts and countries, she helped me to think, read, and write. I thank her for that, for being who she is, and for much else that will remain private.

ITHAKA
New York

1
Introduction

This book is for those who are alarmed by the current state of politics in America. It is a plea for moderation, a defense of our 300-year-old constitutional democracy, a criticism of political extremism, and a warning of the destructive consequences of the politicization of aspects of life that should be left to the discretion of individuals.

A quarter of a century ago I published the twin volumes of *Against Liberalism* and *A Case for Conservatism*.[1] I thought then that liberals and conservatives had fundamental political disagreements. I entered the fray on the side of conservatives. I now realize that I was mistaken. Liberals and conservatives certainly disagreed, but not fundamentally. They agreed about their allegiance to the American political system, to the Constitution, and to their commitment to what they both recognized as the primary importance of the political goods of the rule of law, justice, liberty, legal and political equality, and private property, as well as of defense, education, free market, prosperity, public health, and security. They disagreed mainly about how these political goods should be interpreted and pursued, and how the unavoidable conflicts between them should be handled.

These old times were good times. The Cold War was over. The Soviet Union has disintegrated. Neither China nor terrorism was yet a serious threat. The trauma of Vietnam was healing. The economy wobbled now and then, but was generally in good shape.

---

[1] *Against Liberalism*. Ithaca: Cornell University Press, 1997, and *A Case for Conservatism*. Ithaca: Cornell University Press, 1998.

Throughout all this, the American political system has continued as the oldest constitutional democracy in the world, and America became the only superpower.

Bearing this background in mind, I can now see what I did not see then—that the disagreements between liberals and conservatives were not about ends, but about means to agreed upon ends. They disagreed about the interpretation and the priorities of shared political goods, but the consensus about ends held, even in the face of occasional challenges to it. The challenges were met by politically experienced liberals and conservatives who had good will toward one another. They recognized each other as loyal opponents who were united in their opposition to the extremists whether they were on the left or the right.

These good times have come to an end. China and terrorism have risen and the Cold War has resumed in another form. The weapons became economic, not nuclear. Moderate liberals and conservatives have gradually become small minorities. Both parties have been hijacked by extremists dedicated to the pursuit of their goals regardless of the destructive consequences for the American political system. They now see their opponents as enemies who pursue immoral policies that jeopardize the well-being of the segment of American society the extremists claim to represent. The result is that life in America has become politicized. Moderate liberals and conservatives have not forgotten their disagreements, but they have become allies in deploring what is happening to the American political system. Passionate intensity has replaced the center that no longer holds.

Populists on the right see the political system as a conspiracy to deprive them of liberty. They do not see that the political system sustains and defends the constitutional order that makes liberty and the conditions of its pursuit possible. Egalitarians on the left also see the political system as a conspiracy whose aim is to keep the powerful in power and the oppressed oppressed. Neither populists nor egalitarians realize that the political system and the constitutional order they are attacking protect the conditions in which their grievances could be remedied.

These extremists are alike in their ignorance of the complexities of the rule of law, of the necessity of setting limits to liberty and equality, and of the need to protect the security of the political system against attacks on it by external and internal enemies who aim to destroy it. They are ignorant of the many challenges to the political system other than their own; of the conditions that make prosperity possible; of the long history of trials and errors whose outcome has made and continues to make the American political system the oldest constitutional democracy in the world. They do not understand that politics involves having to choose between limited possibilities, and that making a choice involves giving up some things we want to have in order to have what we want even more. They do not see that making a choice involves not just saying "yes" to a possibility, but also "no" to other possibilities. Extremists see only their grievances, and they are enraged and blinded by them.

The aim of this book is to propose a way of reclaiming the center of the American political system. Moderate Conservatism is the name I have given to the effort to do so. Part of it is a reminder of the political system we have, tend to take for granted, and are in danger of losing. That is the vital center of American politics. It does not depend on politicians but on the everyday lives of the citizens who elect them. Nor does it depend on learned, home-baked, or academic theories about how the political system should be transformed. It depends on the rarely conscious assumptions of the many millions of citizens who live private lives, earn a living, raise a family, mind their own business, protect what they have, and expect the political system to provide the conditions in which they can continue to conduct, within legal limits, their experiments in living. They are the backbone of the American political system, the apolitical majority who has so far been largely unaffected by the poisonous rhetoric of extremists of all stripes.

Moderate conservatives aim to protect the political system of our society only if its citizens willingly support it because it enables them to live as they wish. It does not require a political theory, any political theory, to make people want to protect the living conditions they have found acceptable against imprudent attempts to abandon it in favor of some new and untried possibility. Moderate conservatism is an expression of this elementary requirement of practical good sense. It is neither a mindless attachment to the past, nor the pursuit of some ideal supposed to be of the GOOD that overrides all other considerations.

The justification of the American political system is the voluntary support of those who live in it. They vote for it by staying put when they could opt to move elsewhere. Moderate conservatives know that the protection of such a political system depends on the continuous adaptation of it to changing circumstances. They know as well that it requires flexibility, rather than rigid adherence to any part of the political system. And they also know that the flexibility applies also to the Constitution that has been amended 27 times since 1787 and interpreted and re-interpreted countless times by the Supreme Court.

Protecting our political system is like preserving our house. It requires constant repair, refurbishment, additions if circumstances warrant them, the anticipation of problems and coping with them if they occur unexpectedly, being on good terms with neighbors, and making and keeping it a safe and comfortable place conducive to living in it as we wish. It is a haven to which we can retreat to heal our bruises if life becomes too fractious. But throughout all the necessary changes it remains the house we want to live in. The reason for the changes we make to it is to make living in it better.

Moderate conservatives are not committed to any particular view on the currently hot-button issues of abortion, capital punishment, the economy, euthanasia, gender, gun control, immigration, race, religion, and acceptable sexual practices. It is not a universal theory about the political system all societies should have. It is a practical, political view about how our—the American—political system should in our present context and conditions cope with the adverse contingencies of life, the conflicts between political goods we value, and the compromises we have to make because we cannot have everything we should like to have.

During the last decades political discussions in America have deteriorated into vitriolic polemics. Opponents treat each other as enemies who violate elementary standards of justice and decency. They accuse moderate conservatives of colluding with racism, misogyny, homophobia, and anti-Semitism; of championing the rich, oppressing the poor and women, defending social and economic privilege and white male superiority, intolerance of deviations from Catholic or Protestant orthodoxy; and thoughtless defenders of obsolete practices.

This book is a defense of moderate conservatism that cannot be reasonably accused of holding these deplorable views. It is intended to make explicit and give reasons for the conditions on which the American version of political moderation depends: a pluralistic, non-dogmatic, context-dependent, and practice-oriented interpretation of the political goods we have learned to value in the course of our 300-year history. Its defense aims to show that reasonable people who have political disagreements with each other could still be respectful of their opponents, make an effort to understand the opposing views, and give reasons for their own views and against alternatives to them.

Being reasonable and having reasons for and against political views and evaluations does not depend on a complex theory. It depends on the willingness to take into relevant facts and evaluations, to consider and respond to objections to our views and evaluations, explain why they are preferable to conflicting views and evaluations, and to revise or abandon them if there are weighty considerations contrary to it. Being reasonable is a fallible attitude. It is not a guarantee of anything. But it does have the merit of enabling those who have it to remain critical of their own views and evaluations, and thereby improve them if facts and evaluations contrary to them seem to warrant it.

What is at stake in these political disagreements is the well-being of the society in which all the different kinds of conservatives, liberals, and socialists live together and to which they are all—except the immoderate extremists—committed. They share a common ground that is ultimately more important than their disagreements. And they share as well their commitment to the aim of the American political system, which is to enable members of our society to coexist peacefully and follow their personal conceptions of how they should live.

We are now in the midst of unprecedentedly rapid and momentous social changes brought about by developments in artificial intelligence, communication, the economy, the COVID epidemic, human relationships, international affairs, the internet, medicine, sexual practices, technology, and so forth. The consequences of these developments are unforeseeable. But whatever they may turn out to be, we must find ways of accommodating them somehow in the political system of our society. If we fail, we lose control of our lives. My view is that in the American context, moderate conservatism is a better approach to accommodating these and other changes than the available alternatives to it.

Central to moderate conservatism is understanding why our political system has endured for over 300 years. It is now the oldest continuous constitutional democracy in the world. One of the reasons for its endurance is its flexibility, openness to the revision of parts of it, and toleration of a wide plurality of conceptions of how to live. That it has long endured is a reason for it, but it is by no means a conclusive reason. It may have endured for the wrong reasons, such as coercion, fear, ignorance, indoctrination, lack of alternatives, prejudice, external or internal threats, and so forth. It may, however, have endured for the right reasons.

If members of our society could leave it if they wish; if they have the means of advocating changes to it; if they know of and can opt for reasonable alternatives to it, but they nevertheless continue to live and act within the limits of the political system, then they adhere to it voluntarily. If they are not so deeply dissatisfied with it as to want to leave it; if they cannot reasonably blame their dissatisfactions with their life on the political system, but see them as the result of their personal misfortune or failings, or the criminality, hostility, ill will, or injustice of others, then they can be said to have accepted the political system for the right reasons.

No one should suppose that the right reasons for adhering to our political system have ever been fully met. Most of us now, and most Americans in the past, have been—sometimes reasonably, sometimes not—dissatisfied with some parts of the political system. But if these dissatisfactions have been on balance outweighed by the satisfactions we derive from continued participation in our political system, then it can be said that we have accepted it for the right reasons. Of course accepting it in general is compatible with wanting to change it in particular ways. Questions about what should be accepted and what changed is and has always been a central political question. Answers to it have been and will remain contested. In the chapters that follow I give reasons for the answers that follow from moderate conservatism and reasons against contrary answers.

The first four chapters of the book provide a general overview of the American version of moderate conservatism, of its aims, problems, and of how it can accommodate changes that have to be made to cope with challenges to life in our society. The following five chapters are about the moderate conservative interpretation of the primary political goods of the rule of law, justice, legal and political equality, liberty, and private property. The last chapter is a very brief account of the moderate conservatives attitude to the perennial problems of the ever-changing and often adverse contingencies of life, to the conflicts between primary and secondary political and non-political goods, and to the unavoidable compromises we have to make when following one of our commitments unavoidably precludes following another no less important commitment.

Finally, there are fine histories of American conservatism,[2] but this book is not intended to be one of them. Its aim is to understand and make a case for moderate conservatism in our present context and conditions as the most reasonable approach to coping with the adverse contingencies we face, the conflicts between the political goods we value, and the compromises we have to make because we cannot have everything we reasonably value.

---

[2] See, e.g., Allitt, Patrick. *The Conservatives*. New Haven, CT: Yale University Press, 2009. Bacevich, Andrew J. ed. *American Conservatism*. New York: The Library of America, 2020. Frohnen, Bruce, et al. eds. *American Conservatism*. Wilmington, DE: ISI Books, 2006.

2
From Simplicities to Complexities

The Aim of Moderate Conservatism

The simplicities are what everyone living in our society takes for granted. They are the commonplaces of everyday life, the background of our beliefs, emotions, preferences, and aversions, the shared conventional patterns of our life here and now, part of which is the political system of our society that protects the conditions in which we can live as we think we should. The aim of moderate conservatism is to maintain this political system and the familiar conditions of our lives. Essential to it are the primary political goods of the rule of law, justice, legal and political equality, liberty, private property, and the realization that the interpretation and pursuit of these goods must be flexible and responsive to changing contexts and conditions. If these goods are available, then a substantial number of people in American society can live secure lives protected by economic, legal, moral, and political arrangements. One result of these political goods and arrangements is a consensus about the acceptable and unacceptable ways of coping with the problems caused by adverse contingencies, conflicts between political and non-political goods, and the inevitable compromises we must make since we cannot have all that we reasonably want to have. These contingencies, conflicts, and compromises are perennial problems.

It is in everyone's interest in American society to find ways of coping with these perennial problems because the very possibility of our political system depends on it. Political disputes are about how we should cope with them. The disputes concern the interpretation and the relative importance of the primary political goods and the different ways of coping with these and possibly other pressing problems. Maintaining the American political system depends on maintaining a consensus, by its nature temporary, in the changing contexts and conditions about how these perennial problems could and should be met.

Moderate conservatism is an approach to how this should be done. It is an attitude, not a theory about the supposedly universal requirements that must be met by all good societies and all good lives. Moderate conservatives deny that there is or can be a political GOOD that reason requires all societies to accept and follow.[1] They agree with Adam Smith that the political theorist is so

> enamoured with the supposed beauty of his own ideal plan of government, that ... he seems to imagine that he can arrange the different members of a great society with as much ease as the hand arranges the different pieces upon a chess-board; he does not consider that ... in the great chess-board of human society, every single piece has a principle of motion of its own, altogether different from that which the legislature might choose to impress upon it. ... To insist upon establishing ... in spite of all opposition, every thing which that ... [ideal plan] may seem to require, must often be the highest degree of arrogance. It is to erect his own judgment into the supreme standard of right and wrong.

They think that reasonable approaches to coping with perennial problems vary with societies and individuals. They depend on the context formed of the prevailing and always changing economic, historical, international, physical, psychological, technological, and other conditions. And they are concerned with the evaluation of the reasons for and against alternative ways of responding to these

---

[1] Smith, Adam. *The Theory of Moral Sentiments*. Indianapolis: Liberty Classics, 1853/1969, 380–81.

conditions, given the beliefs, emotions, preferences, aversions, and experiences on which the American political system and individual conceptions of how to live are based. It is an evaluative, contextual, and fallible attitude concerned with the evaluation of reasons both for and against moderate conservatism and the alternatives to it. This chapter is about the attitude itself. The next one is about the approach that follows from it.

Conventional Lives

The Oakes family—mother, father, and three children—live in the old house of her family. She was raised in it, inherited it from her parents, and her husband moved into it when they got married. The children are growing up in it. They all like living in the house and are used to it, but it has many inconveniences. The plumbing and wiring require constant attention, the upkeep is time-consuming, with three growing children it is not spacious enough, the kitchen needs remodeling, another bathroom is needed because the girls hate sharing it with the boy. So they consider looking for a better house. They cannot afford an expensive one, but they could move up a bit. The family has been weighing the pros and cons of moving. They can live with the inconveniences, but they know that another house will also have inconveniences. They get along with their neighbors, the streets are safe, the schools are all right, and they know that all these would change in unpredictable ways if they moved to another house in another neighborhood. On the whole, they like what they have. They know that it could be better, but they are reluctant to take risks, and are not hard enough pushed to have to make a change. After months of discussion, they decide to stay put.

The Oakes prudently aim to protect what they have, make small changes when they are called for, but keep them no bigger than what is needed. On the whole they are satisfied, like their lives, the usual tensions and spats in their family do not run deep and do not leave lasting resentments, they see no reason to make a big change, want to continue the present course of their lives, enjoy their pleasures, do their jobs, earn enough, try to accommodate each other's preferences, and raise their children as well as they can. The Oakes are the salt of the Earth. They illustrate a conventional way of life which, if writ large, points to an attitude—an attitude, not a theory.

Moderate conservatives think that we should do on the larger and much more complex social context of American society what the Oakes do in their personal context. Between the simpler personal and the more complex social contexts there are many intermediate modes of association more or less closer to or farther from the personal or the social end of a continuum. The closer these associations come to the social end, the closer they come to the political attitude moderate conservatives favor. What then is this attitude and what are the reason favoring it?

The attitude is formed by those who in the usual course of life by and large follow the conventional economic, legal, moral, political, and religious modes of evaluation of their society. In normal conditions, their actions are part of generally recognized and accepted patterns, and so are the actions of most people around them. They recognize their responsibility for themselves, their marriage, children, earning a living, doing their work, getting along with friends, neighbors, and colleagues. They want to enjoy their lives, to be secure and respected, to succeed in their activities and to cope with their problems as they occur. The key to this is to recognize, as Hume[2] wrote, that

> this can be done after no other manner, than by a convention enter'd into by all the members of the society to bestow stability

---

[2] Hume, David. *A Treatise of Human Nature*. 2nd ed. Edited by P.H. Nidditch. Oxford: Clarendon Press, 1739/1978, 489.

on the possession of external goods, and leave everyone in the peaceable enjoyment of what he may acquire by his fortune and industry . . . by [this] means we maintain society, which is so necessary to their well-being and subsistence, as well as to our own.

Thus they follow their familiar daily routines, prefer it to experimenting with untried changes whose outcomes are uncertain, opt for security over risk-taking; for the conventional and habitual over changes to them; for the expected over the unexpected; and for what has been tested by experience over what is experimental. This is just what the Oakes family did when they thought about and decided to stay in their old house rather than move to another. Emergencies, threats, important changes in the prevailing conditions may of course disrupt the even temper of such conventional lives, but the disruptions are regarded as unwelcome interferences with their lives, not as impetus for changing them. They realize that sometimes they have to make changes in order to cope with the disruptions, and then they make the necessary ones. But if they succeed, they resume, with as few changes as possible, their customary and habitual lives and actions with relief, rather than resignation. They like what they have more than the uncertain promise of untried possibilities.

Conventional lives are not the whole of the lives of those who are committed to them. The conventions form the outer limits and the range of possibilities of such lives. But within those limits and possibilities there are many different personal attitudes that express many individually different preferences and aversions, for instance, about having and raising children, death, education, faith, family, food, friendship, health, hobbies, money, music, physical exercise, politics, privacy, reputation, sex, status, travel, wealth, work, and so on and on for countless other possibilities available in our society. The conventions are social; the attitudes within the conventional limits are personal.

Moderate conservatism thus leaves ample room for a wide range of different personal attitudes, and also for the choice of whether or not our life should be conventional. It is good for a society if there are in it rebels, skeptics, reformists, and non-conformists who test the limits and challenge the conventions. But moderate conservatives living in American society do think that a society can endure only if a substantial number of those living in the society accept and follow the conventional economic, legal, moral, political, and religious evaluations, not because they are forced to do so, but because these modes of evaluation have become genuine parts of how they see and respond to the world. They could live unconventional lives if they wanted to, or move to another society, but they do not. They are by and large satisfied with their mode of existence and personal attitudes, like the regularity, comforts, and security of their lives, or, less sanguinely, they are not sufficiently dissatisfied with them to want to change them in basic ways.

Cynics see such conventional lives as façades for socially unacceptable urges; romantics scorn them as hidebound denials of the True, the Good, and the Beautiful; sophisticates scorn them as symptoms of ignorance of the complexities of life; deconstructionists claim to see through them with contempt for those who do not; revolutionaries regard them as obstacles to the betterment of the human condition; and idealists pity what they see as the pedestrian lives of timid bean counters.

These knowing unmaskers think that nothing is as it seems to be, that to see is to see through, and to understand is to expose the discreditable urges hidden behind a veil of self-inflicted hypocritical obfuscation. Their knowingness prevents them from understanding that conventional lives are not the whole of the lives of those who live that way, that such lives are the secure basis of our political system, the haven to which we, and the unmaskers as well, return to heal the bruises we get when we venture beyond it. Conventional lives are the center which, if it fails to hold, mere anarchy is loosed upon our world. The unmaskers fail to understand that the commitment to conventional lives may be genuine, not hypocritical, and that the conventionality of such lives is only part of them. The other parts are the great variety of personal attitudes that exist within the conventional limits.

The aim of moderate conservatives is to maintain the difficult balance between the conventional and the personal aspects of lives in the context of American society. This is a balance between providing possibilities and setting limits for the lives and yet leaving sufficient psychological space for the great variety of different beliefs, emotions, and desires of individuals that inform their preferences and aversions about the life they want to make for themselves, given the available possibilities and the restrictions of the limits.

Common Decencies

There is a small but crucial part of life on which the very possibility of conventional lives, personal attitudes, and much else depends. I call it the common decencies. They are the genuinely held and spontaneously acted on simple unsophisticated moral sentiments and actions of most of those who live together in American society. They are to be found in face-to-face encounters in small towns, neighborhoods in large cities, in the routine transactions of everyday life as we shop, bank, wait in waiting rooms, protect children, help the old, pay debts, keep promises, and so on. Here is a randomly selected sample of what I mean by common decencies.

Parents are responsible for their children; breaking a promise requires an excuse; politicians should not lie to the electorate; parents, teachers, physicians, and the clergy should not have sex with those who rely on them; winners should not gloat over losers; the fortunate should not brag to the unfortunate; a life of idleness is a life wasted; eating people is wrong, even when we are hungry; disagreements should not lead to physical violence; handicapped people should not be laughed at; kindness is good and cruelty is bad; we owe loyalty to friends, politeness to strangers, and respect for the privacy of others; we should get the good things we deserve and not the bad things we do not deserve; we should ask permission before borrowing anything; be grateful for the help we get; not cause unnecessary pain to humans or animals; keep confidential information private; tolerate unpopular opinions; regard fortitude, integrity, politeness, and fairness as good and their opposites as bad. And so on and on for hundreds of everyday, undramatic, low intensity spontaneous moral sentiments and actions taken for granted and most of the time acted on by a substantial number of people in our society.

Common decencies make possible political moderation and our peaceful coexistence with others in our society even though we may differ about the relative importance of different modes of evaluation. Regardless of such differences, we can live together in peace and treat each other, if not with respect, then at least with toleration. We acknowledge each other as having a life to live, although it may be different, perhaps even very different, from our own. These generally shared common decencies form a deeper basis than the different often conflicting importance we think different modes of evaluation have. That deeper basis is the reciprocal acknowledgment of the shared humanity, and the basic physiological, psychological, and social needs of those who live together in a society. This forms a bond we share, even as we differ about the relative importance of different economic, legal, moral, political, and religious modes of evaluation, as well as about the particular evaluations that follow from these modes.

It may be said that the common decencies aim to satisfy our basic needs and our commitments to different evaluations aim to satisfy the needs of our individually varied personal attitudes. The common decencies make it possible for us to live together in peace even though we are committed to different evaluations. They enable different people in our society to live a plurality of socially conditioned but individually different lives. Our basic needs are the same. Our more varied needs that follow from our different personal attitudes are different, but they can be met only after our basic needs are satisfied. The needs of our personal attitudes vary with evaluative commitments, contexts, and persons. Both our basic and our varied needs presuppose the possibilities and limits provided by the generally shared modes of evaluation of our society. Sharing it makes it possible for us to coexist in peace and to be guided by our personal attitude to make what we can of our lives, if all goes well. Unfortunately, all often does not go well.

Common decencies are often violated even in the most conventional society and by the most conventional people. But then the violators spontaneously or on subsequent reflection feel some guilt, shame, regret, remorse, or the need to make amends if they could at not too great a cost. There also are complex situations in which these simple evaluations are inappropriate. And it must be recognized as well that in the history of American society there have been deplorable breakdowns of common decencies that required much stronger responses than lamenting actions contrary to them. Moderate conservatives do not and should not ignore these regrettable patterns of actions. They should acknowledge, reflect on, and learn from them. And as we do so, the simplicities are no longer adequate, complexities enter, and we have to struggle with them.

We should then come to understand that the reason why the bad patterns have occurred is that the common decencies have broken down in an alarming way. They were not abandoned, but curtailed by drawing a distinction between "us" and "them." The common decencies were owed to those in our society who were "us," but not to "them," who were not. We can learn from reflection on the past how dangerous that distinction is. And it is the reappearance of that dangerous distinction now that is poisoning the current political situation and threatens us with violence inflicted under the guise of defending the political GOOD deemed to be of such great importance as to override any consideration, including common decencies, that conflicts with it.

I use capitals throughout the book to indicate the overriding importance that the GOOD is claimed by its defenders to have.

If liberty is thought to be the overriding political GOOD, then those who favor curtailing it when it conflicts with legal or political equality or justice are condemned by immoderate political activists as tyrants. If legal and political equality is claimed to be the highest political GOOD, then those who want to restrict it because it undermines liberty and justice are excoriated by the immoderate activists as cruel oppressors who defend unearned privileges. If justice is promoted to be the greatest of all political GOOD, then those who think that it should be limited so as to accommodate the demands of liberty and legal and political equality are condemned by immoderate activists as subversive enemies of law and order. Thus these extremist defenders of the supposedly overriding political GOOD malign their opponents as tyrants, oppressors, and enemies who become "them" because they have violated what are tendentiously assumed to be the limits of civilized life and thereby undeserving of the common decencies that are owed only to "us" who are inside it.

It makes matters even more dangerous that the distinction between "us" and "them" is drawn very differently by political activists with sharply opposing views. Their views have spread from politics to other areas of life, to education, entertainments, friendship, immigration, the internet, literature, the media, medicine, sexual relations, and so forth. Books are published, prizes are awarded, op-ed pieces are accepted or rejected, grants and fellowships are awarded, votes are cast, job applicants are hired, in the educational system salaries, tenure, and promotion depend on political criteria that have little to do with how well or badly people do the job for which they were hired.

Newspapers, television channels and programs, dogmatic left and right wing factions of both of the main parties, and political action committees have come to represent extreme political views that condemn of immorality those who disagree with them. Facts and truth are manipulated to fit the political bias of those who poison reasonable political disagreements by turning them into conflicts between good and evil.

Even neutrality on the heated issues that divide "us" and "them"—such as abortion, affirmative action, capital punishment, discrimination in favor or against chosen groups, healthcare, immigration, levels of taxation, law enforcement—is deplored by the enraged polemics directed against the latest targets of the current invective. It has been said, I am afraid seriously, that there is no such thing as a non-political orgasm; that the political is personal; that not to take sides is to side with "them" and betray "us"; that those who are not with "us" are against "us." This state of affairs is an urgent and pressing reason why common decencies should be observed and strengthened rather than weakened even more by immoderate political activists who abuse of those who disagree with them.

Politicized segments of the news media have come to exercise many of the functions of the secret police in totalitarian countries. They maintain a network of informers, carry out extra-legal investigations, conduct interrogations called interviews on the basis of charges made by anonymous accusers called "sources," and dramatic confrontations are staged in which the guilt of their targets is assumed and no effective defense is allowed. It is an egregious violation of common decencies to condemn and excoriate political opponents as "them" because their conception of the rule of law, justice, legal and political equality, liberty, or private property differs from those of the immoderate dogmatic extremists.

One of my reasons for writing this book is that we are now in the midst of this dangerous condition. Our society has been politicized by extremist political activists who are outraged by what they regard as so bad as to justify them in violating common decencies in the name of whatever they deem to be the overriding political GOOD whose pursuit is far more important in their impassioned opinion than the simplicities of common decencies. I will return to this point in later chapters where I discuss whether the rule of law, justice, legal and political equality, liberty, or private property is defensible as the overriding political GOOD whose importance transcends common decencies.

The point I stress now is that the widespread violation of common decencies by extremist political activists both on the left and the right threaten the conventional lives many of us want to live. Uppermost in their minds is the distinction between "us" and "them." "We" deserve to treat each other with common decency, but "they" do not because their political views are contrary to reason and morality. Extremist political activists disrupt our ordinary encounters with each other in the countless more or less formal and informal non-political transactions of daily life. Our society has been politicized by their vicious attacks on those who disagree with them and abuse them for being enemies of civilized life. But the enemies are the extremists themselves, regardless of whether they are on the left or the right.

The problem with political extremism is not that it challenges conventional evaluations. That may be quite reasonable to do if dissatisfactions with them are widespread. The problem is that the very possibility of reasonable, calm, and civil discussion of reasons for and against conventional evaluations is made impossible by the extremists' abuse of those who disagree with them. It is especially important to observe the common decencies in fraught times, as ours has been in recent years, in order to protect and reaffirm them as the base that must be protected if political or any other disagreements could be discussed peacefully, reasonably, and calmly by people who at least tolerate each other's views even though they disagree with them. If moderate conservatives had their way, they would make politics consist in boring negotiations between elected politicians about the division of chronically insufficient resources, rather than enraged accusations directed at those who disagree with them.

Such a discussion could be conducted only by those who are committed to the modes of evaluation of our society. They share their commitment with others who often do not know each other and may be separated by temporal or spatial distance. Yet they are united by a tacit, unspoken, and typically unreflective agreement that they should be guided by the same sometimes overlapping and sometimes conflicting economic, legal, moral, political, and perhaps religious modes of evaluations. They will disagree about some or many of their particular evaluations, but they will also share many of the important ones; draw many of the same distinctions between good and bad, right and wrong, better or worse; approve or condemn many of the same actions; and pursue many of the same aims. They are likely also to agree about what considerations are and are not relevant to their evaluations, even if they sometimes act contrary to them and even if they disagree about the relative priority of conflicting evaluations. It may be said—metaphorically—that they share an evaluative language, although they may use it to express a variety of conflicting evaluations. I will say that their commitment is to the shared modes of evaluation of their society.

Shared Modes of Evaluation

Shared evaluative language and modes of evaluation are necessary conditions of the continued existence of a society that commands the allegiance of those who live in it. They will, of course, disagree about many of their particular evaluations and about their relative importance. But unless they agree about what modes of evaluation are and are not relevant to how they live and how they treat each other there would be no society in which orderly and peaceful lives could be lived. A society's shared modes of evaluation make possible the coexistence of those who live in it, regardless of how they differ about their particular evaluations, including their political evaluations. Sharing modes of evaluation is more important than disputes about particular political or other modes of evaluation, because without that widely shared agreement there would be no society in which political or any other evaluations could be disputed. This has been recognized by thoughtful people throughout the ages.[3]

In their different ways, all those cited below point at the same thing: the sharing of modes of evaluation is a condition of there being a society in which civilized human lives could be lived. The contents of various modes of evaluation vary from society to society, and so does the relative importance attributed to different modes of evaluation, as well as to different particular evaluations in the same mode. But if a society is to endure, it must be responsive to changing conditions, have shared modes of evaluation, which are flexible enough to respond reasonably to changes in our changing context and conditions. The contents of the particular evaluations

---

[3] "There remains embedded in the very substance of all our thought about the world and about ourselves an inalienable and ineradicable framework of conception, which is not in our own making, but given to us ready-made by society—a wide apparatus of concepts and categories, within which and by means of which all our individual thinking, however original and daring is compelled to move." Cornford, F.M. *From Religion to Philosophy*. New York: Harper & Row, 1912/1957, 44–45.

"One of the broadest and surest generalizations that anthropology can make about human beings is that no society is healthy or creative or strong unless that society has a set of common values that give meaning and purpose to group life, that can be symbolically expressed, that fit with the situation of the time as well as linked to the historical past, and do not outrage man's reason and at the same time appeal to their emotions." Kluckhohn, Clyde. "Culture and Behavior" in *The Collected Essays of Clyde Kluckhohn*. New York: Free Press, 1962, 297–98.

"Inside the general structure or web of human attitudes and feelings ... there is endless room for modification, redirection, criticism, and justification. But questions of justification are internal to the structure or relate to modifications internal to it. The existence of the general framework of attitudes itself is something we are given with the fact of human society." Strawson, P.F. "Freedom and Resentment" in *Freedom and Resentment*. London: Methuen, 1974, 23.

"Our sharing routes of interest and feeling, modes of response, senses of humor and of significance and of fulfillment, of what it outrageous, of what is similar to what else, what a rebuke, what forgiveness, of when an utterance is an assertion, when an appeal, when an explanation—all the whirl of organism Wittgenstein call 'form of life.'" Cavell, Stanley. "The Availability of Wittgenstein's Later Philosophy" in *Must We Mean What We Say?* Cambridge, MA: Harvard University Press, 1969, 52.

will differ since the internal and external conditions of different societies will differ.

These remarks about shared modes of evaluation have been general. But there is no general mode of evaluation, just as there is no general human being. All modes of evaluation are particular, contextual, and respond to different conditions. Different societies have different modes of evaluations; presuppose different metaphysical, moral, scientific, and other assumptions; have been formed by different historical conditions; exist in different circumstances; and change in different ways, for different reasons, and at different rates.

This is true also of the modes of evaluation in the American political system. It is not a rigid structure but a flexible pattern formed of various modes of evaluation that are always in a state of flux. It is responsive to changing conditions and to the dissatisfactions of those who are committed to it. Our economic, legal, moral, political, and religious modes of evaluation are and should be routinely questioned, enlarged, abandoned, or reformed.

Think of what has been happening to our modes of evaluation, given the exponentially growing influence of science and technology; the growth of secularization and the weakening of religious commitments; increasing awareness of threats to the natural environment; the spread of education; the rapidity of communication; and so on. And it is not just the modes of evaluation that are changing, but also the particular evaluations that follow from them. Think, for instance, of our changing and disputed evaluations of beauty, celibacy, culture, debt, faith, honor, loyalty, marriage, modesty, patriotism, privacy, and thrift.

Such changes in the modes and contents of evaluations have always been going on in American society, although they have become more rapid recently than they have been in the past. The well-being of any society, and of course of our own as well, depends on finding ways of accommodating these changes. That must be done if the society is to continue to attract the allegiance of those who live in it. Responding to changes is often difficult, but it is not a fundamental challenge to our political system. The reasons for making the changes are derived from parts of the other modes of evaluation that for the time being hold steady. We continue to value prosperity, simple common decencies, checks and balances, security, and religious harmony, even if we disagree about what exactly they involve and how best to pursue and protect them. We change some of our particular evaluations in order to protect our shared general modes of evaluation that form our political system. R.W.B. Lewis's observation is right:[4]

> Every culture seems, as it advances toward maturity, to produce its own determining debate over the ideas that occupy it: salvation, the order of nature, money, power, sex, the machine and the like. The debate, indeed, may be said to *be* the culture, at least on its loftiest levels; for a culture achieves identity not so much through the ascendancy of one particular set of convictions as through the emergence of its peculiar and distinctive dialogue.

The protection of our modes of evaluation, however, does not mean that all those who are committed to them agree about all their particular evaluations. All particular evaluations in all modes are often questioned. Disputes internal to our modes of evaluation are natural, expected, and healthy challenges to orthodoxy. The danger at the present time is that the invectives of political extremists threaten to destroy the conditions in which reasonable discussions are possible among people with contrary political commitments. The extremist political activists are blinded by their outrage to the harm they are causing as they undermine the very possibility of a context in which reasonable political disputes are possible.

It is against such extremist polemics that moderate conservatives aim to defend the shared modes of evaluation. They recognize the

---

[4] Lewis, R.W.B. *The American Adam*. Chicago: University of Chicago Press, 1955, 1–2.

legitimacy of political disputes between defenders and critics of various versions of conservatism, liberalism, and socialism. But the immoderate political activists are not engaged in such disputes. They are claiming that their opponents, merely because they disagree with the immoderate political views of the activists, place themselves outside the limits of civilized life and therefore do not deserve to be treated with common decency. John Stuart Mill is right about this:[5]

> The worst offense . . . which can be committed by a polemic is to stigmatize those who hold contrary opinions as bad or immoral men.

Shared commitments to modes of evaluation leave ample room for serious disputes. Personal attitudes differ about the relative importance of economic, legal, moral, political, and religious evaluations. Immigration, multiculturalism, and secularization are transforming our society. If we share modes of evaluation, we are united by our commitment to it and may be divided by our particular evaluations. Some of us care little, others a great deal about economics. Many are ignorant of the complexities of the law, others are preoccupied with them. We may have different moral views about particular virtues and vices, obligations to others, sexual practices, punishment, responsibility, and so forth. Some are content to leave politics to politicians, others are passionately engaged in it. Some have deep religious commitments, others have none.

Regardless of these differences, those of us who are committed to the shared modes of evaluation of our society have a bond, even if some of our particular evaluations are disputed, or changing, or our priorities shift. Yet the hold on us of our shared modes of evaluation is very strong, because we rely on it to distinguish between what

---

[5] Mill, John Stuart. *On Liberty*. Indianapolis: Hackett, 1859/1978, 51.

is good and bad, better or worse, important and unimportant. We depend on it to provide the possibilities we might pursue and to set the limits within which we should pursue them. We derive from it many of the evaluations that have become parts of our personal attitude. We make sense of how we want to live partly in terms of the possibilities and limits our modes of evaluation provide.

It would be wonderful if life would be guaranteed to go well for us if we were reasonable in our evaluative commitments and in disputes about them. Unfortunately life is not like that. Not even our best efforts to evaluate the reasons for and against the alternatives between which we have to choose would guarantee that we will succeed in making an acceptable life for ourselves. We are often dissatisfied with our lives because we are not sufficiently reasonable, and then the fault is our own. But no matter how reasonable we are, there is no guarantee that we will be satisfied with the life we have because we face unavoidable perennial problems that are part of the conditions of life, but not of our making.

The various political goods—not the GOOD of the extremist—we value are plural and conflicting, our evaluations are contextual and the contexts change, the conditions to which we have to respond are permeated with unforeseeable contingencies and changes, and the result is that we have to make compromises because we cannot have all that we reasonably value. These perennial problems leave us uncertain about how we should respond to them. No improvement in our modes of evaluation, personal attitude, or political system could guarantee that all would go well enough if only we were reasonable enough. These conflicts have centrally important political consequences for all versions of conservatism, liberalism, and socialism. I will discuss what they are and what consequences they have in the next chapter. One main reason for moderate conservatism is that, for reasons I will give in what follows, its approach to coping with the political consequences of unavoidable perennial problems is more reasonable than those of alternatives to it.

Sources of Complexities

Let us assume, contrary to the facts, that in contemporary American society the political requirements are adequately met: many of us live conventional lives, common decencies are generally observed, and there are widely shared modes evaluation, even if we often disagree about the particular evaluations that follow from them. If meeting these conditions were accepted as necessary for the defense of the American political system, it would still not be sufficient to make our society one in which we would want to continue to live. Why?

Because not even the purest good will, the selfless pursuit of the common good, and the dedicated following of the primary political goods would be enough to cope with the perennial problems of adverse contingences, conflicts, and the compromises we must make because we cannot have everything we reasonably want. We must face adverse contingencies caused by external and internal threats, natural disasters, scarcity of resources, hostile enemies, over which we have no control. We must cope with conflicts between political goods; between political and non-political goods; between political and non-political modes of evaluation; and between evaluations that follow from our personal attitude and those that follow from the modes of evaluation of our society. And we must compromise our own reasonable evaluative commitments because they are often incompatible. Politics is a necessary part of civilized life, political evaluations are crucial to it, but we do not live by politics alone. Even if our political system were perfect, which it certainly is not, we would still have to face and cope with perennial problems. Moderate conservatives respond to this somber realization by accepting that no matter how reasonable we are, we must live with perennial problems, and that we cannot have all we want, not even if what we want is reasonable.

One of the difficult problems moderate conservatives must face and respond to is having to decide what we should actually do—not in theory but in practice—when we know that perennial problems are unavoidable and that however we respond to them we will have significant losses of political goods we value. However wise or foolish our acceptance may be, it does not help us decide what we should do to minimize our losses. Whatever choices we make, we will lose something we need and want to have.

This is not a problem only for moderate conservatives. It needs to be faced and responded to by defenders of all political views. They all are vulnerable to contingencies and conflicts, and they all have to make compromises by giving up some of the goods they value in order to have other goods they value more. This is not just a political problem. It is a problem that affects all of our evaluations regardless of our political views. The problem of finding such a response will take a variety of forms depending on contexts, conditions, and the nature of the goods that are either defended or compromised. The various problems to which we have to reconcile ourselves may be aesthetic, historical, literary, moral, personal, political, psychological, religious, scientific, tragic, and so forth. But this book is about politics, and I consider only two of the main political responses to it. One involves the rejection of the most widely followed response. The other is the one favored by moderate conservatives. I consider first the widely favored one and the reasons for rejecting it and then turn to a preliminary indication of the moderate conservative response which will be developed throughout the book.

The widely accepted way political theorists cope with these conflicts is to claim that the political GOOD is so important to the well-being of a society that it should always, in all conditions, override whatever political good conflicts with it. The question is which of the political goods is supposed to have this overriding importance. Political theorists disagree about it. Here are some examples, drawn from many, of the disagreements between some well-known contemporary political theorists.

According to Berlin "only rights can be regarded as absolute."[6] Dworkin says that "equal concern is the sovereign virtue of political community."[7] Rawls claims that "justice is the first virtue of social institutions . . . the rights secured by justice are not subject to political bargaining."[8] In Raz's words: the "overriding aim [is] to secure the political conditions that are necessary for the exercise of personal freedom."[9] In Williams's view "every citizen, indeed every human being . . . deserves equal consideration. . . . there is nothing more basic in terms of which to justify it."[10]

These are fine words expressing the heartfelt sentiments of these influential theorists, but they mean very little unless their defenders consider how much of other political goods they are willing to have less of in order to have more of the one they regard as overriding. If rights were really the overriding political GOOD, then the rights of criminals could not be curtailed, not even in an emergency; and it would require their defenders to go far beyond the borders of their society in defense of the overriding rights of people in Tientsin, Teheran, and Timbuctoo. If equal consideration were the overriding political GOOD, how would resources be distributed among the billions all over the world to whom equal consideration would have to be extended? Do dictators and their victims, benefactors and scourges of humanity, torturers and the tortured deserve equal consideration? If personal freedom were the overriding political GOOD, it would require the protection of the personal freedom of enemy

---

[6] Berlin, Isaiah. "Two Concepts of Liberty" in *Four Essays on Liberty*. Oxford: Oxford University Press, 1969, 165.

[7] Dworkin, Ronald. *Sovereign Virtue*. Cambridge, MA: Harvard University Press, 2000, 1.

[8] Rawls, John. *A Theory of Justice*. Cambridge, MA: Harvard University Press, 1971, 3–4.

[9] Raz, Joseph. *The Morality of Freedom*. Oxford: Clarendon Press, 1986, 2.

[10] Williams, Bernard. "Philosophy as a Humanistic Discipline" in *Philosophy as a Humanistic Discipline*. Edited by A.W. Moore. Princeton, NJ: Princeton University Press, 2006, 194–95.

soldiers in war, of the diseased in an epidemic, of criminals all over the world, and the release of everyone from all jails in the world.

The fineness of these words will lose its sheen as soon as we ask what their defenders would be willing to give up in order to have what they claim is or should be overriding, and thus prevailing against all conflicting considerations. If they really mean that the political GOOD they favor overrides all conflicting considerations, then no reasonable person who understands the far-reaching political consequences of acting on these fine words would accept them. If, however, these theorists accept that the political GOOD to which they are committed may sometimes be curtailed, then they could no longer claim that it is absolute, or a sovereign or first virtue of social institutions, or not subject to political bargaining, or that it is overriding.

Moderate conservatives recognize that rights, legal and political equality, liberty, and respect are political goods. But they do not accept that any of them is so important as to override any other political good that may conflict with it regardless of what the conflicting good is, and what the contexts and conditions are. It makes a serious difference to how such conflicts are resolved whether they occur in the midst of war or peace, in an epidemic or in robust public health, in an environmental disaster or bumper harvest, in a disintegrating or booming economy, or in a law-abiding or crime-ridden society. And why should any political good override not just all other political goods, but also non-political goods, which may be legal, moral, religious, or some other kind that conflicts with the supposedly overriding political good?

Let us suppose, however, that contrary to disputes about it all through the millennia, there is a generally accepted and overriding political GOOD. The ones often proposed here and now are liberty, equality, and justice. This would achieve very little because all the many questions of interpretation about the permissible possibilities and the acceptable limits of the political good remain open. Aristotle saw this[11]:

> All men think justice to be a sort of equality... they say that what is just is just *for* someone and that it should be equal for equals. But there still remains a question: equality or inequality of what? Here is the difficulty which calls for political speculation.

And so did Burke[12]:

> I should... suspend my congratulations on... liberty... until I was informed how it had been combined with government; with public force; with the discipline and obedience of armies; with the collection of an effective and well-distributed revenue; with morality and religion; with the solidity of property; with peace and order; with civil and social manners. All these (in their way) are good things too; and without them liberty is not a benefit.

It is fine and good to stress the overriding importance of liberty, equality, or and justice. The serious work begins when we struggle with such question as, What are the limits of liberty? Equality or inequality in what respect? Is it criminal, distributive, or international justice that is supposedly overriding? And what about the adjudication of torts? Will that be also overriding? And who on what basis would adjudicate disputes about what is and what is not just? The heart of the matter is how we answer such questions. These theorists should recognize that order, private property, the rule of law, or security must in some ways limit the unquestionable

---

[11] Aristotle. *Politics*. Translated by Benjamin Jowett. *The Complete Works of Aristotle*. Vol. 2. Edited by Jonathan Barnes. Princeton, NJ: Princeton University Press, 1984, 1282b16–22.

[12] Burke, Edmund. *Reflections on the Revolution in France*. Indianapolis: Liberty Fund, 1790/1999, 93–94.

importance of liberty, equality, and justice, however they may be interpreted.

The history of political thought is a history of conflicting theories about the supposedly overriding political GOOD. Each of these theories favors some overriding political GOOD. Many political disputes are between defenders and critics of these theories. Their disputes often turn into immoderate polemics because parties to them see themselves as defending the overriding political GOOD on which the well-being of individuals and their society depends. They think that the political GOOD they regard as overriding is endangered by their opponents, and they see themselves as reacting with justified outrage to those they malign for being enemies of the GOOD.

Moderate conservatives differ from all these theorists because they deny that there is an overriding political good that is always in all conflicts and in all contexts more important than any of the others. If there is no political good that always overrides any of the others that may conflict with it, then the question needs to be answered: how should we cope with perennial problems that beset the primary political goods of the rule of law, justice, liberty, legal and political equality, and private property? There is a short and long answer to this question. The long one is the subject of this book. It will be gradually worked out in the chapters that follow. The short one is merely a brief indication of what the long answer is.

The short answer is that how we should cope with perennial problems is always particular, never general. It depends on the context and the conditions in which we have to contend with adverse contingencies, with conflicts between political goods that are essential for the protection of the American political system, and with the compromises we have to make because we cannot have all that we reasonably want. And we should realize that contexts and conditions change, that the contingencies, conflicts, and compromises we have to face differ as these changes occur, and that not even the most reasonable response we can formulate at one time will carry over to another time when we will have to contend with perennial problems that recur in different contexts and conditions.

Moderate conservatives think that this is not the fault of our political system, nor a consequence of our limitations, but the inescapable human condition. We can and should look for ways of coping with perennial problems. There are better and worse, more and less reasonable ways of doing so, but it is an illusion to suppose that there is a redemptive political GOOD whose pursuit would relieve us from having to cope with perennial problems. What we need to do again and again, in forever changing contexts and conditions, is to find the best available way of coping in our particular context and conditions. The rest of this book is about how we should go about finding that way.

3
Perennial Problems

Overview

I approach perennial problems by way of a quick survey of the moderate conservative political view to make explicit the background against which perennial problems arise and to which moderate conservatives respond. This book, then, is about the political conditions of our well-being in the American context. There is, of course, more to our well-being than politics. Two distinctions are central to understanding what more is needed. One is between the universal and the contextual conditions of our well-being. The universal conditions are the same for everyone. The contextual conditions vary with times, places, and societies. The other distinction is between the politics of limits and the politics of possibilities. The politics of limits aims to protect the universal conditions; the politics of possibilities is concerned with protecting the contextual conditions.

The universal condition has to do with requirements that all human beings have regardless of their identity and the context in which they live: the satisfaction of basic needs. This is a necessary condition not just of our well-being but also of our continued existence. I call this the humane requirement. It is not always met. Sometimes ill will or incompetence prevents it. At other times, the obstacles are natural conditions beyond our control, such as the scarcity of resources, epidemics, or natural disasters. Whatever the causes are, it is a universal requirement of the adequacy of all political systems that they should do what they can to satisfy the humane requirement of their subjects and protect them from violations.

This is the point at which the universal condition of well-being and the politics of limits should coincide. The first should provide what is needed; the second should prohibit interference with it. What should happen, however, often does not. An essential aim of moderate conservatism is to assure that in American society the humane requirement is met. The various kinds of conservatives, liberals, and socialists who disagree about many things, agree about this much. They also agree that it would be good to meet the humane requirement and to extend the politics of limits to all human beings in all societies. Regrettably, there are serious practical and political obstacles to doing so. It remains a controversial question whether and how these obstacles could be surmounted in other societies.

However, even if the humane requirements were generally met, it would still not be sufficient because human well-being also depends on a plurality of contextual conditions. In our context there are deep disagreements about the relative importance of the various conditions and of the various possibilities of life we may try to realize. One source of these disagreements is that not only is there a plurality of contextual conditions of human well-being, but also a plurality of conceptions of well-being itself. Their plurality is a plain fact of life in different societies, as we know from anthropology, history, literature, philosophy, and religion. I mention, by the way, that this casts serious doubt on efforts to defend any theory that is committed to a universal context-independent ideal of human well-being.

Whatever may be the case in other societies, the political conditions in our society include the constitutional protection of the primary political goods of the rule of law, justice, liberty, legal and political equality, and private property. They also include the protection of secondary political goods, such as adequate defense, education, order, law enforcement, prosperity, public health, security, and so forth. I call this the contextual, as opposed to the universal, requirement because societies differ about what their primary and secondary political goods are and how their contextual requirements should be protected.

This book is about politics, and moderate conservatism is an approach to American politics. That is why I have focused on the political conditions of well-being in our context. But our well-being depends also on various non-political conditions, which may be aesthetic, cultural, economic, historical, legal, moral, personal, political, prudential, religious, and so forth. Moderate conservatives do not suppose that the protection of the primary and secondary political goods would be sufficient to assure everyone's well-being in our society.

One reason why they are not sufficient is that there are many and often conflicting political goods. Ideal theorists,[1] who may be liberal, socialist, or non-moderate conservative, think that there is a context-independent, universal, highest political GOOD, although they differ about what it is. But whatever it may be, its importance for human well-being is supposed by ideal theorists to be so great as to override any consideration that hinders its pursuit. Since moderate conservatives deny that there is a highest political or any non-political GOOD that always has such overriding importance in all contexts and conditions, how then do they respond to conflicts between political goods? They do so by evaluating their relative importance from the point of view of the protection of the entire political system of our society. Its protection depends on how well the universal and contextual conditions of the well-being of members of our society meet the test of time. The resulting evaluations are disputable, but not arbitrary, matters of political judgment. In this moderate conservatives follow Hume:[2]

The test of time is the moderate conservative alternative to all ideal theories, regardless of what their favored GOOD is supposed to be.

---

[1] I take the term from Rawls, John. *A Theory of Justice*. Cambridge, MA: Harvard University Press, 1971. See the Index for references to ideal theory.

[2] Hume, David. "Idea of a Perfect Commonwealth" in *Essays Moral Political and Literary*. Edited by Eugene F. Miller. Indianapolis: Liberty Press, 1741/1985, 512.

The ideal is of some universal, context-independent, theoretical conception of the GOOD that overrides whatever consideration may hinder its pursuit. In sharp contrast, the test of time is pluralistic, social, contextual, and practical. It is the product of the historical experience of a people. The flexible and changing standard on which we, in American society, rely as we try to cope with the ever-changing contingencies, conflicts, and compromises that are obstacles to living according to the wide plurality of different conceptions of well-being we individually try to realize. In this we follow Hume

> An established government has an infinite advantage, by that very circumstance, of its being established; the bulk of mankind being governed by authority, not reason, and never attributing authority to any thing that has not the recommendation of antiquity. To tamper, therefore, in this affair, or try experiments merely upon the credit of supposed argument and philosophy, can never be part of the wise magistrate, who will bear a reverence to what carries the marks of age; and though he may attempt some improvements for the public good, yet will he adjust his innovations as much as possible to the ancient fabric, and preserve the chief pillars and supports of the constitution.

The prevailing political arrangements of our society meet the test of time if we have good reasons for continuing to participate in it; our humane requirements are met; we could move to another society, but we do not; there are familiar and sufficiently varied possibilities of life available to us; we are, within lawful limits, free to try to realize them; our dissatisfactions with some of the prevailing political arrangements are on the whole outweighed by the satisfactions we derive from them; and we have the means of expressing our dissatisfactions and advocating changes to the prevailing political arrangements. If these considerations are met, they jointly tilt the balance of reasons in favor of our continued participation in our political system.

It is central to understanding moderate conservatism that the protection of the humane requirement by the politics of limits is necessary but not sufficient for our well-being. For that depends also on a plurality of various non-universal contextual primary and secondary political goods. These political goods, if all goes well, are protected by the politics of possibilities. But we need still more for our well-being. We need to have access to some aesthetic, economic, historical, literary, moral, personal, political, religious, or other goods beyond the satisfaction of our basic needs. And we need to rely on the politics of possibilities to protect the conditions that enable us to pursue some of the great plurality of non-political goods and thereby enrich the possibilities of life available to us and enable us to conduct our experiments in living.

In an ideal world, if we followed moderate conservative policies and both the universal and the contextual conditions of our well-being and the politics of limits and possibilities were protected, then our well-being would be assured. The mere availability of these conditions, however, would not guarantee that we could take advantage of them because perennial problems may prevent it. They are the problems to which the title of this chapter refers: the *contingencies* of life, *conflicts* between our evaluative commitments, and the *compromises* we have to make in order to live as we want to be.

They are perennial because they are unavoidable and recurrent by-products of our nature and conditions. They are problems we have to live with, like aging, social changes, vulnerability to disease, or getting along with others. These problems cannot be solved once and for all, partly because all possible solutions are vulnerable to the contingencies, conflicts, and compromises to which they are intended to respond. We have to learn to live with them as long as our basic nature and conditions remain as they have been since time immemorial. We have reasonable policies, approaches, and attitudes toward them, but they are disputable because they involve controversial judgments about the relative importance of the reasons for and against our various possible responses to the contingencies, conflicts, and compromises we have to make in our particular conditions and contexts. We have to contend with the disputable and disputed evaluations of the relative importance of the reasons for and against various ways of responding to these problems. Our knowledge of the relevant facts is imperfect; the situations are fluid and often change; and we must decide how to respond to them. Doing nothing would be worse than doing something. We are influenced by our past experiences and by the immediate pressures of the conditions we face, and we must estimate the short and long range consequences of the various decision we might make. The complexities and ambiguities of these considerations make us uncertain about what we should do.

Should we go to war or compromise our interests? How should we respond to an economic crisis or to the scarcity of essential resources? Can we trust foreign military or commercial powers in negotiations with them? Should we increase the already considerable tax burden of citizens? Can we count on compliance if we raise taxes enough to cover necessary expenses? How should we respond to widespread criminality or addiction? How far can we go in making compromises before we betray our principles? These are some of the political situations in which we come up against and have to respond to perennial problems. I begin with contingencies.

Contingencies

Two and a half thousand years ago Euripides asked (in *Hecuba*, 489–92) a question about us and our world that has not ceased to be asked again and again throughout the ages:

> ... do we, holding that the gods exist,
> deceive ourselves with unsubstantial dreams
> and lies, while random careless chance and change
> alone control the world?

One contemporary answer to it has been given by Bernard Williams:[3]

> We know that the world was not made for us, or we for the world, that our history tells no purposive story, and that there is no position outside the world or outside history from which we might hope to authenticate our activities. We have to acknowledge the hideous costs of many human achievements that we value, including this reflective sense itself, and recognise that there is no redemptive Hegelian history or universal Leibnizian cost-benefit analysis to show that it will come out well enough in the end.

If so, then chance and change do indeed control the world.

John Cottingham[4] has given a contrary answer to the same question. The dream is not unsubstantial because

> the religious perspective ... offers the possibility of meaningfulness by providing a powerful *normative framework* or *focus* for the life of virtue. ... The morally good life is indeed one which enables us to fulfil our human nature. But what the religious dimension adds is a framework within which that nature is revealed as ... pointing to the condition that a Being of utmost benevolence and care that we can conceive of desires us to achieve ... a moral order that the cosmos was created to realize.

If chance and change do control the world, then contingencies are perennial problems. Whatever we do, however good and reasonable our intentions and efforts may be, they may fail or lead to unintended bad consequences. If we accept this, it would make our efforts pointless, hopes chimerical, and life meaningless. And that

---

[3] Williams, Bernard. *Shame and Necessity*. Berkeley: University of California Press, 1993, 166.
[4] Cottingham, John. *On the Meaning of Life*. London: Routledge, 2003, 72.

dispiriting possibility might make us receptive to the belief that the dream of a cosmic moral order is not unsubstantial and what seem to us as contingencies have a deeper purpose which we do not understand.

Yet the bad things in the world, the horrors of history, man's inhumanity to man, and the endless acrimonious controversies about what the moral order supposedly includes and excludes make us suspect that the dream is no more than the expression of our hope for a better world than ours seems to be. We will then ask why we should not believe that the dream is just a consoling stratagem for avoiding despair. The answer, if there is one, will have to do more than assert the possibility that the cosmos was created to realize a moral order.

Why should we believe that the cosmos was created at all rather than a name we give to the immensity that includes everything? or that it has an aim? or that its aim, if it has one, is the creation of a moral rather than an indifferent or an immoral or a Manichean order? or that the cosmos is beyond our understanding? or that different parts of it have different aims? or that the aims change? We will need better founded answers to such questions than the mere assurance that the dream is not unsubstantial. It seems, then, that Williams's and Cottingham's answers to Euripides's question leave us with a choice between disillusion and illusion.

Moderate conservatives deny that we have to make such a stark choice. We should descend from the height of theoretical speculations about the nature of the cosmos. Instead of making theories about whether there is a moral order inherent in the cosmos, we should consider the implications of a realistic scenario that illustrates how the contingencies we can neither foresee nor control in our actual context make us vulnerable.

A commercial jet with many people aboard is flying over the ocean. It runs into a unexpected storm, lightning strikes it, its engines catch fire, it crashes, and everyone dies. This is certainly an unforeseen contingency and it is bad. Now consider two of the passengers who died. One is a psychopath specializing in torture, at which he is very good. The other is an expert in the prevention of tropical diseases and is on the way home after having saved many lives that would have been lost if it had not been for his know-how. We will not grieve for the psychopath, but we will lament the death of the life-saver.

Thinking about this case allows us to distinguish between two kinds of contingencies. One is factual. It is a contingency we could have prevented if we had known more about weather prediction, make airplanes more resistant to lightning, finding less risky routes to fly over, and so on. We should not infer from factual contingencies that the cosmos is out to get us. It is neither our friend, nor our enemy. It seems to be just there in its immensity. We should accept instead that we are vulnerable to such factual contingencies because we have cognitive limits. The growth of our knowledge may enable us in small ways to make our cognitive resources less limited. I have no idea how far we can go in this direction. But we know that we can go quite a way beyond where we now are because we have done it in the past and continue to do it now, as the growth of science and technology shows.

The other kind of contingency is evaluative. Natural conditions are what they, but our economic, historical, legal, medical, moral, personal, political, religious, and other evaluations are human constructions based on our assumptions about what is favorable or detrimental to our well-being. Natural conditions, like the storm, are indifferent to how they affect us. Yet the evaluative framework of our society depends on and has insufficient control over the natural conditions on which our evaluations and well-being depend. There is much that affects our well-being and yet we cannot foresee all the many adversities to which we may become vulnerable. The dependence of our well-being on natural conditions over which we have insufficient control is the perennial problem of contingencies.

Moderate conservatives acknowledge the problem, but deny that either disillusion or illusion is an acceptable response to it. Against disillusion counts the fact that although all societies are vulnerable to contingencies, some respond to them much better than others. Some, like ours, continue to meet the test of time, while others collapse under the weight of the dissatisfactions of those who are forced to live in unacceptable conditions. Williams is impressed by the fact that we are vulnerable to contingencies, but takes no account of the no less significant fact that there are better and worse ways of responding to them. We cannot be free of contingencies, but we can cope with them sometimes more and at other times less successfully. We are challenged, but not doomed by contingencies. We know from the history of our society that sometimes—only sometimes I say—we have managed to cope with them creditably, for instance by discovering the benefits of air conditioning, anesthesia, dams, religious toleration, sanitation, the separation of powers, none of which have hideous costs. Williams rightly stresses some of the costs we have incurred, but forgets about the benefits that far outweigh their costs.

Against Cottingham's illusion that following one of the many religious ideals will make the human condition meaningful, morally inspired, and fulfilled stand the sobering contrary facts. Religious ideals promise to make life meaningful, good, and give us hope, but all of them have been rejected by defenders of other religious ideals and by non-religious skeptics who believe that meaning, goodness, and hope may be found in non-religious art, history, literature, morality, music, and (yes!) even in the rule of law, justice, legal and political equality, liberty, and private property. We know as well that religious societies, whatever their favored religion may be, are just as vulnerable to contingencies as non-religious ones. And we should not forget the lamentable fact that in the long history of religious ideals of the GOOD much harm has been done by defenders of their ideal to those who had other religious ideals. Why should we suppose that a society's favored ideal must be religious? Why not cultural, historical, moral, or political? Disillusion and illusion are both based on abstract generalizations about the nature of the cosmos and the human condition, but they are inconsistent with the concrete reality of the contrary facts.

Distrusting abstract generalizations about *the* human condition, moderate conservatives ask: why suppose that given the great variety of human beings, cultures, epochs, and conditions there is only one human condition rather than many different ones that vary with societies and circumstances? There certainly are some universally human conditions, such as the physiology our body, basic needs, our social nature, the division of labor, and so on. But these universal human conditions are only some among the many different non-universal conditions that must be part of the great plurality of quite different conceptions of human well-being. Why suppose that all-embracing abstract generalizations can be made about the great variety of particular human conditions?

Some of us may be quite reasonably disillusioned with the conditions of our lives, and seek different conditions without the risk of thereby losing our humanity. Others have nurtured illusions about a better future, which turned out to be realizable. And there are many others who find the conditions of their lives here and now livable and improvable, and then proceed to improve it. It is a mistake to think that all the conditions of human well-being must be universal.

Illusions and disillusions alike are the products of the thousands of years old search for a theory of everything: an all-embracing world view about the cosmic moral order. Some think that they have found that it is GOOD and that nothing is more important than living according to it. They then have to face the disillusioning fact that their actual experience of the world is contrary to their own view of it, and also the further fact that untold number of thoughtful, historically informed, morally committed, and politically experienced people see the world very differently. Others are overpowered by a sense of doom because there is no theory that makes sense of everything, and then lose hope, and become disillusioned. Those who have succumbed either to an illusion or to a disillusion fundamentally disagree with each other, but they share the assumption that making sense of life depends on finding the theory of everything.

Moderate conservatives reject this assumption. They think that making sense of life depends on making sense of our own life and of the lives of those we care about in our context and prevailing conditions. Only a few dedicated philosophers, theologians, ideologues, moralists continue to search for a theory of everything. But even they have to apply what they think they have found to the complexities of their daily life and then, just as do those who live without such a theory have to rely on their own practical experience to consider how the choices they might make would affect their well-being. The connection, if there is one, between a theory of everything and daily life has to be bridged by complex intermediate considerations that vary with changing context and conditions. There is no simple way of bridging the gap between a theory of everything, be it metaphysical, moral, personal, philosophical, political, or some other kind, and everyday life.

Moderate conservatives are centrally concerned with how we might cope with these complexities in the political system of American society. This is a practical and political matter, not a theoretical, universal, and impersonal one. One main reason for it is that whatever view we have formed has to be applied, and that depends on our personal evaluative commitments. Moderate conservatives are concerned with the complexities of the contingencies and adversities we face, with the obstacles in our way, and with how to cope with them.

Abstract theoretical generalizations are irrelevant to how most of us try to cope with the problems we face. Few of us have or need a theory of everything that includes among the multitude of complexities the nature and conditions of all human societies and lives. We are rarely encouraged by illusions or discouraged by disillusions about the prospects of all of humanity or about the conditions of the cosmos. It neither is nor does it need to be part of one of the many and various contexts in which all of us live. As Adam Smith put it:[5]

> The administration of the great system of the universe, however, the care of the universal happiness of all rational and sensible beings, is the business of God, and not of man. To man is allotted a much humbler department, but one much more suitable to the weakness of his powers, and to the narrowness of his own comprehension—the care of his own happiness, of that of his family, his friends, his country: that he is occupied in contemplating the more sublime, can never be an excuse for neglecting the mode humble department.

We are engaged in our lives, pursue our projects, face adversities, care about the conditions of the society in which we live, do what we can to cope with them, endure failures, and celebrate successes. How we might reasonably go about doing that leads to the difficult personal question of how we should live. This book is about politics and I set personal questions aside.[6]

Moderate conservatives think that there is an intermediate realistic response between cosmic illusion and disillusion. It is based on the possibility of increasing our limited control over the conditions of our lives. Nothing we could do would free us from contingencies. But we can maintain a steady critical, constructive, flexible, and practical attitude in order to correct the political arrangements of our political system by making them less vulnerable to both natural and evaluative contingencies. The key to doing this is to be responsive to the generally felt dissatisfactions of members of our society. In order to make appropriate changes to

---

[5] Smith, Adam. *The Theory of Moral Sentiments*. Indianapolis: LibertyClassics, 1853/1976, 386.

[6] I discuss it in *Enjoyment*. Oxford: Oxford University Press, 2008; *How Should We Live?* Chicago: University of Chicago Press, 2014; *Hard Questions*. New York: Oxford University Press, 2019; *Wisdom*. New York: Oxford University Press, 2020.

the prevailing political arrangements, we rely on the primary and secondary political goods of our political system. And a perpetual responsiveness to such dissatisfactions is the aim and the justification of the primary and secondary political goods of our political system.

In one way or another, the contingencies of life will impinge on us no matter what we do. Our attitude toward them, however, is to some extent within our control. There can be no theory, rule, or ideal that could guide what we should personally do to increase the limited control we have. What we could and should do depends on the prevailing conditions, the nature of the adversities we face, the alternative possibilities open to us, and on our fallible evaluations of their relative importance.

In this way moderate conservatism offers us in our society an alternative response to both disillusion and illusion. It is the continued participation in our political system that has so far met and is committed to keep meeting the test of time. It protects the conditions in which we can pursue our personal conceptions of well-being. And that is why our political system deserves our continuing personal support. It is true that both the political system and our evaluations are vulnerable to contingencies. But it is also true that we are not helpless because we can continue to rely on our political system, on its primary, secondary, and non-political goods embedded in our evaluative framework, and on our historical experience that enables us to distinguish between better and worse ways of responding to the contingencies that threaten our well-being. We can draw that distinction by evaluating the relative importance of the available responses we have for responding to contingencies. For that there is no abstract, theoretical, universally applicable rule, principle, or standard. Their relative importance depends on the nature of the contingencies to which we have to respond, on the prevailing context and conditions, on the political, moral, and personal commitments of those who have to make the relevant decisions, and on whatever guidance we may get from the successes and failures of efforts that have been made in history of our political system.

Our 300-year-old political system has not always done as well as it could and should have, but all in all it has enabled us to cope with the contingencies that threatened our well-being. We have sustained our losses in various wars; weathered economic crises; maintained order and prosperity with some ups and downs in trying circumstances; and corrected, albeit belatedly, the wrongs that have been done and allowed to be done to some members of our society. The success of that critical, constructive, flexible, and practical approach on which we can rely to evaluate what is more and what is less important in coping with contingencies is the reason why we should neither succumb to disillusion, nor nurture the illusion that if we tried harder, then we could become invulnerable to the perennial problem of contingencies.

Conflicts

"Conflict" is an imprecise term. It ranges from simple matter-of-fact choices we have to make all the time between incompatible actions (e.g., walking or driving to work) to complex choices whose consequences have serious implications for how we go on living after we have made the choice. Complex conflicts become perennial problems if they compel us to choose between incompatible commitments we regard as important to living as we think we should. Such conflicts are, for instance, between commitments to public and private life, ambition and integrity, comfort and discipline, courage and security, autonomy and family life. These are usually important, wrenching personal conflicts between our own commitments.

Moderate conservatism is a political view. Its main concern is not with personal but with perennial political conflicts and in the American context. Some of these conflicts are internal to the political mode of evaluation and occur between the primary political goods. Other conflicts are between secondary political and non-political goods, which may be economic, legal, medical, moral, personal, prudential, religious, and so forth. In the normal course of events, if the primary goods of the rule of law, justice, liberty, legal and political equality, and private property conflict with secondary political or non-political goods, then priority is given to the primary ones because they protect the conditions in which other political and non-political goods can be pursued. And in particularly complex conflicts of this kind, we rely on the Constitution and the best interpretation of it we can arrive at in the context and the conditions in which the conflicts occur.

However, the normal course of events is routinely disrupted by contingencies, such as environmental crises, epidemics, a flourishing illegal economy, foreign military aggression, natural disasters, scarcity of essential resources, internal social unrest caused by widespread criminality, the illiteracy and/or addiction of substantial numbers of the electorate, and the resulting serious dissatisfactions with the entire political system. These contingencies threaten the very survival of our political system and thereby the possibility of pursuing any of the political or non-political, primary or secondary goods on which our well-being in American society depends. When this happens or threatens to happen, we face a far more serious conflict than merely having to choose between conflicting evaluative commitments within our political system.

It would be a mistake to dismiss this as a remote possibility. It happened again and again in the course of history: to Athens as a result of the ill-fated Syracusan expedition; to the Roman Empire when Christianity replaced the ancient Greco-Roman civilization; to the manifold Asian civilization devastated by the Mongolian invasion; to Europe decimated by the Black Death; to the rapid rise and slow fall of the Ottoman Empire; to the destruction of the civilizations of South and Central America in the 16th century by the conquistadores. The perennial problem of political conflicts sometimes has a resolution, but it is not always a felicitous one.

How then should we respond to the perennial problem of political conflicts? This is a particularly acute question for moderate conservatives because they reject the answer ideal theorists give to it. If there were an overriding political ideal of the GOOD, then conflicts between it and other political goods could always be resolved in favor of the GOOD. But if there is no such GOOD, and if the various lesser goods conflict, as we know that they do, then we need an explanation of how conflicts between primary political goods could be resolved.

The key to the moderate conservative approach to such conflicts is to change how we think about them. We should treat them as unavoidable parts of political life, not as indications of a crisis, or of a deep flaw in our political system, or of a contradiction in our thinking. This has been a theme in Stuart Hampshire work, and in this respect I follow him. Here is a succinct statement of it:[7]

> Neither in the social order, nor in the experience of an individual, is a state of conflict the sign of a vice, or a defect, or a malfunctioning. It is not a deviation from the normal state of a city or of a nation, and it is not a deviation from the normal course of a person's experience. To follow through the ethical implications of these propositions about the normality of conflicts ... a kind of moral conversion is needed, a new way of looking.

He writes elsewhere[8] that part of the new way is to recognize the significance of the fact that

---

[7] Hampshire, Stuart. *Justice Is Conflict*. Princeton, NJ: Princeton University Press, 2000, 33–34.

[8] Hampshire, Stuart. "Morality and Conflict" in *Morality and Conflict*. Cambridge, MA: Harvard University Press, 1983, 155.

we know that we in fact have essential divisions within us as persons and that we experience moral conflicts arising from them. A person hesitates between two contrasting ways of life, and sets of virtues, and he has to make a very definite, and even final, determination between them. This determination is a negation, and normally the agent will feel that the choice has killed, or repressed, some part of him.

Moderate conservatives go on from recognizing perennial conflicts and the need for a new way of looking at them, and actually suggest a new way. It is to see conflicts not as problems but as catalysts for a deeper understanding of our political system. These conflicts are between our commitments to political and non-political goods we value as essential for the protection of our political system. Since they are essential, it would be disastrous for us to give either of them up. The alternative is to recognize that we do not have to make a final and irrevocable choice between these political or non-political goods. We can remain committed to both. What we are conflicted about is their relative importance in the particular context and conditions in which we encounter their conflict. But contexts and conditions change. As a result, conflicts between political and non-political goods will have different particular and practical resolutions in different contexts and conditions. And our evaluations of the relative importance of the conflicting goods will change accordingly.

If we understand conflicts as catalysts, we will realize that our evaluations of their relative importance does not commit us to what we or anyone else should do in the future when we or they once again come up against the conflict between primary, secondary, political, and non-political goods. Our evaluation will be of their relative importance in the context and conditions we face then and there. Contexts and conditions are all too likely to change, and then the relative importance of the conflicting goods will also change. To see the conflicts as catalysts is to see them as calling for practical and particular evaluations, not theoretical and universal evaluations that ideal theorists suppose all reasonable people will have to accept.

What, then, do we have to do to come to see the perennial problem of conflicts as catalysts? To begin with, we have to accept that many of the conflicts we face have no simple solutions. The conflicts are perennial and recurrent. They have no once-and-for-all solutions. We have to respond to them again and again as they recur in slightly different ways. They are, like the contingencies of life, unavoidable consequences of our political system in which there is a great plurality of primary, secondary, political, and non-political goods, conceptions of personal well-being, a constantly changing context, and varied conditions both external and internal to our political system.

If we accept this, we must abandon the effort to find an ideal theory that will provide a standard on which we could rely for a simple solution based on an overriding GOOD that reason, morality, politics, religion, metaphysics, and all other modes of evaluation require everyone to accept and follow. It is to accept that we know of no GOOD, no ultimate principle, no once-and-for-all solution, no authority in this world or out of it on which we could confidently rely for conclusive guidance to how we should respond to our conflicts. It is to accept that perennial problems are perennial as long as the world and human lives are as they are.

The constructive approach of moderate conservatism to perennial political problems follows from seeing them as catalysts. It is a moderate because it occupies the middle range of a continuum. At one end of it are the views of various ideal theorists. At the opposite end are the views of relativists who think that to see is to see through what they regard as our illusions and to see that, having seen through, what we find is that there is nothing there. Moderate conservatives think that what occupies the middle range of the continuum is our political system that has stood the test of time. It is guided by the Constitution and the 300-year-old political experience on which we rely as we face the complexities of the problems that arise in the ordinary lives and practical affairs or ordinary people who do what they can to live as they think they should. We rely on our political system, as Karl Popper writes,[9] for the tradition that has

> the important double function of not only creating a certain order or something like a social structure, but also giving us something upon which we can operate; something that we can criticize and change.... If we wipe out the social world in which we live, wipe out the traditions and create a new world on the basis of blueprints, then we shall soon have to alter the new world, making little changes and adjustments. But if we are to make these little changes and adjustments, which will be needed in any case, why not start them here and now in the social world we have? Since we will always have to make them, it is very much more sensible and reasonable to start with what happens to exist at the moment, because of these things we at least know where the shoe pinches. We at least know of certain things that they are bad and that we want them changed.

What, then, should we actually do to cope with the perennial problem of conflicts if we accept, as moderate conservatives think we should, that conflicts are catalysts that prompt us to consider the relative importance of the reasons we have for and against conflicting important goods we value? We should begin by abandoning the search for a universal and context-independent GOOD to which we could appeal to resolve conflicts between particular goods. And we should realize that even if there were such a universal and context-independent GOOD, it would have to be applied to resolve conflicts in particular contexts and conditions.

---

[9] Popper, Karl R. "Towards a Rational Theory of Tradition" in *Conjectures and Refutations*. New York: Harper & Row, 1968/1948, 130–31.

How to do that unavoidably varies with contexts and conditions, and the GOOD, being universal and context-independent, could not tell us how to apply it. It could tell us only that we should apply it, but not how.

If we give up the futile search for the GOOD, then we could realize that coping with conflicts need not require us to make an all-or-nothing choice between important goods we value. We could then respond to conflicts between them by evaluating their relative importance in our particular context and conditions and make a choice between them by having more of one and less of the other. We may then respond to the conflict for example between the rule of law and liberty, or justice and equality, or security and prosperity by deciding to have more of one and less of the other. And then the conflict will catalyze us to decide which of the conflicting goods is more important in a particular context and conditions. Sometimes the conflicts will not be between primary or secondary political goods, nor between them and non-political goods, but between different ways of coping with contingencies like war, social unrest, natural disasters, criminality, economic crises, and the like.

There will, of course, be disagreements about the relative importance of the conflicting goods. In these cases we will have a standard—which will not be the GOOD—by which we can decide the relative importance of the conflicting goods. That standard is the protection of our entire political system. The reasonable choice will favor the primary or secondary political or non-political good that is more important for the protection of our entire political system that has met the test of time for 300 years than any of the goods that form part of the system. Some of these decision will be difficult because they may require decision-makers to give priority to some good or consideration other than the one to which they have an evaluative commitment. In such cases, politicians have to make difficult choices and the rest of us have to live with the consequences. The choices, however, have to be made by particular persons. All choices, political or non-political, are personal choices, even if the choosers act in their official capacity. And the choosers, being human, will be conflicted about the relative importance of the conflicting political and non-political goods. They will be motivated by the often conflicting beliefs, emotions, desires, and experiences they have formed over the years and those they have in the present in response to the immediate situation they face. They will have to decide the relative importance of the conflicting goods.

If reasonable, their decisions will be based on their understanding and evaluations of the prevailing context and conditions, the foreseeable consequences of the various available possibilities, and the likely compliance or resistance of those who will be affected by the alternatives among which they have to choose one of those currently available. None of the available alternatives will be good, because all of them will involve having less of some good they value. It is not unusual in our political system that politicians have to make such difficult choices on the basis of imperfect information and uncertainty about the consequences. The choices they make are likely to be disputed because whatever they decide will involve having less of some political or non-political good that it is their responsibility to protect. Even if they make the best possible choice in a particular context and conditions, some important good will be diminished.

In such conflicts, personal and political evaluations will be interdependent and inseparable. Embedded in them will be three different points of view. One is of the political system of the society whose protection is the responsibility of those who have to make the choices. The other is of the personal commitments from which follow the possibilities and limits of the actions that the choosers can in good conscience act on and live with. Their political and personal commitments however conflict. And then, since they have to choose to do something, there will be a third point of view in which either the personal or the political commitment will dominate the other. There will therefore typically be a threefold conflict about how to respond to difficult conflicts in difficult contexts and conditions.

Personal conflicts will be between the chooser's often conflicting beliefs, emotions, desires, and experiences that may lead them to respond differently to the choices they have to make. Political conflicts will be between the conflicting primary and secondary political goods on whose protection the political system of the chooser's society depends. And there will be a complex mixture of the often conflicting personal and the political evaluations that it is the responsibility of the decision-maker to resolve and act on.

Added to the complexities of these three kinds of conflicts will be the fact that the context and the conditions in which the choices have to be made will unavoidably change because of changing external threats to the society by enemies, competitors, and natural conditions. They will also be changing as a result of the dissatisfactions with the prevailing political arrangements by members of the society. Such dissatisfactions may be caused by crime, disease, scarcity, and by the ongoing economic, environmental, legal, medical, prudential, scientific, and technological changes that affect the society and to which appropriate responses need to be found. These are the difficulties, choices, and complexities that make conflicts perennial problems. Coping with them requires the choosers to make compromises by acting contrary to some of their own commitments. And that leads to the third perennial problem.

Compromises

Reasonable responses to contingencies and conflicts require us to evaluate of the relative importance of the available responses. The more important ones will override the less important. But if we are committed to both, then whichever we act on will involve acting contrary to the other. And the more important the unmet commitment is to being the kind of person we want to be, the worse we will feel about compromise we have to make. This will be so even if are convinced that we have done the best we could in the context and conditions in which we had to make the choice. That certainty will not annul our regret for failing to be true to one of our own commitments. The undeniable fact remains that we have knowingly and deliberately failed to act as our commitment requires us to do. We were not true to our word, loyal to those we love, conscientious in the performance of our duties, kind to those in need, and, in political contexts, we have failed to protect one of the other primary goods of the rule of law, justice, liberty, legal and political equality, or private property. No matter how good our reasons were for acting as we did, we will rightly feel that we have failed to be true to one of our own commitment.

If, say, there is an alarming increase in the murder rate and my political responsibility is to do something about it, then I may have to do what I can to strengthen the rule of law and justice. But that unavoidably requires me to curtail the liberty of those over whom I have authority. It then becomes my political responsibility to implement repressive policies: impose a curfew, increase surveillance, post undercover agents, recruit and pay informers, take resources needed elsewhere and use them to strengthen law enforcement, and so forth. Suppose that my considered judgment is that I have to enforce these repressive policies, and I do so. I will thereby act contrary to my commitment to liberty, feel responsible for it, and regret curtailing the liberty of the many innocent people who are affected by my repressive policies. I may think that I had good reasons for acting contrary to my commitment to liberty, but that does not change the fact that I have compromised my commitment to it.

If I do not regret my failure, then my commitment to liberty could not have been genuine. Even if I acted as I did and knowingly chose the lesser of two bad alternatives, and even if others agree that I have done the best I could in that wretched situation, the hard fact remains that I have failed to act according to my commitment to liberty. In such situations my commitments motivate me to act in incompatible ways. Whichever I choose to act on, I will compromise my commitment to one of them. I did what I had to do, but it was *I* who did it contrary to my own commitment. This is no longer merely the political problem of finding and implementing the best policy. It becomes my personal problem, because I am not an abstract political agent but the particular person who chose and implemented the repressive policy. It will be *I* who compromises my commitment to liberty.

Assume that I accept that from the political point of view I did the best I could; everyone who knows the relevant facts thinks that I did the right thing; and anyone in my place would have opted for repressive policies rather than liberty. From the political point of view, I did the right thing. But from my personal point of view, I have become an agent of repression and compromised my commitment to liberty. That I did it because the situation called for it does not change the fact that I have failed to be true to my commitment to liberty. Have I or have I not then failed to be the kind of person I am committed to being? The perennial problem of compromises is that the personal and political points of view diverge. This is not an abstract theoretical problem. It becomes my personal problem because although I acted in a political context, the two points of view are embedded in my commitments, and my personal evaluations that follow from them are incompatible.

The problem is not what I should do. I have decided that. It is rather that doing it has damaging consequences for being the person I think I should be. Contexts and conditions may occur in which I may have good reasons to lie to my beloved child, break a solemn promise I have made to a friend, betray a confidence, abandon my cause, or reject my country. But by acting contrary to such commitments that are formative parts of the person I am and want to be, I will be compelled to think and feel that I have failed to be true to the person I could respect.

This is a serious problem for moderate conservatives, but not only for them. It is a problem for all those who have a plurality of evaluative commitments, regardless of what they may be. It is not a new problem. The contemporary name for it is the problem of dirty hands. It derives from Jean-Paul Sartre's play[10] whose title, in translation, is "Dirty Hands." In an influential article Michael Walzer[11] initiated the extensive contemporary discussion of it. However, I will not follow this usage because the problem is very old indeed. Abraham faced it when God told him, according to *Genesis* 22, to sacrifice his beloved, son Isaac. Kierkegaard discussed Abraham's predicament as the teleological suspension of the ethical.[12] What has subsequently been called the "Pauline Principle" is clearly implied in *Romans* 3:8, 6:1, and 15 as: do nothing bad so that good may come of it. A fine discussion of it is by John Finnis.[13]

Now whatever may be said for and against doing bad for the sake of good, it is standard practice in politics. Politicians routinely act in ways that are normally regarded both by others and themselves as morally reprehensible. They tell outright lies, weasel out of telling an unpopular truth, mislead the electorate and the press, make promises and then break them, violate treaties, act contrary to the principles they avow, falsely claim to have virtues, religious commitments, moral probity, or a happy family life, which they do not have. These are mostly self-serving falsifications. But not all falsifications are self-serving.

There are important occasions on which it is the political responsibility of decision-makers to act in morally bad ways in order to bring about politically important good consequences. Politicians who are unwilling to do this, should not be in politics. In politics, as

---

[10] Sartre, Jean-Paul. "Dirty Hands" in *Three Plays*. Translated by Lionel Abel. New York: Knopf, 1946.

[11] Walzer, Michael. "Political Action: The Problem of Dirty Hands" in *Philosophy and Public Affairs* 2(1973): 160–180

[12] Kierkegaard, Soren. *Fear and Trembling*. Translated by Walter Lowrie. Princeton, NJ: Princeton University Press, 1843/1941.

[13] Finnis, John. *Fundamentals of Ethics*. Oxford: Clarendon Press, 1983, 113.

in all other areas of life in our society, different modes of evaluation may conflict and in some contexts and conditions the evaluations that follow from one mode may override evaluations that follow from another mode. When this happens we have to decide which should override which in that context and conditions. This is part of the perennial problem of conflicts about which I have already said what I could. The perennial problem of compromises is not the problem of contingencies and conflicts, but a consequence of them.

It is the personal problem of how we should go about deciding the relative importance of our personal and political commitments. This is a problem that all of us living in our society and its political system have to face whether or not we know and acknowledge it. Living in our context, being subject to its changing, contingent, and often conflicting conditions, and trying to be faithful to our commitments depends on finding and maintaining a balance between our commitments and the possibilities and limits of what we can do set by primary and secondary political goods. The problem is that we have to maintain this balance in changing contexts and conditions because both the contents of our commitments and the available possibilities and limits constantly change.

Our commitments change because our beliefs, emotions, desires, experiences, and evaluation change in response to new experiences, to what we have learned from our past successes and failures, to how we are favorably or unfavorably impressed by the lives and actions of those we encounter personally or vicariously by way of the media, books, conversation, and imaginative reconstructions of what it might be like to live in ways other than our own. And, of course, it is not just we personally who change, but also the economic, international, legal, moral, political, religious, scientific, and technological conditions that make the conditions of our society and lives what they are. As a result, the personal and the political conditions of our lives are unavoidably and inseparably connected, reciprocally influence each other, and jointly form the unstable complex conditions in which we have to make decisions about the relative importance we attribute to our personal and political commitments and the actions that follow from them.

All of us in our society have to contend with these complexities. Yet when we face actual situations in which we have decide about the relative importance of our personal and political commitments, we are rarely overwhelmed by these complexities. This is not because we can rely on an abstract theory that applies to all contexts and conditions. We do not and cannot have such a theory. We can manage to deal with the complexities if we recognize that we are called upon to make practical decisions in particular situations relying on our evaluation of the relative importance of the available possibilities.

Such evaluations depend on comparing the possibilities by asking such particular questions as: how does acting on either the personal or the political evaluation affect the humane requirements of the people involved? how seriously would our political system be affected if we gave priority to either our personal or political evaluation? would either of the difficult decision we might make be acceptable to members of our society? is the extent to which we would have to compromise our personal evaluations be serious enough to warrant our resignation from our political office? should we sacrifice our good opinion of ourselves for the good of our society? can we give a reasonable explanation to others why we have decided to act in one way or another? All of these questions are difficult and complex, but there are answers to them. Our task is to give the most reasonable answer we can in our particular context and conditions, acknowledge that it may be mistaken, and yet accept the possibility of failure. This is our condition. The perennial problem of having to make compromises is an inescapable part of it. Reasonable responses to it depend on the context and the conditions in which we have to evaluate the relative importance of the particular evaluative commitments we have made.

Since I began I also end with Isaiah Berlin's words:[14]

> To demand more than this is perhaps a deep and incurable metaphysical need; but to allow it to determine one's practice is a symptom of an equally deep, and more dangerous moral and political immaturity.

---

[14] Berlin, Isaiah. "Two Concepts of Liberty" in *Two Concepts of Liberty*. Oxford: Oxford University Press, 1969, 172.

4
The Problem and the Response

The Problem

At the end of the previous chapter I concluded that the perennial problems of adverse *contingencies, conflicts* among goods we reasonably value, and the *compromises* we have to make since we cannot have all that we reasonably value are unavoidable in human life. I concluded as well that we cannot cope with perennial problems by relying on any ideal theory that aims at an ideal of the GOOD. This leaves defenders of moderate conservatism with the problem of explaining how we should respond to perennial problems. This chapter is about that problem and the moderate conservative response to it.

I turn to the lovely concept of VUCA situations for a better understanding of the nature of the problem. Coping with VUCA situations is part of the training of British marines, and I borrow the term from their training manual. VUCA is an acronym for situations characterized by *v*olatility, *u*ncertainty, *c*omplexity, and *a*mbivalence. An important part of the training of marines is to recognize VUCA situations in which they have to act; cannot count on outside help; inaction has unacceptable consequences; all available responses involve serious risks and losses; and their task is to find the response that involves the least risk and loss in their particular context and conditions that is volatile, uncertain, complex, and make them ambivalent.

Perennial problems unavoidably create for American society and its political system VUCA situations. We need to face unforeseeable adverse contingencies, like natural disasters, scarcity of much-needed resources, epidemics, and the threat of foreign military and/or economic aggression. We need to find ways of coping first with conflicts between the primary political goods of the rule of law, justice, legal and political equality, liberty, private property. Second, between these primary political goods and quite different secondary ones, such as order, peace, prosperity, public health. And third, between general modes of evaluation, which may be aesthetic, economic, historical, literary, personal, religious, scientific, and so forth. We need to accept the necessity of making compromises between the various goods and modes of evaluation we reasonably value, and to accept as well that our compromises unavoidably involve having less of some good we reasonably value in order to have more of some other good we value more.

These VUCA situations are *volatile* because the conditions are in a state of flux as a result of causes we do not fully understand; we are dissatisfied because even our best laid plans are frustrated by unforeseeable obstacles; the available alternatives open to us are typically untried, risky, and consequently *uncertain*; the situation is *complex* because we have reasons for and against many of the available responses; and yet it is urgent that we do something, even though our knowledge of the relevant facts and of the consequences of our actions is incomplete. This makes us *ambivalent* toward all the available possibilities. These are some of the perennial problems we often face in VUCA situations.

The apparently simple ways of responding to VUCA situations are in fact not at all simple. Trying to apply the lessons we have learned from our own or others' past responses to similar situations are doomed to fail because the past contexts and conditions have been altered by the forever changing contingencies, conflicts, and compromises. We cannot look outside of VUCA situations for some overriding ideal of the GOOD because all the proposed ones are just as much subject to volatility, uncertainty, complexity, and ambivalence as the one to which we are trying to find a response. And even if, unlikely as that is, there were an uncontroversial overriding

GOOD to which we could appeal, it would still have to be applied to evaluate the relative importance of the available responses in the present VUCA situation. But for that we need to answer the just as controversial question of why the selected response is preferable to other available responses.

The volatility, uncertainty, and complexity of VUCA situations make us ambivalent because the relative importance of the possible responses to them depends on the point of view from which they are selected. That point of view may be economic, historical, legal, moral, personal, political, prudential, religious, scientific, or some other possible mode of evaluation. And the question needs to be faced and answered why that mode of evaluation, whatever it may be, is preferable to the others. How, then, according to moderate conservatives, should we go about finding reasonable responses to perennial problems that occur in VUCA situations?

A step toward identifying reasonable responses is to give up the illusion that there can be a simple answer to this question. No matter how reasonable a response may be, adverse contingencies, conflicts among the goods, and the compromises we have to make will affect all the available responses and are likely to complicate how we might identify the most reasonable one. However, even though there is no simple way of identifying the most reasonable response, there is a way. It depends on the evaluation of the relative importance of the various goods we hope to realize in the context and conditions in which we are confronted with perennial problems in VUCA situations.[1]

---

[1] "All political questions are infinitely complicated, and . . . there scarcely ever occurs, in any deliberation, a choice, which is either purely good, or purely ill. Consequences, mixed and varied, may be foreseen to flow from every measure: And many consequences, unforeseen, do always, in fact, result from every one. Hesitation, and reserve, and suspense, are, therefore, the only sentiments [the philosopher] . . . brings to this . . . trial. Or if he indulges in any passion, it is that of derision against the ignorant multitude, who are always clamorous and dogmatical, even in the nicest questions, of which from want of temper, perhaps still more than of understanding, they are altogether unfit judges."
Hume, David. "Of the Protestant Succession" in *Essays Moral Political and Literary*. Indianapolis: Liberty Press, 1741/1999, 507

The reasonable answer is to give priority to the most important of these goods. That, of course, depends on deciding which of them is in a particular context and conditions more important than the others. Given the plurality of many different modes of evaluation and many different kinds of goods, it is bound to be arbitrary to assume that one of the many goods will always be more important than the others regardless of how contexts and conditions may change.

There is however another and different evaluation that is neither hopeless nor arbitrary. It is to identify and give priority to the good that in that particular situation would minimize our unavoidable losses of other goods caused by the contingencies, conflicts, and compromises we face. Identifying that good will not depend on making a yes-or-no decision about the relative importance of the goods involved in that situation. It will be a decision about which of the goods we should have less of in order to have more of the others. We will suffer losses. The reasonable response is the one that minimizes our losses.

Moderate conservatives think that reasonable responses to perennial problems in VUCA situations are to be found in three increasingly general contexts and conditions. There is in each a standard on which we can rely for the evaluation of the relative importance of available responses, but none of these standards is universal and overriding as the standard set by a supposed GOOD is supposed to be. All the goods affected by perennial problems in all VUCA situations are plural and vary in their relative importance as contexts and conditions vary. And as they vary, so do the relevant standards on which reasonable evaluations of their relative importance depend. These standards increase in generality as we consider, first, the relative importance of the primary political goods; then of all the goods be they primary, secondary, political or non-political, and last of the great variety of often incompatible modes of evaluation. These are the complexities we have to contend with as we make decisions in VUCA situations. We do so by relying on one of the multiplicity of conceptions of how we should live that in changing contexts and conditions guide our personal attitudes. This is one of the consequences of evaluative diversity:

> The region of the ethical is a region of diverse, certainly incompatible and possibly practically conflicting ideal images or pictures of a human life, or of human life; and it is a region in which many such incompatible pictures may secure at least the imaginative, though doubtless not often practical, allegiances of a single person. Moreover this statement itself may be seen not merely as a description of what is the case, but as a positive evaluation of evaluative diversity. Any diminution in this variety would impoverish the human scene. The multiplicity of conflicting pictures is itself the essential element in one's pictures of man.[2]

Strawson rightly notes that any diminution in this multiplicity diminishes the riches of our lives, but he does not mention that with the riches come the complexities of perennial problems and VUCA situations. Moderate conservatives stress that just as conflicts between the goods we value is not a symptom of irrationality but a catalyst spurring us to decide what we regard as of more and what of less importance for how we live, so the complexities of possible responses to VUCA situations enrich the possibilities open to us as we contend with perennial problems in changing contexts and conditions. Ideal theorists who rely on some conception of the GOOD do not understand that their ideal impoverishes human possibilities. They see evaluative complexities and multiplicity as regrettable consequences of faulty personal attitudes. Moderate conservatives see them as welcome consequences of the riches of human possibilities.[3]

[2] Strawson, P.F. "Social Morality and Individual Ideal" in *Freedom and Resentment*. London: Methuen, 1974, 29.
[3] "Neither in the social order, nor in the experience of an individual, is a state of conflict the sign of vice, or defect, or malfunctioning. It is not a deviation from the normal state of a city or of a nation, and it is not a deviation from the normal course of a person's experience.

Just as it would be destructive of art if there were such a thing as the perfect work of art that artists can only try to approximate, so it would be destructive of human possibilities if there were such a thing as the GOOD that we should all try to approximate. It is life-enhancing that art, history, literature, and science are open-ended, and so it is an enrichment of our lives that the evaluative dimensions of human lives are open-ended. Open-endedness liberates, closure impoverishes. Moderate conservatives recognize the need to set limits, but they value the open-endedness of the possibilities of political and non-political goods, of modes of evaluations, and of personal attitudes. The politics of the ideal of the GOOD limits the possibilities as well.

Complex Evaluations

According to moderate conservatives, political and non-political views must contend with the complexities that follow if they acknowledge that reasonable evaluations of the relative importance of incompatible goods, modes of evaluation, and personal attitudes depend on complex more-or-less, not simple yes-or-no, evaluations. In this respect, Moderate conservatives follow Aristotle.[4] These complex evaluations need to be made in particular VUCA situations, and in three different contexts.

To follow through the ethical implications of these propositions about the normality of conflict... a kind of conversion is needed, a new way of looking at all the virtues."
Hampshire, Stuart. *Justice Is Conflict.* Princeton, NJ: Princeton University Press, 2000, 33–34.

[4] "The whole account of matters of conduct must be given in outline and not precisely... matters concerned with conduct and questions of what is good for us have no fixity.... The general account being of this nature, the account of particular cases is yet more lacking in exactness; for they do not fall under any art or precepts, but the agents must in each case consider what is appropriate to the occasion."
Aristotle. *Nicomachean Ethics*, 1104a1-6. Translated by W.D. Ross. Revised by J.O. Urmson. In *The Complete Works of Aristotle*. Edited by Jonathan Barnes. Princeton, NJ: Princeton University Press. c.340 BC/1984.

In the first, the evaluation is of the relative importance of the primary political goods of the rule of law, justice, legal and political equality, liberty, and private property. In the second, more general, context, the evaluation is of the relative importance, not of goods, but of the modes of evaluation from which economic, legal, moral, personal, political, religious, and other goods follow. In the third, the evaluation is of the relative importance of the personal attitudes of members of American society and of the protection of the entire American political system that includes all the various political and non-political goods, modes of evaluation, and personal attitudes. On each level, there is a standard to which reasonable responses should conform, but all the standards, as well as the political and non-political goods, modes of evaluations, and personal attitudes depend on the prevailing context and conditions. In the contexts and conditions of other societies, the relative importance of the goods, modes, of evaluations, personal attitudes, and of the entire political system is all too likely to be evaluated differently. This is one of the reasons why the ideal theorists' appeal to the supposed standard of the GOOD is doomed to fail.[5]

Consider then the familiar question on the first level about the relative importance of two primary political goods, for instance between liberty and the rule of law, or between justice and equality. The beginning of a reasonable response is to get away from the abstractions of theories. The question arises in the context and conditions of our society here and now. We have a strong

---

[5] "To assume that all values can be graded on one scale, so that it is a mere matter of inspection to determine the highest, seems to me to falsify our knowledge that men are free agents, to represent moral decision as an operation which a slide-rule could, in principle, perform. It is more humane because it does not (as system builders do) deprive men, in the name of some remote, or incoherent, ideal, of much that they have found to be indispensable to their life as ... self-transforming human beings. In the end, men choose between ultimate values; they choose as they do ... by fundamental moral categories and concepts that are ... part of their being and thought and sense of their own identity; part of what makes them human."
Berlin, Isaiah. "Two Concepts of Liberty" in *Four Essays on Liberty*. Oxford: Oxford University Press, 1969, 171–72.

commitment to both of the conflicting goods and have to evaluate their relative importance in our particular and changing conditions. They are important personally to each of us and generally for the protection of our political system. We need to understand how we and others would be affected if our liberty were curtailed, if the rule of law broke down, if we could not count on justice, and if our legal or political equality were in jeopardy. And then we become defenders of the violated political good and oppose those who appeal to another political good that is supposedly more important than the one we feel strongly about.

Such disputes about the relative importance of primary political goods often become impassioned, and those on opposing sides of it come to see each other as enemies. Such passions blind us to the fact that the primary political goods are all necessary for the protection of the American political system on which our own as well as everyone else's well-being in our society depends. Instead of excoriating each other, we should moderate our animosity and acknowledge that preferring one primary political good to another need not be a perverse or a wicked choice, but one that may be supported by thoughtfully arrived at reasons. If no primary political good is always the overriding GOOD, then there may be contexts and conditions in which any of the primary political goods may prove to be more important than any one of the others. And it complicates matters even more if we bear in mind that coping with adverse contingencies in some cases, as in natural disasters, foreign aggression, scarcity of necessary resources, and so forth, may be more important than any protection of the primary political goods.[6]

Reasonable and politically experienced people in American society would not think that such decision involve denying the

---

[6] "There is no consideration of any kind that overrides all other considerations in all conceivable circumstances."
Hampshire, Stuart. *Innocence and Experience*. London: Allen Lane, 1989, 172.

importance of any of the primary political goods. They would understand that the well-being of our society and of our own depends on the primary political goods and on our evaluations of their relative importance. And that, in turn, depends on finding some compromise that involves having more of one and less of the other. We have to decide in particular contexts and conditions how much we can give up of one in order to have more of another. The resulting compromise will leave us dissatisfied, because any compromise we might make would unavoidably secure less of the political good we would like to have more of.

If we are reasonable, we will realize that the compromise is nevertheless worth making because it would make us less dissatisfied than we would be if we had neither of the primary political goods we favor. Reasonable and experienced politicians recognize and accept that we frequently have to make such compromises and that they are everyday facts in political life. Ideal theorists and politically naïve people fail to accept it, talk about betrayal and the loss of integrity, and that makes their political judgments dangerously misguided.[7]

The political mode of evaluation that has emerged in the course of the history of the American political system involves a cumbersome decentralized process of give and take in trying to find compromises that defenders and critics of the primary political goods both find acceptable, even as they rue having to do so. The search for it is decentralized because it will yield different results in different contexts, conditions, localities, cities, states, and occasionally in the country as a whole. This is just the nature of the political mode of evaluation in American society. Its results will always

---

[7] "The virtue assigned to the affairs of the world is a virtue with many bends, angles, and elbows, so as to adapt itself to human weakness; mixed and artificial, not straight, clean, constant, or purely innocent. . . . He who walks in the crowd must step aside, keep his elbows in, step or advance, even leave the straight way, according to what he encounters . . . according to the time, according to the men, according to the business." Montaigne, Michel. *The Complete Works of Montaigne*. Translated by Donald M. Frame. Stanford: Stanford University Press, 1588/1943, 758.

and unavoidably leave many of us dissatisfied. But if we understand the reasons for our dissatisfactions—a big if—and if we are not so deeply dissatisfied as to want to leave our society, then the political mode of evaluation can be relied on to lead to a way of evaluating the relative importance of primary political goods when we cannot have as much of both as we would like.

This, however, is far from the end of the matter because there will be perennial problems also on the second level. It will not be between political goods, but between economic, legal, moral, political, religious, and other modes of evaluations, among which the political mode is only one. The evaluation of the relative importance of the goods that follows from these different modes of evaluation will often differ. No matter how important political goods are supposed to be from the point of view of the political mode of evaluation, their importance is likely to seem very different from the point of view of an economic, legal, moral, or religious mode of evaluation. So the complexities of coping with first level conflicts between primary political goods lead to even greater complexities on the second level between modes of evaluation.

Once again, the relative importance of various modes of evaluation depends on the context and the available alternatives among which a choice has to be made. It makes a great difference whether the context of the evaluation is raging inflation, or the urgent need to control crime syndicates, or the case for and against legalizing drugs, or decriminalizing voluntary euthanasia, or religious intolerance, and so on and on. Whichever mode of evaluation is given priority in a particular context and its conditions, it remains controversial how far its priority can reasonably go in overriding conflicting evaluations that follow from other modes of evaluation that defend other political or non-political goods.[8]

---

[8] "The basic concern of morality is with how to conduct ourselves in our relations with other people. Now why should *that* be, always and in all circumstances,, the most important thing in our lives? No doubt it is important; but, so far as I am aware, there is no convincing argument that it must invariably override everything else."

Political theorists respond to such disputed questions of priority by claiming that one of the primary political goods is always, in all contexts and conditions, more important than any of the others. They then need to single out the particular primary political good that they claim should be recognized by all reasonable and adequately informed people as one that is in all conflicts, contexts, conditions, and at all times and places is more important than any of the others. The problem with this response is to give reasons for the "should" in that claim.

The "should" cannot be reasonably thought to follow from any one of the goods or modes of evaluation because the question is why any good or any mode of evaluation should always have priority over the others. That question cannot be answered by the mere assertion that one of them should be. Why should any one of the primary political goods of the rule of law, justice, legal and political equality, liberty, or private property *always* be more important than any of the others? There is no way of telling what adverse contingencies may arise in the future, or what consequences it may have in other contexts and conditions to give priority to one of the primary political goods. Perhaps the evaluation of its importance rests on factual mistakes, or on ignorance of available alternatives, or on overwrought emotions, or on inconsistent or unexamined preferences or aversions, or have incalculable and possibly dangerous consequences.

Moderate conservatives deny that a reasonable context-independent and unconditional priority could or should be given to any of the primary political goods. In the changing contexts and conditions of perennial problems in VUCA situations there is no *always*. There is at best a particular reasonable evaluation that gives priority to one of the primary political goods in a particular context and conditions, but it cannot be generalized to other contexts

Frankfurt, Harry G. *Taking Ourselves Seriously & Getting It Right*. Stanford, CA: Stanford University Press, 2006, 28.

and conditions. For this and the preceding reasons, the problem of coping with reasonable but disputed evaluations of the relative importance of primary political goods remains open on the second level.

However, the problems can be approached on the third level from the point of view of the American political system in its entirety. That point of view includes the protection of all the political goods and all the shared modes of evaluations that have come to be regarded as having primary importance in the course of the history of our society. Resolving disputes between reasonable but disputed evaluations of their relative importance is always difficult because choosing between them depends on informed political evaluation, hands-on political experience, and the realistic weighing of the reasons for and against the available alternatives.[9]

This is not a hopeless problem if we bear in mind two considerations. One is that everyone's well-being in our society depends on maintaining our political system. The other is that we do have a guide for the evaluation of the alternative possibilities and limits: the Constitution. This is a crucial step toward the reasonable evaluation of the relative importance of conflicting goods and modes of evaluation, but it is not the end of the perennial problems that we must recognize and cope with. There will still remain two points of view from which we can evaluate the relative importance of various goods and modes of evaluation: the well-being of the society as a whole and the well-being of individual members of American society.

---

[9] "The conditions of deliberation are, then, an agent. . . not knowing for certain what the future will be. . . . The materials at [his] disposal . . . are prudential maxims, 'opinions about things that could happen otherwise,' or they may be general precepts of indeterminate relevance, or mythical beliefs about the world he inhabits, or homemade conclusions about the persons and circumstances concerned. They may be more or less reliable, but they are not flickering shadows of necessary truths or premisses from which conclusions can be deduced. They are aids to deliberation, guesses of varying generality, made with different degrees of confidence and drawing upon evidence of varying quality."

Oakeshott, Michael. *On Human Conduct*. Oxford: Clarendon Press, 1975, 44–45.

This is perhaps the most difficult of all the problems of the evaluation of the relative importance of primary political goods and modes of evaluation. For the choice we have to make is whether we want to continue to live in the society that has been our home for a long time, or leave it for another. This is a choice we all make, whether we realize it or not. For if we stay, we thereby choose to put up with the many dissatisfactions caused by the compromises we and others in our society have to make between the various conflicting goods, modes of evaluation, and the various extents to which we are willing to change our personal attitude to conform more closely to the political system of our society. If we understand that having to face this existential VUCA situation is part of life in our society, then we will be less likely to abuse those who evaluate the reasons for and against the compromises we all have to make differently from the way we do it. Reasonable people in VUCA situations may be guided by different personal attitudes and evaluate differently whether they should remain in their society and put up with their dissatisfaction with its political system, or leave their society and move elsewhere. What approach then do moderate conservatives recommend we should follow when we face a VUCA situation in which our personal attitude and political system motivate us to act in contrary ways?

Personal Attitudes and Our Political System

The point of departure for moderate conservatives in our present context and conditions is the obvious observation that although we participate in our political system there is very little we can do to change it, were we to wish to do so. We can certainly vote and express in various ways such dissatisfactions as we have with it, but we have no realistic hope of changing the elephantine system and its all-pervasive bureaucracy we encounter in innumerable aspects of our life. There is no doubt that we are all dissatisfied with it in various ways. If we take the trouble to think beyond our dissatisfactions, we will also remember the countless satisfactions we derive from its overall, but far from faultless, protection of the rule of law, justice, legal and political equality, liberty, private property. We count on the political system to continue to provide the conditions in which each of us can live according to our personal attitude.[10]

This is not to deny that we have various dissatisfactions with it, and that some of us have reasons to be more dissatisfied than others. The fact remains, however, that our satisfactions with it far outweigh our dissatisfactions. The great majority of Americans every day of their lives cast their votes in favor of the political system, whether they know it or not. They do so by their continued voluntary participation in it when they could leave it and move elsewhere if they wished to do so. And this has been so for a long time during which millions of immigrants have opted to live in it and very few indeed have chosen to leave it for another political system. These facts are the moderate conservative's point of departure. I will refer to it by saying that our political system has met the test of time.

If our personal attitudes to how we should live are reasonable, then we acknowledge these facts and go on from them to think about the sources of the undoubted dissatisfactions we all share as a result of having to face perennial problems in VUCA situations. These dissatisfactions are part of the human condition in general, not just the products of our political system. They are and will continue to be part of human lives regardless of what political system we participate in. And they would persist even if it were possible—which it is not—to construct a political system that is dedicated to the pursuit of the final and incontrovertible ideal of the GOOD.

---

[10] "Human beings have done many more fetching and elegant things than invent and routinize the modern democratic republic. But, in the face of their endlessly importunate, ludicrously indiscreet chaotic and always potentially murderous onrush of needs and longings, they have, even now, done few things as solidly to their advantage."
Dunn, John. *The Cunning of Unreason*. New York: Basic Books, 2000, 363.

What then do moderate conservatives think should the relation be between our personal attitude and political system? This question is as old as politics. The history of political thought is a history of the reasons that have been given why one should dominate the other. Moderate conservatives deny that either should be dominant. They recognize that the evaluations that follow from personal attitudes and those that follow from the political system of our society are both necessary for living as we reasonably think we should, and that neither is alone sufficient for it. Yet our personal attitudes often lead us to be dissatisfied with our political system and political evaluations often set limits to the possibilities our personal attitudes may lead us to value. This is one main reason why we may be dissatisfied with our political system.

Moderate conservatives acknowledge the dissatisfactions but deny that coping with them requires us to give priority to one or the other. They deny that the reasonable approach to coping with our dissatisfactions depends on relying a standard like the categorical imperative, natural law, the authority of a great thinker or of a great treatise, the common good, individual or general happiness, or on being guided by virtue, faith, or altruism. And they deny as well that if these or some yet to be discovered principle, rule, theory, or authority is spurned, then we are doomed to sink into irrationality and its awful consequences. How then should we respond to our dissatisfactions with our political system?

Moderate conservatives think that we should look for a way of finding a balance between the evaluations that follow from our personal attitude and political system.[11] Finding it depends on understanding the prevailing conditions, the relative importance of the

---

[11] "To balance a large state or society . . . is a work of so great difficulty, that no human genius, however comprehensive, is able, by the mere dint of reason and reflection, to effect it. The judgments of many unite in this work: Experience must guide their labour: Time must bring it to perfection. And the feeling of inconveniences must correct the mistakes, which they inevitably fall into, in their first trials and experiments."
Hume, David. "The Rise of Arts and Sciences" in *Essays Moral Political and Literary*. Edited by Eugene F. Miller. Indianapolis: LibertyClassics, 1777/1985, 124.

personal and political evaluations, and whether the consequences would change our personal attitude and the political system of our society for the better or the worse. As moderate conservatives see it, one main aim of our political system is to maintain this balance in ever-changing conditions between our personal and political evaluations. If found, it would follow from it how far the political system should go in curtailing our personal attitude, and how far our personal attitude should go in following our own evaluations even if they conflict with the evaluations that follow from our political system. There is no general answer to the question of what the reasonable balance is. It can be found, but it is always a particular one that depends on the prevailing conditions, on the actual contents of the particular personal and political evaluations, and on the available alternatives in the context in which the balance is sought. Finding that balance in difficult times is what makes politicians into statesmen. This is what the Federalists and Lincoln succeeded in doing.

Finding that reasonable balance between them is not as difficult as it may seem because our personal attitude and the political system of our society overlap, and because, although some of our personal evaluations are directed inward and concern mainly ourselves, some of the others are directed outward and concern not just ourselves but also others and our society. In many cases, personal and political evaluations are inseparable. We are born into both a family and a political system. As we grow up, we are taught hundreds of evaluations of what we can and cannot, should and should not do; how we should treat others and they us; how to distinguish between what is ours and what is not; who are and who are not family members, friends, and strangers; we learn about what is and what is not important, about sickness and health, private and public, debts and gifts, time and distance, truth and lies; about rules, exceptions, and impossibilities; and so on for hundreds of categories, distinctions, evaluations, expressions, and identifications.

As we learn all this, we simultaneously develop the rudiments of our personal attitude and learn about the simpler elements of the political system of our society. During our childhood they are for us indistinguishable. As we grow up, we gradually learn to distinguish between them and to question some or many of the various evaluations we have been taught and learned. But we do not just question them. We question some while relying on others that we at least temporarily do not question. Many of the evaluations we learn in our early years stay with us throughout our lives. So the connections between our personal attitude and the political system are not usually ones in which we must opt either for one or the other. In countless everyday contexts, personal and political evaluations coincide, rather than diverge.

Sometimes, however, they do diverge, and then we routinely evaluate their relative importance in the context in which they diverge without inflating their divergence into tragic conflicts. We do decide without great difficulty whether we should make a political contribution or take a vacation; tell the truth or obfuscate it for political reasons; continue to support a cause even though we suspect that it has been corrupted; and so. Only rarely do we have to face momentous conflicts in which we have to make a difficult choice between remaining true either to our personal attitude or to the political system of our society. In such conflicts, no compromise is possible. But few of us who live in a civilized society ever encounter them. This in fact is one of the advantages of living in our society.

It misrepresents everyday connections between personal and political evaluations to inflate them, as self-dramatizing people do, into tragic conflicts, like those faced by Oedipus, Antigone, or Orestes. Unlike tragic figures, we often fudge our everyday conflicts, acknowledge both personal and social evaluations, and use innocuous socially acceptable anemic phrases—adjustment, coming to terms, making do, splitting the difference—to describe reasonable compromises we make between them. In doing this, we are prudent, not hypocritical. Ideal theorists tend to spurn such prudent compromises, but by doing that they disqualify themselves from participation in reasonable political life.[12]

Nevertheless, sometimes we do have wrenching conflicts between important evaluations that follow from our personal attitude and political evaluations that follow from our political system. Reasonable responses to unfudgeable conflicts between our important evaluations, depend on considering the consequences of the decisions we might make about how we should respond to them. On the whole, our political system is better protected by the primary political goods and public opinion than our personal attitudes. Advocates of the re-evaluation of all values, legal, moral, political, and religious fanatics usually and fortunately have few followers in our society. Moderation leads prudent people to avoid extremes and to be reluctant to endanger the life they have made for themselves.

Personal attitudes are far more fragile than the political system of our society. The consequences of our violation of one of our own important moral, political, or religious evaluations may diminish our self-respect, make us feel ashamed, guilty, gnawed by regret, and degrade our personal attitude. We can, if we must, become indifferent to being condemned by others, but we cannot be indifferent to our own condemnation of ourselves. In most ordinary conflicts between personal and social evaluations, when the decisions we have to make concern mostly our personal affairs, not the political conditions of our society, the balance of evaluations tilts toward giving priority to our personal evaluations over the political ones.[13]

---

[12] "The virtue assigned to the affairs of the world is a virtue with many bends, angles, and elbows, so as to join and adapt itself to human weakness; mixed and artificial, not straight, clean, constant, or purely innocent. . . .whoever escapes with clean breaches from handling the affairs of the world, escapes by a miracle."
Montaigne, Michel. *The Complete Works of Montaigne*. Translated by Donald M. Frame. Stanford: Stanford University Press, 1588/1943, 758–59.

[13] Few would disagree with Smith's eloquent observation that "the care of the universal happiness of all rational and sensible beings is the business of God, and not man.

This view is embedded in the political system of our society. It assumes that we are guided by our personal attitude and that it includes social evaluations that follow from the modes of evaluation of our society. Our personal attitude is our own. It embodies our sense of what is and what is not important, or what is more or less important. But it is not personal in the quite different sense that it is directed only inward toward what we regard as our own interests or happiness. Of course we care about that, but we also care about some of our economic, legal, moral, political, religious, and other social evaluations that are directed outward, and often have only indirect and remote bearing on our own well-being.

No matter how reasonable and well-ordered is our personal attitude, how well-attuned it is to our political system, how well the political system meets the test of time, we will remain vulnerable to the perennial problems of adverse contingencies; to conflicts between the political and non-political goods and the modes of evaluation to which we are committed; and we will have to compromise some of our evaluative commitments. We will therefore be dissatisfied.

Moderate conservatives think that such dissatisfactions are unavoidable part of life even in the best of all contexts and conditions. We expect it to be otherwise, but this widely shared expectation will not be met. We remain vulnerable to perennial problems, and that is the deepest source of our personal and political dissatisfactions. What, then, we should do about it? We should teach ourselves to abandon the expectation and cultivate instead negative capability.

To man is allotted a much humbler department, but one that is much more suitable to the weakness of his powers, and to the narrowness of his comprehension—the care of his own happiness, of that of his family, his friends, his country: that he is occupied in contemplating the more sublime, can never be an excuse for his neglecting the more humble department."
  Smith, Adam. *The Theory of Moral Sentiments*. Indianapolis: LibertyClassics, 1853/1976, 386.

Negative Capability

The phrase is from a letter of that great wordsmith, John Keats.[14] Negative capability is an attitude of the acceptance of the complexities of life. It is the very opposite of a theory. It is the realization that we often have to make serious decisions about our life in VUCA situations on the basis of imperfect knowledge, mixed emotions, and often confused desires. We know that the decision is important, that it is ours to make, and that it will have consequences we have to live with. Such a decision, in Bacon's apt phrase, is a "wager of thought." We cannot get out of making the wager by turning to a theory, any theory, for help. Theories are by their very nature general and our decision is unavoidably personal and particular. It depends on our evaluation of what is and what is not important for us then and there in that situation. We have to decide what combination of which of our various beliefs, emotions, and desires we should act on, and whether we could and would wish to live with the possible consequences of the decision we might make. Negative capability is to accept that this is how it is for many of us at important junctures of life. It is to accept that[15]

> such is the disorder and confusion of human affairs, that no perfect or regular distribution of happiness and misery is ever, in this life, to be expected. Not only the goods of fortune, and the endowments of the body (both of which are important), not only these advantages, I say, are unequally divided between the virtuous and the vicious, but even the mind itself partakes, in some degree, of this disorder, and the most worthy character, by

---

[14] "I mean *Negative Capability*, that is, when a man is capable of being in uncertainties, Mysteries, doubts, without any irritable reaching after fact and reason."
Keats, John. Letter to George and Thomas Keats, December 21, 1817. Cited in Walter Jackson Bate, *John Keats*. Cambridge, MA: Harvard University Press, 1963, 249.

[15] Hume, David. "The Sceptic" in *Essays Moral Political and Literary*. Edited by Eugene F. Miller. Indianapolis: LibertyClassics, 1777/1985, 159–60.

the very constitution of the passions, enjoys not the highest felicity.... In a word, human life is more governed by fortune than by reason ... and is more influenced by particular humour, than by general principles.

It may be said against this that Hume underestimates the resources of reason. Reasonable people will accept that reason is fallible and that fortune—moral luck, in the current idiom—in the form of perennial problems is part of life. But they will also say that we can rely on reason to respond to these familiar facts of life. Now moderate conservatives certainly accept that we should rely on reason in doing the best we can to respond to perennial problems. The acceptance of that, however, is a useless attitude unless it specifies what reliance on reason guides us to do when we face perennial problems in a particular VUCA situation that is volatile, we are uncertain about the complex possibilities of action, and that makes us ambivalent about what we should do. The injunction to rely on reason is vacuous verbiage as useless as it is to be told that we should do our duty, be guided by good will, aim at the common good, or act virtuously. What we do not know is what these inspiring spurs to action actually prompt us to do in a VUCA situation. Unless we are told what specific action would be an appropriate expression of reason, we are left in the same state of indecision as we were before we were given this uplifting talking-to. If we knew what we should do, we would not need to be told to search for and then act as reason commands. And if we do not know what we should do, telling us that we should rely on reason is an irritant, not a helpful suggestion.

Another unsatisfactory answer, as I have argued again and again, is to rely on the GOOD, and suppose that it is the standard to which we can appeal to decide what is and what is not reasonable. We cannot do that because the standard to which we appeal must itself be reasonable. How do we find out then what the reasonable standard is? How do we tell the difference between reasonable and unreasonable standards? If we press these questions, as reason requires, whenever yet another putative standard of reason is provided, then we realize that the proposed standard needs also to be shown to be reasonable, and so on *ad infinitum*. And then we come up against Hume's devastating point that

> if reason be considered in an abstract view, it furnishes invincible arguments against itself.[16]

What, then, do Moderates suggest, since they certainly are committed to reason? They suggest that we should not consider reason in an abstract view. We should not ask what makes a particular action reasonable. We should ask what makes a particular decision reasonable in a particular context and conditions.

Reason considered in an abstract view treats "reason" as a noun, implying that there is an object to which "reason" refers. So reason is reified, and then the search for it begins the never ending questioning of what makes the latest candidate really reason. Moderates do not think of "reason" as a noun that refers to an object. They think of it as an adjective, as in a "reasonable" action. Reason, then, is understood by Moderates as a desirable characteristic of reasonable actions. And the question becomes how we can tell whether an action is reasonable. An answer to it is the well-known and influential one given by Donald Davidson.[17] Another is given by Moderates.

As I understand it, Davidson is not proposing a theory of rationality, nor is he appealing to any conception of the GOOD. He is concerned with answering the question of how we should go about

---

[16] Hume, David. *Dialogues Concerning Natural Religion*. Indianapolis: Hackett, 1779/1980, 8.
[17] Davidson, Donald. "How Is Weakness of Will Possible?" in *Essays on Actions and Events*. Oxford: Clarendon Press, 1980, 21–42, and "Paradoxes of Irrationality" in *Philosophical Essays on Freud*. Edited by Richard Wollheim and James Hopkins. Cambridge: Cambridge University Press, 1982, 289–305.

making a reasonable decision about what we should do. And he approaches it indirectly by asking what would make an action unreasonable. He asks, rhetorically,[18]

> Why would anyone perform and action when the thought, everything considered, another action would be better? . . . [And he answers] if the question is read, what is the agent's reason for doing *a* when he believes when he believes that it would be better, all things considered, to do another thing, then the answer must be: for this, the agent has no reason.

Davidson's answer is that we act reasonably if we take into account all relevant considerations and decide on that basis what we think would be the best thing to do. His answer is contextual, conditional, and allows that an action that is reasonable in one situation may not be reasonable in another. And an action is unreasonable if we fail to take into all relevant considerations. This view has the great merit of not reifying reason, not deriving it from a theory, or a universal standard of rationality, or of appealing to an ideal of the GOOD. It avoids relying on a standard, which then needs be justified by another standard, and thus it avoids Hume's skepticism about reason. And another of its great merits is that it recognizes that reasonable decisions vary with contexts and conditions, and, at the same time, provides a clear explanation of what makes decisions reasonable or unreasonable. Nevertheless, Davidson's view is flawed, and it strengthens the Moderate view to understand where Davidson's goes wrong.

It promises that if we consider all things and decide on that basis what is best thing to do, then we will arrive at what would be a reasonable action. But this promise will not be met. It goes wrong because it fails to realize that when we take into account all relevant considerations in order to evaluate what the best thing to do is, then

---

[18] "Weakness," 40.

our evaluation will depend on the mode of evaluation from which are evaluating what is the best. What that is supposed to be will vary whether we are asking it from the point of view of an economic, legal, medical, moral, political, prudential, religious, or scientific mode of evaluation. So we need an additional reason to explain why the particular mode of evaluation from whose point of view we evaluate what is the best is the right mode of evaluation. The search for a reasonable explanation of that encounters two problems that it cannot satisfactorily meet.

One is that whatever the mode of evaluation is from whose point of view we evaluate what the best is, our evaluation may be based on advertising, dogmatism, haste, impatience with complexities, indoctrination, prejudice, propaganda, and so on. We may be convinced that we have considered all things, but in fact we have not because the evaluation we arrive at is not ours, but foisted on us by the increasingly sophisticated techniques used by the expert manipulators of Amazon, Twitter, Facebook, TV, and the press. We may think that we have considered all relevant things and we have arrived at an evaluation of what is the best thing to do—which is usually to buy something—and we may be mistaken. What seems to us is the best may not be the best. And even if we managed to escape all this manipulation, what we think is the best may be based on our own dogmatism, ignorance, prejudice, self-deception, stupidity, or misunderstanding. We cannot know that we have considered all things because the belief that we have done so would have to be based on the consideration of all things, and so endlessly on.

The other problem with Davidson's view is that if we have managed to avoid the first problem, then we encounter perennial problems in VUCA situations that are volatile, uncertain, complex, we are ambivalent, and we do not know what, so to speak, the best is. If we declare that *a* is the best, then we have to explain what makes what we take to be the best really the best. And then we are back at Hume's problem of needing a standard that makes the best the best, and then we start sliding down the slippery slope of infinite regress that Hume says is an invincible argument against reason. Davidson's answer is flawed because it ignores the difficulties created by the perennial problems of adverse contingencies, conflicting evaluations, and having to compromise what we think is good in order to protect something else we think is also good.

Davidson's view therefore is not an acceptable response to the realization that we often have to face inescapable perennial problems in VUCA situation. Negative capability is to realize and accept that this is part of life, a consequence of the plurality of political and non-political goods, of modes of evaluation, and of the changing contexts and conditions in which we must live, if we live at all. How then should we go about making reasonable decisions about how we should live if we give up the futile pursuit of the GOOD and cultivate negative capability?

Toward Reasonable Actions

We should accept, first of all, that this question does not have a simple and general answer that will point at *the* reasonable action. What that is depends on the nature of the situation, on what particular adverse contingencies we face, on the particular goods and modes of evaluation that conflict, on what the goods are that we may compromise and the ones that we aim to protect. And that, in turn, it depends as well on the balance of our beliefs, emotions, desires, and experiences that have formed our personal attitude, and on our particular dissatisfactions with the political system of our society. The answer to the question is therefore complex and varies with contexts, conditions, and persons.

The complexity of the answer, however, does not prevent us from acting reasonably in the countless situations of everyday life. This is so because we can rely on the political system of our society that has met the test of time; we can participate in the conventional life of our society; most of the time know what we owe to others and they to us; count on common decencies based on modes of evaluation we share with the many people to whom we are connected informally or formally, intimately or casually, personally or socially. We are not usually at war with each other. Nor are we usually assailed by wrenching conflicts in our inner lives. We certainly are vulnerable to perennial problems and we do have to struggle with making reasonable decisions in VUCA situations, but the great merit of our society is that most of the time we can rely on our political system to protect the conditions that enable us to live as we want and on the personal attitude we have formed by a process of trial and error that we began in childhood and end only when we do.

The most important aim of the politics of moderation that this book is intended to defend is the protection of this vital center of our political system and our personal attitudes to how we should live. And its protection is from immoderate political activists who indefensibly arrogate to themselves the pretended moral authority to make fundamental changes to our 300-year-old political system in which we do what we can, for better or worse, more or less reasonably and successfully to live as we think we should. They claim to know better than we do how we should live, and they condemn those who disagree of being enemies of the GOOD.

Moderate conservatives follow Aristotle[19] in responding to political immoderation:

> Those who think that all excellence is to be found in their own party principles push matters to extremes; they do not consider that disproportion destroys a state. A nose which varies from the ideal of straightness to a hook or snub may still be of good shape and agreeable to the eye; but if the excess is very great, all

---

[19] Aristotle. *Politics*, 1309b22-27. Translated by J. Solomon. In *The Complete Works of Aristotle*. Edited by Jonathan Barnes. Princeton, NJ: Princeton University Press, c.340 BC/1984

symmetry is lost, and the nose at last ceases to be a node at all on account of some excess in one direction or defect in the other.

None of this is intended to deny that we do face perennial problems, that sometimes we do find ourselves in VUCA situations, that neither our political system, nor are our personal attitudes free of adverse contingencies, conflicts, and compromises. It is to remind ourselves what we should protect and, if need be, correct; why it is crucial to do so; and to seek reasonable ways of doing it. The most important of these ways is the protection of the primary political goods of the rule of law, justice, liberty, legal and political equality, and private property on which both our political system and personal attitudes depend. The five chapters that follow are about how we can reasonably contend with the contingencies, conflicts, and compromises that endanger these primary political goods.

5
The Rule of Law

There is a body of exceptionally high quality and yet controversial jurisprudential work on how the concept of the rule of law should be understood.[1] I am indebted to it, learned from it, and gratefully acknowledge it. What follows in this chapter draws on it, but it is not intended as a contribution to it. It has the modest aim of understanding the importance of the Constitution and the rule of law in the American political system:

> This Constitution, and the laws of the United States which shall be made in Pursuance thereof, and all the Treaties made, or which shall be made, under the Authority of the United States, shall be made, under the Authority of the United States, shall be the supreme law of the land.[2]

I start with outlining the approach to it by moderate conservatives.

The Approach

The rule of law is one of the primary political goods. Its aim is to maintain order and define the rights and responsibilities of those living in American society. The Constitution and the laws consistent

---

[1] For a general overview and bibliography, see Waldron, Jeremy. "The Rule of Law" in the *Stanford Encyclopedia of Philosophy*: https://plato.stanford.edu/archives/sum2020/entries/rule-of-law, and McIntyre, Kenneth B. *Nomocratic Pluralism: Plural Values, Negative Liberty, and the Rule of Law*. Cham, Switzerland: Palgrave/Macmillan, 2021.
[2] *Constitution of the United States of America*. Article VI, 2nd paragraph.

with it specify some of the basic conditions that enable us to follow our conception of how we should live. The laws are justified if they do protect these conditions. If all goes well, these conditions are met. But all often does not go well. There usually are more or less widely shared dissatisfactions with some of the laws that define the possibilities and limits of permissible personal conceptions of how to live. Some of these dissatisfactions are reasonable, others are not. If they are reasonable, they can and should be ameliorated by abandoning or revising either the laws or the personal conceptions.

Dissatisfactions, however, may be caused by unforeseeable contingencies whose occurrence is beyond the possibility of control: natural disasters, epidemics, scarcity of resources, or hostile enemies bent on the destruction of our society. Neither the rule of law nor personal conceptions of how to live should be blamed for the resulting dissatisfactions. The reasonable response is to attribute them to adverse conditions and respond to them as well as possible, while protecting the rule of law insofar as it is consistent with the Constitution, the laws, and the various conceptions we have of how we should live. If the dissatisfactions are nevertheless widespread, they threaten the sustainability of American society.

The rule of law specifies the requirements that the promulgation of particular laws should meet. Part of the justification of particular laws is that they meet these procedural requirements. Experts at jurisprudence disagree about many things, but they agree that these requirements are that the laws should be made public; generally known; clear and simple enough to be understood by those who are subject to them; not more demanding than what average people could in the course of normal life follow; consistent with other laws; apply only to the present and the future, but not retroactively to the past before the laws were promulgated; and be flexible enough to allow for meeting changing conditions and for possible exceptions and excuses.

Moderate conservatives add to these procedural requirements the further one that the laws should be consistent with the

Constitution and, insofar as it is possible, also with the much wider and more varied evaluative framework participation in which forms the complex web of attitudes and feelings that continues to meet the test of time and commands the widespread allegiance of those living in American society. In Hart's words,[3] they jointly

> form part of the generally accepted picture of the life which individuals are expected and indeed assumed to live.

That accepted picture of life, as Strawson put it:[4]

> is a condition of the existence of any form of social organization, of any human community, that certain expectations of behaviour on the part of its members should be pretty regularly fulfilled: that some duties, one might say, should be performed, some obligations acknowledged, some rules observed. We might begin by locating the sphere of morality here. It is the sphere of the observance of some rules, such that the existence of some such set of rules is a condition of the existence of a society.

There is a presumption in favor of the rule of law that meets these procedural requirements, but it is defeasible if changing or unusually threatening conditions require it for safeguarding the society and its evaluative framework. The rule of law, therefore, is a primary political good, but it is not an overriding one. It has been amended 27 times in the course of 300 years.

The rule of law thus understood should not be confused with justice. The rule of law is a primary political good that specifies the procedural requirements that the promulgation of particular laws should meet. Justice is also a primary political good, but it specifies

---

[3] Hart, H.L.A. *The Concept of Law*. Oxford: Clarendon Press, 1961, 177.
[4] Strawson, P.F. "Social Morality and Individual Ideal" in *Freedom and Resentment*. London: Methuen, 1974, 30.

what the particular criminal, distributive, administrative, civil, or possibly international laws should be. The rule of law is general, the laws of justice are particular. The violation of a particular law of justice is an offense. It injures in some way particular persons and their legitimate interests. Actions that attack the entire Constitution and the system of laws consistent with it are seditious. They injure everyone in our society by threatening the conditions that enable us to follow our conception of how we should live.

Advocating minor or major changes to particular laws or to the rule of law itself is neither criminal nor seditious. Acting on what is advocated may be condemned, justified, or excused. What condemnation, justification, or excuse may be acceptable needs to be decided case by case. It depends on the conditions, on the nature and context of the action in question, on the evaluation of the reasons for and against the action, and on how the consequences of the actions affect the evaluative framework of American society.

As we have seen in the preceding chapter, political goods and the political mode of evaluation are part of the evaluative framework, but no more than parts. Other parts are economic, legal, moral, religious, and other goods and modes of evaluation. The evaluative framework is much wider than just the political goods and the political mode of evaluation. The evaluations that follow from these various political and non-political goods and modes of evaluation may conflict, and that is relevant to deciding whether the actions that follow from these conflicting evaluations are or are not contrary to the Constitution and the rule of law, and whether they should or should not be condemned, justified, or excused.

One of several reasons for regarding the rule of law as a primary political good is that it provides procedures for resolving conflicts between political and non-political goods and modes of evaluation without assuming that any of them does or should always override conflicting ones. The moderate conservative view is that the evaluation of all goods, modes of evaluation, the political system, the evaluative framework itself, and the conflicts between them are contextual, complex, and defeasible. Reasonable approaches to such evaluations and conflicts are not to be found in the speculations of theorists but in the historically accumulated social experiences of the society as a whole. They are embedded in the continuing way of life formed of customs, practices, and institutions that have endured because they met the test of time.

Theorists can describe, criticize, or justify this way of life, but they cannot make or unmake it. They can describe it from the outside and give a reliable account of what matters to those who live that kind of life. But only if they share or imaginatively reconstruct their sense of what is more and what is less important can the theorists understand why they care as much as they obviously do that the rule of law should protect the evaluative framework and the order, peace, and security that unites those living in a society and enables them to follow their conception of how they should live. They conceive of their lives in terms of the possibilities and limits the rule of law and the evaluative framework of their society provide.

This lack of understanding of the sense of importance those living in the society share is the main reason why no purely descriptive account of the rule of law can be sufficient for understanding the force of the commitment to the Constitution and the laws consistent with it. Without sharing that understanding the rule of law seems like overbearing legalism. Sharing it is the ultimate source of the sense of importance that those living in American society rarely consciously and mostly habitually share. The motivating force of the commitment to the rule of law cannot be captured by likening it to a commitment to the categorical imperative, or to the general happiness, or to some metaphysical ideal of the GOOD. It is a complex contextual attitude formed of shared—widely shared!— beliefs, emotions, desires, and experiences that unite those who see their lives and society in terms of that attitude. Depending on conditions, adversities, and challenges, sometimes one component of it is dominant, and sometimes the emphasis shifts in response to changing personal or social conditions. Taken in its entirety it is part of their conception of how they should live. If, but only if, all goes well!

It is this shared attitude to the rule of law that makes it a primary political good. It is not just one among the multitude of laws that jointly form the legal system, but a unifying force that connects those living in a society. And because it is a shared attitude, and not a theory, that it is a mistake to over-systematize and over-intellectualize it by ignoring the formative importance of the interlocking and reciprocally reinforcing web of beliefs, emotions, desires, experiences, habits, customs, and the remembered past that jointly form allegiance to the rule of law.

It would be a misunderstanding to suppose that those who share the attitude have no serious disagreements. As Strawson puts it[5]:

> inside the general structure or web of human attitudes and feelings ... there is endless room for modification, redirection, criticism, and justification internal to it. The existence of the general framework of attitudes itself is something we are given with the fact of human society.

Disagreements within it may actually strengthen the web if they concern how best to maintain its evaluative framework. If the web is frayed, if a society's entire evaluative framework is questioned, if the dissatisfactions of its participants are many and serious, then the shared attitude becomes uncertain, and so does what is good and bad, right or wrong, important or unimportant. And then the attitude that hitherto united its participants is collapsing. In these conditions, the rule of law could not and should not try to protect it.

We know from the bitter experience of people in other societies that the rule of law can fade, be abused, or ridiculed by knowing cynics, and then it can no longer protect the conditions that make

---

[5] Strawson, P.F. "Freedom and Resentment" in *Freedom and Resentment*. London: Methuen, 1974, 23.

it possible for people to follow their different conceptions of how they should live. This happened to Athens as a result of the disastrous Sicilian expedition; to Rome and the Byzantine Empire when they could no longer resist invaders; to 17th-century Europe as a result of the religious hatred that led to the 30-year war that killed one-third of the population of Europe; to Tsarist Russia when communism destroyed its already enfeebled order; to the collapse of the Chinese administrative system that lasted for thousands of years; to Germany as a result of Nazism; and to Italy, Spain, and Portugal when Fascism put an end to the old regimes.

And it is because dissatisfactions are widespread that all does not go well for us now. The American political system is threatened by acrimonious political disagreements and the politicization of aspects of life—for instance about child-rearing, education, marriage, public health, sex, and so on—that have traditionally been free of politically motivated intrusion. This threat adds urgency to the contemporary moderate conservative defense of the rule of law and of the integrity of non-political areas of life.

I turn now to the basic question of how the rule of law should be understood and to the reasons for understanding it as moderate conservatives think it should be understood: Is the rule of law procedural or substantive?

Procedural or Substantive?

The question is whether the rule of law should only be a procedure that specifies how any particular law should be promulgated regardless of what its substantive content may be, or whether it should not be only procedural, but also specify some substantive content that particular laws should have. There can be no serious doubt that the rule of law must have a procedural component specifying how laws, any law, should be promulgated. There are all sorts of rules, regulations, commands, and requirements that may be formulated, but they acquire the force of law only if they conform to the procedural requirements described earlier. But is there also some substantive content that all laws should have? The answer is controversial.

One answer is that the rule of law should be only procedural. According to Hayek,[6]

> The rule of law is therefore not a rule of the law, but a rule concerning what the law ought to be, a meta-legal doctrine.

Oakeshott has the same view:[7] the rule of law is a human association

> not in terms of doing and the enjoyment of the fruits of doing, but of procedural conditions imposed upon doing: laws. Relationship, not in terms of efficacious arrangements for promoting or procuring wished for substantive satisfactions (individual or communal), but obligations to subscribe to non-instrumental rules.

And Waldron partly quotes and partly characterizes Raz's claim that:[8]

> the Rule of Law is a purely formal/procedural ideal . . . and that the rule of law is just one of the virtues which a legal system may possess and by which it is to be judged,

and that we should not read into it other considerations about democracy, human rights, and social justice.

These answers seems to me untenable for four reasons. First, the procedural and substantive requirements of the rule of law are not

---

[6] Hayek, Friedrich A. *The Constitution of Liberty*. Chicago: Regnery, 1960, 206.
[7] Oakeshott, Michael. "The Rule of Law" in *On History and Other Essays*. Oxford: Blackwell, 1983, 148.
[8] Waldron, Jeremy. "The Rule of Law" in the *Stanford Encyclopedia of Philosophy*: https:// plato.stanford.edu.entries/rule-of-law, and Raz, John. "The Rule of Law and its Virtue" in *The Authority of Law*. Oxford: Oxford University Press, 1977.

separable. There are different procedures for promulgating laws that follow from different conceptions of law. The English conception of common law is one. The conception in Roman law is another. In societies ruled by kings, aristocrats, religious leaders, tribal elders, the military, or ideologues, the procedures for promulgating laws differ. And since the procedures depend on the authority of the law-makers and the historical and political conditions of the society, they unavoidably have some substantive content derived from the past, present, and desired future conditions of the society whose rule of law it is.

Such contextual contents are often taken for granted and remain unexpressed by law-makers, but they are nevertheless there. It is, for instance, a substantive assumption of common law that elected law-makers have the authority to promulgate laws, but the clergy, physicians, generals, and teachers have none. And that is a substantive assumption, whether or not it is conscious or articulated, that forms part of the substantive component of the rule of law.

Second, the rule of law has an aim and a context. As Finnis points out,[9] the relevant

> actions, practices, etc., can be fully understood only by understanding their point, that is to say their objective, their value, their significance or importance, as conceived by the people who performed them, engaged in them, etc. And these conceptions of point, value, significance, and importance will be reflected in the discourse of those same people, in the conceptual distinctions they draw and fail or refuse to draw. Moreover, these actions, practices, etc., and correspondingly these concepts, vary greatly from person to person, from one society to another, from one time and place to other times and places. *How, then, is there to be a general descriptive* theory of these varied particulars?

---

[9] Finnis, John. *Natural Law and Natural Rights*. Oxford: Clarendon Press, 1980, 3–4.

This is a pivotal question. The answer moderate conservatives give to it is that no purely descriptive theory can be sufficient for understanding the evaluative force of these social practices. That is why there cannot be general, context-independent purely procedural requirements of the rule of law. The requirements are partly substantive and contextual. As Hart puts it:[10]

> The basic character of such rules may be brought out by the question: If there were not these rules what point could there be for beings such as ourselves in having rules of *any* kind? The force of this rhetorical question rests on the fact that men are both occasionally prone to, and normally vulnerable to, bodily attack. . . . This fact . . . makes obvious the necessity of mutual forbearances and compromise which is the basis of both legal and moral obligation.

If the point of having laws at all is understood, it becomes obvious that the laws must have some substantive content which they aim to secure. What that aim is partly depends on the context of the society in which rule of law is intended to hold. The aim may be to protect order, security, justice, liberty, or something else. Whatever it may be, it gives substantive content to the rule of law, a content that depends on the history, conditions, and evaluative framework of the society. Since contexts vary with societies, so do the aims of the rule of law. How these rules are promulgated and how extensive is their range partly depends on the context in which they should hold. There can be no adequate concept of the rule of law without specifying what its aims are. And because some aims vary with contexts, there are many conceptions of law, and their substantive content partly depends on the context in which it should hold. Hart calls his book, rightly regarded as a classic, *The Concept of Law*. It would have been more accurate, however, to call it *Our*

---

[10] Hart, H.L.A. *The Concept of Law*. Oxford: Clarendon Press, 1961, 190, 191.

Concept of Law. The recognition that the rule of law is contextual does not diminish its authority. It provides a better understanding of the source of its authority.

The third reason against thinking that the rule of law is only procedural is that if laws had no substantive content, then *any* law that was promulgated by following the required procedure would thereby become legitimate, no matter how immoral, irrational, or tyrannical it may be. No reasonable person who realized that this would follow from regarding the rule of law as purely procedural could find this acceptable. If the rule of law were purely procedural, it could not exclude inhuman, vicious, and destructive laws. Part of the aim of the rule of law is the regulation of the possibilities and limits of human actions. It cannot be a matter of indifference to law-makers how the laws they make affect the human beings to whom they apply. Law-makers may be mistaken about what they suppose the effects of the laws will be, but they cannot fail to take into account the consequences of the laws on those who are subject to them. So the laws must have some substantive content.

The fourth reason why thinking of the rule of law as purely procedural is mistaken is the inconsistency of those who claim to be committed to it. Hayek claims that the rule of law is a meta-legal doctrine. And then goes on to write a whole book defending liberty as a necessary part of the rule of law. Oakeshott calls it a purely formal/procedural ideal, but he stresses that the importance of the rule of law is that it enables human beings to make what they can of their lives, and that is certainly a substantive consideration. And Raz defends the rule of law as a procedural ideal, while unaccountably forgetting about his defense of what he calls the political morality of liberalism in which the rule of law is committed to protecting liberty. I conclude that the reasons for regarding the rule of law as both procedural and substantive are much stronger than the reason against it.

Doubts about Priorities

It is tempting but mistaken to conclude simply that the rule of law must have some substantive content, and then leave it at that. If we do that, Waldron rightly cautions,[11]

> we open up the possibility of the Rule of Law's having a substantive dimension, we inaugurate a sort of competition in which everyone clamors to have their favorite political ideal incorporated as a substantive dimension of the Rule of Law. Those who favor property rights and market economy will scramble to privilege their favorite values in this regard. But so will those who favor human rights, or those who favor democratic participation, or those who favor civil liberties or social justice.

That competition has been raging with great fervor between theorists who are committed to the priority of the political good they favor. Here are some examples:
Berlin claims that[12]

> no power, but only rights, can be regarded as absolute... [and] there are frontiers, not artificially drawn, within which men should be inviolable... defined in terms of rules.

Dworkin writes:[13]

---

[11] Waldron, Jeremy. "The Rule of Law" in the *Stanford Encyclopedia of Philosophy*: https://plato.stanford.edu.entries/rule-of-law/, 11/19.
[12] Berlin, Isaiah. "Two Concepts of Liberty" in *Four Essays on Liberty*. Oxford: Oxford University Press, 1959/1969, 165.
[13] Dworkin, Ronald. *A Matter of Principle*. Cambridge, MA: Harvard University Press, 1985, 11.

the power of the state should never be exercised against individual citizens except in accordance with rules explicitly set out in a public rule book available to all.

And elsewhere he claims that[14]

No government is legitimate that does not show equal concern for the fate of all those citizens over whom it claims dominion.... Equal concern is the sovereign virtue of political community.

According to Hayek,[15]

Not only is liberty a system under which all government action is guided by principles, but it is an ideal that will not be preserved unless it is itself accepted as an overriding principle governing all particular acts of legislation.

Rawls begins his immensely influential book with the rousing declamation:[16]

justice is the first virtue of social institutions... the rights secured by justice are not subject to political bargaining.

Each of these theorists claims that the primary political good he favors should be included in the rule of law and should always have priority to other primary political goods that may conflict with it. Of course every primary political good is important. But none of these theorists explains why any one of them should always, in all

---

[14] Dworkin, Ronald. *Sovereign Virtue*. Cambridge, MA: Harvard University Press, 2000, 1.
[15] Hayek, Friedrich A. *The Constitution of Liberty*. Chicago: Henry Regnery Company, 1960, 68.
[16] Rawls, John. *A Theory of Justice*. Rev. ed. Cambridge, MA: Harvard University Press, 1971/1999, 3–4.

conditions, at all times, in face of all contingencies be more important than whatever primary political good conflicts with it. Why assume that rights are *absolute*? that equal concern is the *sovereign* virtue? that the protection of liberty is the *overriding* principle of legislation? Why is justice—by which Rawls means distributive rather than criminal justice—the *first* virtue? Why do they ignore the obvious fact that there have been, are, and in the future are likely to be conditions in which the protection of order, peace, or security may be more important for their society than the protection of the rights, equal concern, liberty, or distributive justice?

In the influential books from which I have been citing these passages, the priority of a favored political good is asserted at the very beginning, taken for granted, and its nature is elaborated in the hundreds of pages that follow, but, as far as I can tell, not justified. There are ample reasons given for the importance of the most favored political good. And there is no doubt that it is important. But why is it always more important than any political or non-political good, or any other consideration that may conflict with it? To that question these theorists give no answer. What has happened is that the theorists accept that the rule of law cannot be only procedural, recognize that it must have some substantive content, and then, less self-critically than they should and contrary to moderate conservatism, offer their own substantive candidate for that content and insist that it should always take priority over any other substantive content that may be offered as an alternative to it.

Moderate conservatives ask them: Why should the rights of terrorists, drug dealers, or dictators be absolute? Why should our society have equal concern for its benefactors and scourges, for torturers and the tortured, or for competent and incompetent surgeons? Why should liberty have priority to all other political goods? Why might not justice, equality, or prosperity in some conditions have priority to liberty? Why should distributive justice be the first virtue of social institutions? Why are not order, peace, or security just as important virtues of social institutions as distributive justice?

These questions are not answered by these theorists or their followers because they take themselves to be defending the political good on whose priority all other political goods and the entire society depends. But why should rights have to be absolute, liberty unconditional, equal concern the sovereign virtue, and distributive justice the first virtue? Why should not order, peace, and security be acknowledged to be just as important in some contexts as rights, liberty, equal concern, or distributive justice? Why insist on the implausible and immoderate claim that there is one political good that should always, in all contexts have priority over whatever may conflict with it? I have tried hard, but I have not found a satisfactory answer to this question in the voluminous works of Berlin, Dworkin, Hayek, and Rawls.

The approach of these theorists is reminiscent of learned disputes about how many angels can dance on the head of a pin. The disputants assume that there are angels and then earnestly discuss what they can and cannot do. The angels of these political theorists are absolute rights, sovereign or first virtues, and liberty that is the foundation of all good things in life. And then they and the army of their followers earnestly debate how their angel would or should respond to various contingencies of life.

This is an unsatisfactory state of affairs and it threatens the political system of American society. If the rule of law cannot be purely procedural, and if its substantive content leads to endless disputes and immoderate claims about which political good should have priority to all other political or even non-political goods that may conflict with it, then the rule of law cannot be a reliable guide to what the laws of American society should be. Then the Constitution and the laws consistent with it have to be interpreted, but it has become apparent that their interpretations are from the conflicting political views of law-makers and theorists who disagree about which political good should have priority to the others. Is there a way of avoiding this morass of conflicting dogmatisms? Moderate conservatives think that there is. I call it the moderately substantive requirement.

The Moderately Substantive Requirement

Formulating this requirements depends, in the first instance, on recognizing that there are some centrally important procedural and substantive requirements of the rule of law. A procedural requirement that should be added to the ones discussed earlier is that the rule of law should not include laws that favor particular political causes. It should be a neutral instrument that is not be used by judges, law-makers, or politicians to impose their partisan political views on others. Nevertheless, the rule of law should not be only procedural. It should have some politically neutral but nevertheless substantive content. The difficult question is how this moderately substantive requirement could avoid being political.

It could avoid it by recognizing that laws have unavoidable consequences that for better or worse affect those who are subject to them. The moderately substantive requirement is that they should aim to have better rather than worse consequences. Waldron rightly warns against the danger of the political abuse of this requirement. What is regarded as better or worse is likely to involve political considerations. The moderately substantive requirement avoids the danger of this abuse by specifying that the politically neutral requirement should be that no law is promulgated that prevents the satisfaction of the basic physical, physiological, and psychological needs of that all those have who are subject to the rule of law.

What those basic needs are is in the great majority of cases obvious to everyone. In a minority of cases it may be unclear whether a need is basic or merely important for a person or a group. The answer in such cases is factual, usually medical or scientific, not a matter of either political or non-political evaluation. Whatever the basic needs exactly are, all subjects of the rule law have them quite independently of their conception of how they should live and whatever may be the political views of other people, judges, law-makers, and politicians. This then is the moderately substantive requirement that the rule of law should specify for the promulgation of laws. It goes beyond purely procedural requirements, it holds equally for everyone in that society, and it is not, and should not become, subject to political disagreements.

There is a tendency to refer to the satisfaction of basic needs as rights, or as human rights. Moderate conservatives agree that basic needs should be satisfied and that no law should deprive anyone in a society of their satisfaction. Rights, however, are often supposed to imply more, namely that the requirement that basic needs should be satisfied is universal, impartial, impersonal, and context-independent. And that moderate conservatives doubt. They agree, of course, that it would be good if everyone's basic needs were always satisfied. They deny, however, that it should be made a substantive requirement of the rule of law. The rule of law should require only what is possible, and the satisfaction of everyone's basic needs is often impossible because it is prevented by adverse contingencies.

This is not a trivial point. The manifold contingencies of life, such as accidents, natural disasters, epidemics, scarcities, external enemies, internal subverters of the rule of law cannot be legislated out of existence. Life would certainly be better without adverse contingencies. We can reasonably wish that life should be better, but the rule of law should not be thought of as an expression of wishful thinking. It would be absurd to make it a requirement of the promulgation of laws that they should require that there be no contingencies that prevent the satisfaction of the basic needs of those who are subject to the rule of law.

It is beyond the possibility of human control to prevent all contingencies that may affect us. It must be possible for subjects to follow the rule of the law, but it is quixotic to make it a requirement of the rule of law that its subjects should not affected by contingencies. So the law should not require the satisfaction of basic needs, since adverse contingencies may make it impossible to satisfy them. It would, of course, be good if basic needs were satisfied, but making sure that they will be satisfied is not within human control, so no law should require it. It is a procedural requirement of inclusion in the rule of law that it should be possible to satisfy it. It is a contingent matter whether the resources for satisfying basic physical, physiological, and psychological needs are or can be made available, whether they can be distributed in a timely manner so as to be available for everyone who needs it, or whether the resources could be preserved until needed, and so on. To require that the rule of law should include such laws is wishful thinking, not reasonable legislation. This is one reason why Bentham called rights nonsense upon stilts.

What is not wishful thinking, but a reasonable and moderately substantive requirement of the rule of law that it should exclude any law that would prevent the satisfaction of basic needs. I stress this obvious point about the rule of law because it has immediate consequences for all political theories that make it a substantive requirement of the rule of that the political good they favor should always override any other primary political good, or, indeed, any other consideration that may conflict with it. As we have seen, the inclusion of this unacceptable substantive requirement of the rule of law is claimed by Berlin for rights, Dworkin for equal concern, Hayek for liberty, and Rawls for distributive justice. Whether they realize it or not, all of these theorists are committed to the impossibility of exempting the rule of law from the contingencies of lawlessness, civil or foreign war, or the insecurities caused by contingencies that threaten the entire society.

If they were not committed to exempting the rule of law from vulnerability to such adverse contingencies, they would not claim that rights were *absolute*; or that equal concern was the *sovereign* virtue of all political communities; or that rule of law depended on liberty even if those who are subject to the rule of law used their liberty to undermine the rule of law; or that distributive justice was the *first* virtue of social institutions. Social institutions could not function if the rule of law broke down because of anarchy, war, criminal conspiracies, or uprising. Social institutions depend on order, peace, and security.

And only if they are protected by the rule of law is it possible to protect rights, equal concern, liberty, and distributive justice.

These influential political theorists are not exceptions, but models followed by countless other theorists who are endeavoring to make a case for the indefensible substantive requirement that the rule of law should be committed to the priority of whatever political good they favor no matter what the contingencies are that their society must meet. They are committed to making the rule of law an instrument for enforcing the political good they pursue. They fail to see that they could not pursue it if the rule of law did not first protect their society from anarchy, war, internal or external enemies, or indeed from intolerant dogmatists who make the pursuit of rights, equal concern, liberty, or distributive justice impossible. They do not realize that the rule of law is a condition on which the pursuit of whatever political good they favor depends. By politicizing the rule of law, they endanger it, and thereby jeopardize their own political aims.

By way of a summary of what moderate conservatives think are the procedural and substantive requirement of the rule of law, here is a brief statement of them. One set of procedural requirement is that laws should be public, generally known, clear, simple, not too demanding, consistent with other laws, and prospective, not retrospective. These requirements are, I think, generally accepted.

Moderate conservatives in the American context add to them the requirement that the laws should be consistent with the Constitution and that part of the evaluative framework of American society that has met the test of time. That test is met if there is a continued general and voluntary support of those who are subject to them. It is likely that there will be dissatisfaction with particular laws and with parts of evaluative framework, but if the dissatisfactions are not so strong as to lead those living in our society to reject substantial portions of the Constitution, the laws, and the evaluative framework, then they continue to meet the test of time. We cast our tacit vote in favor of these procedural requirements by continuing to adhere to most of them, even though we have the option not to do so.

In addition to these procedural requirements, the laws should meet some moderately substantive requirements. First, the laws should be politically neutral in that they do not require that any of the political or non-political goods or modes of evaluation should always override any other political or non-political good or mode of evaluation that may conflict with it. Laws should recognize that political and non-political goods and modes of evaluation may conflict, and should not require that their conflicts be always resolved in favor of any particular one of them. Second, the laws should not require what is impossible. In particular they should not require the satisfaction of the basic needs of all those who are subject to them have, because their satisfaction depends on contingencies that may prevent their satisfaction. Third, the rule of law should exclude laws that prevent the satisfaction of basic needs. And fourth and last, there is the requirement that has been implicit in all preceding procedural and substantive requirements, namely that this conception of the rule of law and particular laws should hold only in American society, apply to all and only to those who live in it, and should not be required to hold anywhere else, no matter how desirable it may be that it should. The rule of law should regulate the possibilities and limits of the actions of those who live in American society.

Moderate Conservatism and the Rule of Law

I have been endeavoring to make as strong a case as I could for the importance of the rule of law in the American political system. But its importance should not lead to supposing that it is an unconditional good. Commitment to the rule of law, as Finnis nicely put it,[17] is not a suicide pact. The justification of the rule of law in our

---

[17] Finnis, John. *Natural Law and Natural Rights*. Oxford: Clarendon Press, 1980, 275.

political system is that conformity to it enables us to follow our conception of how we should live, given that the possibilities and limits of the Constitution, the laws consistent with it, and the evaluative framework of American society continue to meet the test of time. There may be conditions in which this justification breaks down.

One such condition is that the rule of law becomes too demanding or too permissive and conflicts with other primary political goods, such as justice, legal and political equality, liberty, private property, which are just as important as the rule of law is. Another is that conditions may occur in which acting according to the rule of law has destructive consequences for our society and ourselves. This may happen if the society is attacked by enemies and successful resistance to them requires actions contrary to the rule of law. Yet a further possibility is that the preponderance of the members of our society become dissatisfied with the rule of law, think that it no longer meets the test of time, and reject it because they find it too simple-minded, or demanding, or hidebound to respond successfully to new conditions. They may be right about this, and then the rule of law would no longer protect the conditions that enable them to follow their conception of how they should live. Or they may be wrong about it because they have been indoctrinated by a destructive ideology, or by some kind of economic, legal, moral, political, or religious dogma, or they may have allied themselves with enemies who are bent on the destruction of the society. If this were to happen, whether for good or bad reasons, American society would be seriously threatened.

The rule of law is a centrally important primary political good, but moderate conservatives recognize that its importance depends on the prevailing conditions. They think that its importance arises out of and must be understood against the background of the Constitution, the laws consistent with it, and the evaluative framework of a society that has met the test of time. If these conditions hold and if there are no immediately threatening conditions, then the rule of law is justified because it protects the conditions that enable those who are subject to it to follow their conception of how they should live. It is possible to tell whether this condition is met if those who are subject to the rule of law follow it voluntarily, while having a reasonable option of not following it by leaving their society.

They may of course be dissatisfied with the social conditions of their lives, with some or more of prevailing laws; with the rule of law in its entirety; with the evaluative framework of which the rule of law is a part; or with the Constitution itself. Or their dissatisfactions may be with what they have made of their lives given the possibilities and limits of their social conditions. Whatever the causes may be of their dissatisfactions, if they stay in their society, although they have the option of leaving it, is a strong presumption in favor of the justification of the rule of law as it is.

This is not say that it is fine as it is. There may be countless ways in which it could and perhaps should be improved. But if the imperfections of the rule of law and the dissatisfactions of those who are subject to it are not so great as to compel many to leave it, then the presumption in favor of the justification of the rule of law is stronger than the presumption against it. How strong or weak that justification is depends on how defective the laws are, how dissatisfied are those who are subject to the laws, and how well the entire political system of American society can cope with the contingencies, conflicts, external and internal enemies, and the dissatisfactions of those living in it. The evaluation of the strength of this justification and the reasons for and against the presumption is an exceptionally difficult matter of judgment about which reasonable and experienced people are all too likely to disagree. I am not one of these people, but I nevertheless express an opinion without claiming for it more than that it is my personal opinion.

I think that our political system is seriously threatened because numerous areas life have become politicized by immoderate political activists who see themselves as defenders of what they claim is overriding political ideal, and demonize those who disagree with them as enemies of humanity because they are opposed to what they regard as the ideal. They fantasize that their ideal is under attack by those who ignorantly or viciously pit themselves against it. They claim to know that what is bad in our society is caused by enemies of their overriding ideal. Correcting what is bad depends on protecting the ideal by any means necessary.

Their ideal may be nationalist or internationalist, religious or secular, white or black racist, egalitarian or elitist, misogynist or feminist, libertarian or authoritarian, but they are alike in being motivated by an immoderate moralistic fervor and indignation at the history of the wrongs that have been done to those they suppose themselves to be defending. They see themselves as crusaders fighting a war of liberation from oppressors who are enemies of the overriding ideal on which everyone's well-being depends. And that makes them immoderate and intolerant; blind to the complexities of moral and political evaluations; to the constraints set by the available alternatives; to the demands of competing needs and the scarcity of resources; they are unaware of external threats and of the domestic necessity of maintaining order, peace, and security; they do not acknowledge the importance of defending the society from criminals, terrorists, and from foreign ideologues whose moralistic fervor is as destructive as those of immoderate domestic political activists. They spout slogans about liberty, equality, and justice, while aiming to deprive their opponents of them; they try to make the rule of law a weapon against their opponents, and compel others to follow what they suppose is the overriding ideal rather than their conception of how they should live. They aim to subvert the Constitution, make radical changes to the evaluative framework and the political system of the society that has met the test of time, and they cause all this harm in the name of what they claim to be the overriding ideal. Moderate conservatives think that the spread of such immoderate moralistic political activism is the major threat to the American political system that has so far stood the test of time and sustained what has become the oldest constitutional democracy in the world.

The alternative to responding to that threat is to acknowledge that some dissatisfactions are justified, that some reforms need to be made, and then make them moderately, gradually, and cautiously; to make peace, not war; to understand the dissatisfaction, not to vilify those who have them; to treat opponents with civility, not with contempt. And, as Lincoln memorably said a little before he was killed by one of the immoderate political activists at a time as fraught as our own time is now: respond with malice toward none, with charity for all, with firmness in the right, with the will to do the work that needs to be done, and to try to heal the nation's wounds.

6
Justice

Justice as Desert

This chapter is about the moderate conservative conception of the primary political good of justice. I call it justice as desert.[1] Contemporary discussions of justice are dominated by John Rawls's liberal theory of justice. The conception of justice as desert differs from it in significant ways.[2] In the last part of this chapter I discuss the reasons why moderate conservatives reject Rawls's theory of justice. One main reasons for this is that Rawls's conception of justice is a theory, and moderate conservatives think that there can be no acceptable theory of justice if it aims to defend justice as a context-independent, universal, and unconditional political ideal that always takes priority to all considerations that may conflict with it. Moderate conservatives think of justice as one of several possible responses to VUCA situations in which we have to respond to perennial problems of adverse contingencies, conflicting evaluations, and compromises we have to make in always changing contexts and conditions. In such situations we have to weigh the relative importance of all the various primary and secondary political goods, as

---

[1] This chapter is a heavily revised version of my "Justice," *Social Philosophy and Policy*, 23(2006): 88–106.
[2] For a very good anthology of centrally relevant works on justice in general, see Solomon, Robert C., and Mark C. Murphy, eds. *What Is Justice?* New York: Oxford University Press, 2000. For overviews and bibliographies, see Miller, David. "Desert and Merit" in the *Routledge Encyclopedia of Philosophy*: https://www-rep-routledge/articles/thematic/desert-and-merit/; Miller, David. "Justice." https://plato.stanford.edu/entries/justice/. Feldman, Fred, and Brad Skow. "Desert." https://www.rep.routledge.com/articles/thematic/desert-and-merit/v-1. One excellent account of the concept of desert is by George Sher, *Desert*. Princeton, NJ: Princeton University Press, 1987.

well as of non-political goods, and, while justice is centrally important, it is only one of the centrally important goods we have to take into account. There can be no theory that specifies that regardless of differences in all contexts and conditions reason requires giving priority to justice. Hume recognized that:[3]

> All political questions are infinitely complicated, and . . . there scarcely ever occurs, in any deliberation, a choice, which is either purely good, or purely ill. Consequences, mixed and varied, may be foreseen to flow from every measure: And many consequences, unforeseen, do always, in fact, result from every one. Hesitation, and reserve, and suspense, are, therefore, the only sentiments [the philosopher] . . . brings to this . . . trial.

Rawls, however, thinks his theory of justice provides a simple answer:[4]

> Justice is the first virtue of social institutions . . . laws and institutions no matter how efficient and well-arranged must be refined and abolished if they are unjust. Each person possesses an inviolability founded on justice.

Moderate conservatives, in agreement with Hume, think that Rawls's theory is a futile attempt to do what is impossible. I say this at the beginning of this chapter to make clear that the moderate conservative conception of justice is very different from Rawls's theory. I will now concentrate on discussing what that conception of justice is and giving reasons for it. Only after that is done will I return to Rawls's theory.

---

[3] Hume, David. "Of the Protestant Succession" in *Essays Moral Political and Literary*. Edited by Eugene F. Miller. Indianapolis: LibertyClassics, 1777/1985, 507
[4] Rawls, John. *A Theory of Justice*. Cambridge, MA: Harvard University Press, 1971, 1.

The simple commonsense view of justice is that it requires that we should get what we deserve and not what we do not deserve. It is part of what I have called in Chapter 2 common decencies. We are outraged if vicious murderers are acquitted on technicalities or if speculators make a fortune from the financial disaster they have caused to others. Miscarriages of justice undermine our trust in the political system by which we live in our society.

All this needs a great deal of explanation and qualification, but according to moderate conservatives, the basic idea of justice as desert is right: we deserve to get what we are entitled to based on our relationships, agreements, and actions, and we do not deserve what is contrary to them. This way of understanding justice has a long history. It has been stated and re-stated by many different thinkers who lived in different contexts and at different times.

Here is a sample of them:

Old Testament: "Give every man according to the fruit of his doings." *Jeremiah* 17.10.

Plato: "It is just . . . to render each his due." *Republic* 331e.

Aristotle: "it is by proportionate requital that the city holds together. Men seek to return either evil for evil . . . or good for good." *Nicomachean Ethics*, 1132b2-5-1133a1.

Justinian: "Justice is a constant and unceasing determination to render everyone his due." *Institutes*, I.iii.1.

Aquinas: "Justice is the constant and abiding will that renders each person his desert." *Summa Theologiae*, 2a2ae.58.1.

Smith: "As every man doth, so it shall be done to him." *The Theory of Moral Sentiments*, 160.

Mill: "It is universally considered just that each person should obtain that (whether good or evil) which he *deserves*; and unjust that should obtain a good, or be made to undergo evil, which he does not deserve." *Utilitarianism*, 242.

Understanding the conception of justice as desert depends on an account of what is deserved and on how we can tell in any particular case whether or not something is deserved. I begin with some clarifications. First, it may not be unjust if we get what we do not deserve. It may be a generous gift from a friend or a parent, a lottery prize, or the lucky escape from a contagious disease or a car accident. Second, it may not be unjust if we do not get what we deserve. Whether it is unjust depends on why we do not get it. We may die before we could get it, or it is there waiting for us to get it, but for some reason we do not want it, or because scarcity or some natural disaster prevents it. Third, not getting what we deserve is sometimes good and not unjust, because others may deserve it even more, or because we forgo our entitlement to it in favor of others. Fourth, getting a scarce good thing we deserve in old age may be unjust if it makes little difference to us, whereas it would make a great difference to someone early on in life who needs it very much and deserves it.

Moderate conservatives think that justice as desert is one of the crucially important primary political goods. However, being moderate, they do not think that its claims are unconditional. According to them, no political or non-political good should always take priority to and override any contrary claim that may conflict with it. The claims of justice as desert may on some occasions be justifiably overridden by more urgent claims of benevolence, compassion, generosity, love, prudence, or other-regarding sentiments. Furthermore, in cases of emergency, crises, foreign attacks, and adverse conditions the requirements of justice may also be overridden by the need to protect the entire political system of our society in which justice is only one, undoubtedly important primary political good. There also are other, no less important, political goods, and in some cases they may be even more important than the distribution of good and bad things according to desert. Moderate conservatives think that this is true of all political goods, not only of justice. In the context of politics, there is no consideration of any kind that should always takes precedence over whatever consideration may conflict with it.[5]

Clarifications are therefore needed of the conditions in which the requirements of justice should be met or suspended. One of these conditions is that it should be possible to get what we deserve and not what we do not deserve. The claims of justice are not of good or bad things caused by natural conditions, such as immunity to a disease or having excellent memory, or bad things like losing our sense of taste or going blind. The good or bad effects on us of facts beyond the possibility of human control—matters of good or bad luck—are excluded from the context of justice as desert. It may be unfortunate if we suffer from the bad contingencies of life, or fortunate if good contingencies happen to favor us, but neither is a matter of justice as desert. The context of justice as desert is formed of interactions between human beings or human institutions that have it in their power to act or refrain from acting in ways that affect other human beings by benefiting or harming them. What is just or unjust, then, is getting the good or the bad things we deserve as a result of human interactions. I turn now to two questions about the nature of these interactions.

Suppose you have to choose between living in one of two societies. The amounts of good and bad things are exactly the same in both societies, but they are distributed differently. In one, the good and bad things are distributed randomly across the population. In the other, good people get the good things and bad people

---

[5] "Nothing universal can be rationally affirmed on any moral, or any political subject. Pure metaphysical abstraction does not belong to these matters. The lines of morality are not like the ideal lines of mathematics. They are broad and deep as well as long. They admit of exceptions; they demand modifications. These exceptions and modifications are not made by the process of logic, but by the rules of prudence. Prudence is not only the first in rank of the virtues political and moral, but she is the director, the regulator, the standard of them all."

Burke, Edmund. "An Appeal from the New to the Old Whigs" in *Further Reflections on the Revolution in France.* Edited by Daniel E. Ritchie. Indianapolis: Liberty Fund, 1791/1992, 91.

the bad things. Call the first random and the second ordered society. The first question is: which of the two societies would you choose to live in? I have asked this question on numerous occasions from numerous people and I have yet to meet one who would choose to live in the random society.

Analytically minded people will quibble. They will say that my question is poorly formed because it ignores complexities: good and bad things are often mixed; what is good and bad changes with contexts; and there are many disagreements about what things are good and bad. I accept all this. I stipulate that the choice is between the random and the ordered distribution of the most favorable good-to-bad ratio, whatever the chooser thinks are the good and bad things. As to disagreements, there certainly are plenty of them, but not about all good and bad things.

No reasonable person disputes that in normal conditions—not on the last days of humanity, or in a lifeboat, or a torture chamber—and from our personal point of view, it is better to be healthy than sick, happy than miserable, have enough to eat rather than starve, live in a secure and prosperous society than in an anarchic and impoverished one, and so on for the satisfaction or the frustration of the basic requirements of living a normal human life as we in our context understand it. So I stipulate further that the choice is between living in one of two societies in which the uncontroversially good and bad things are in normal conditions distributed either in a random or in an orderly manner. It is extremely unlikely that anyone who understands what is at stake would actually choose to live in the random rather than the ordered society.

My second question is: why is living in an ordered society preferable to living in a random one? It is preferable because in the ordered society we are far more likely to get what we deserve and not what we do not deserve than in the random society. The trouble with the random society is that if we lived in it, we would have no reason to believe that our actions would lead to our goals. Hard work, planning, intelligent choices, and self-control, for instance, would have exactly the same chance of success as sloth, stupidity, and self-indulgence. In the ordered society, there are good reasons for thinking about what we should do, forming intentions, making choices between alternatives, and aiming at results, even if sometimes the contingencies of life or the ill will of others may frustrate us no matter how reasonable may be our intentions, choices, and aims. In the random society, no one could have any reason to connect choices with outcomes, efforts with aims, planning with success. The conception of justice as desert is that in the ordered society justice is more likely to prevail and we are far more likely to get what we deserve and not what we do not deserve than in the random society where both justice and desert will be unpredictable matters of chance.

Justice understood in this way fits naturally into the politics of moderate conservatism because it aims to make the good or bad things we deserve proportional to how well or badly we meet the responsibilities of our relationships, agreements, and actions. It is by reliably meeting our expectation of proportionate requital that our society is held together. Only then can it be reasonable for us to want to live in a just society, make plans, think about the likely consequences of our actions, act on our beliefs, form intentions, have goals, feel secure, and be able to depend on the cooperation of others because they depend on us to do the same. In the ordered society it is more likely that in our interactions with others we get what we deserve and not what we do not deserve, while in the random society, the likelihood of it is unpredictable.

Why Should We Get What We Deserve?

Consider a simple sequence of motivation leading to an action. I am hungry, want to eat, decide to go home for lunch, and walk there. Implicit in this sequence is that I have a set of beliefs: my house is in walking distance, there is food in the fridge, and there are no obstacles in the way of getting there. I also have a set of capacities: I can walk, rely on my memory, estimate distance, and so on. The components of the sequence are motive, belief, capacity, goal, and action. Each component in such a sequence may in a variety of ways and for reasons be mistaken. Suppose, however, that none of them is mistaken and I take the action. I expect, then, that my action will achieve my goal. In simple sequences of this sort, normally all of us have good reason to believe that our expectation will be met.

It would be comforting if such simple sequences would assure that in general we achieve our goal, but this is not so. We have to contend with perennial problems in VUCA situations. Complexities often arise because it is difficult to tell whether a component of the sequence is mistaken. Our motives may conflict; beliefs may be based on faulty information; capacities may be limited or obstructed by fatigue, inattention, or shifting interest; we often have several goals and the pursuit of one may conflict with the pursuit of another, and then we have to decide which is more important; and what seems more important at one time may change because we or our conditions change. We have to judge how these contingencies may affect our goals and our motivation to pursue them. This requires getting the facts right and evaluating their relative importance. Good judgment about such complexities is often difficult because we may misjudge their relative importance, or because conditions beyond our control disrupt simple sequences. Either way, we do not achieve our goal.

Suppose however that we have successfully coped with such complexities and our judgment is good. Might we reasonably expect then that our actions will be successful? No, because others may justifiably prevent us from succeeding. Most of the time our success depends on the tacit or active cooperation of others. But they may have more important concerns; or want what we want and are better at getting it; or what we want may run counter to the interests of others, or of an institution, cause, or group that others want to protect; or they may be motivated by ill will. More is needed therefore before we can reasonably expect to achieve our goal and get what we deserve. This is true of everyone in our society.

We all have to take into account that we live with others and depend on their cooperation. The terms of cooperation, therefore, have to be clear and familiar, so that we can count on them being generally met. They include what I have called common decencies in Chapter 2, as well as the rule of law, and also, as I will shortly discuss, numerous conventional terms of cooperation that include but go beyond the rule of law. In the great majority of complex sequences, we can get what we deserve only if these conditions are met in our society. Terms of cooperation are among these conditions, and they may be more or less adequate for maintaining the optimum conditions in which most of us in our society can get what we deserve.

Can we reasonably expect that our actions will be successful if they are unobstructed by contingencies, conflicts, and unavoidable compromises, our judgments are good, and we participate in the terms of cooperation in our society? The answer is still no, for two reasons. One is that the prevailing terms of cooperation may be defective. Let us assume for the moment that they are adequate. The other reason is that not even adequate terms of cooperation can eliminate competition. We may fail to achieve our goals because we lose out in a competition with others who, like us, are not obstructed by adverse contingencies, have good judgment, and participate in the terms of cooperation. Only one person can win the race or the prize, get the job, be elected, be the first to make a discovery, break a record, solve a problem, marry the beloved person, and so forth. For each of those who succeed, there are many who try and fail. Not all goals are competitive, of course. Having a good marriage, enjoying nature, developing a historical perspective, or appreciating chamber music are fine non-competitive achievements. But many are competitive, and because of them, even if we meet the required conditions, we may still fail to achieve our goals.

Putting all this together, the following requirements of successful action emerge: having good judgment; conforming to adequate terms of cooperation; and, if the goal is competitive, then prevailing in the competition. The expectation of success is reasonable only if these requirements are met. This finally allows me to make clear the point of the preceding discussion. What I mean by saying that we should get what we deserve is that we should get it provided our expectation of success is reasonable.

The "should" expresses a requirement of practical reason. This is the use of reason that guides us to form and act on reasonable sequences of reliable motives, beliefs, capacities, goals, and actions. In this way, the use of practical reason makes our lives better by living in a society in which it is more likely that we get the good things we deserve, and not the bad things we do not deserve. This is what makes a society ordered. And this is why an ordered society is preferable to a random one in which the use of practical reason will not make lives better. Justice as desert, then, prevails if the requirements of practical reason are met. This is at once the aim and the justification of justice as moderate conservatives understand it.[6]

It is up to each one of us personally to try to do as well as we can to cope with adverse contingencies; our conflicting evaluations; the compromises we have to make; improve our judgments; form reasonable sequences of beliefs, goals, and decisions; and make appropriate efforts to increase the likelihood that we will achieve our goals, especially when the goals are competitive. Although such efforts are necessary, they are still not sufficient. We live together

---

[6] "The essential condition of stability in political society, is a strong and active principle of cohesion among the members of the same community.... We mean a principle of sympathy, not of hostility; of union, not of separation. We mean a feeling of common interest among those who live under the same government.... We mean, that one part of the community do not consider themselves as foreigners with regard to another part; that set a value on their connexion—feel that they are one people, that their lot is cast together, that evil to any of their fellow-countrymen is evil to themselves."
Mill, John Stuart. *A System of Logic*, Book VI, Chapter X, par. 5 in *Collected Works of John Stuart Mill*, vol. 8. Indianapolis: Liberty Fund, 1898/2006, 923.

with others and must participate in adequate terms of cooperation with them. Only by the combination of successful personal efforts and adequate terms of cooperation can justice in our political system prevail. So I turn to the question of what terms of cooperation are adequate.

Terms of Cooperation

There are countless formal and informal, lasting and episodic, personal and institutional, private and public, conventional or evolving terms of cooperation situated, as it were, in the social space between informal and undemanding common decencies and the demanding legal requirements of laws. It would be futile to try to list all terms of cooperation, especially since they vary with societies, contexts, and times. I proceed instead by calling attention only to three kinds of conventional terms of cooperation central to American society, and then consider what they imply. They include but go beyond common decencies and the shared modes of evaluation that inform the habits, customs, practices, and the more and the less clearly formulated formal and informal rules that have historically been and continue to be part of the political system of American society. The terms change, but usually slowly. Implicit in them are evaluations that range along a continuum between the two extremes of good and bad, and include many intermediate evaluations closer to or farther from the two ends of the continuum.

The resulting evaluations praise or condemn whatever appropriately falls within the domain of one or another term of cooperation. The terms imply responsibilities that those living in American society are expected but may fail to meet, and from which, in specifiable conditions, they may be exempted or excused. These terms of cooperation can continue to exist only if there is a reasonable and widely held expectation that the relevant responsibilities will be generally met. Actions that meet or fail to meet these responsibilities and expectations form one of the bases on which good and bad things, benefits and harms, rewards and punishments are or should be distributed in American society. The terms of cooperation are social conventions that guide what we should or should not do in familiar areas of life that are well known to all who have been living in this society.

One of these terms of cooperation concerns personal or institutional relationships. Married couples, lovers, competitors, friends, colleagues, parents and children, teachers and students, judges and defendants, physicians and patients, merchants and customers are connected by conventional ties. Embedded in them are reciprocal responsibilities and expectations of how those related in these ways should treat one another. Some of these relationships are symmetrical, others are not. Married couples, friends, colleagues typically have many of the same reciprocal responsibilities and expectations. But the responsibilities and expectations of parents and children, physicians and patients, teachers and students are asymmetrical because one party in the relationship has some kind of authority over the other, or one provides a service the other needs, or produces or sells something the other wants to have.

Another term of cooperation has to do with agreements, such as contracts, promises, loans, appointments, memberships in organizations, employment, or being licensed to drive a car, teach in a school, practice medicine or law, build a house, act as a judge, referee, or competitor, and so forth. Some such agreements are formal, the responsibilities and expectations are governed by written rules and are legally binding. Others are informal. What is owed and expected rest on the tacit uncodified understanding of both parties of such matters as gratitude, respect, reciprocity, acceptable forms of excuse, recognition of important precedents, when bargaining is acceptable, and when it is unseemly, and so forth. The basis of such informal agreements is the shared trust and the good will of the parties toward each other.

A third term of cooperation concerns actions that affect the security of others. A society cannot endure unless it protects the security of those living in it. But how far the protection should extend and what kind of actions it includes or precludes vary with contexts, times, and conditions. And it varies also what violations of security are permissible, excusable, or prohibited; what counts as cruelty, negligence, accidental injury; whether security should be understood in economic, legal, medical, moral, political, psychological, religious, or other forms; and when punishment in some form is or is not appropriate. Civilized societies must have conventions about the protection of life, liberty, private property, legitimate authority, the limits of punishment for transgressions, what is and is not private, acceptable and unacceptable risks, the treatment of illness, injury, suicide, dead bodies, and so on.

Part of the importance of these conventional terms of cooperation, and of many others I have not mentioned, is that they guide what people in our society deserve. That is what according to the terms of their relationships, agreements, and actions that affect others they should get. And they do not deserve to get what would be contrary to these terms of cooperation. Thus the terms of their cooperation provide concrete reasons for the responsibilities and expectations that those living in our society have toward each other. I stress that they are concrete responsibilities and expectations, not theoretical abstractions about the general will, the common good, or the categorical imperative. Children deserve a decent upbringing from their parents because that is how the responsibilities of parenthood are understood by us. Incompetent physicians deserve to lose their license because physician are expected by us to be able treat ill health well. Murderers, thieves, muggers, deserve to be punished because that is how we go about protecting security.

These terms of cooperation are conventional, but they are not merely conventions we happen to hold. They are connected with how we in our society conceive of the general requirements of a life worth living. It requires that children be prepared for adult life, that illness be treated, and that security be protected. The particular ways in which they are done are conventional, but it is not conventional that in a human society they must be done in some way. If they were not done in our society, it would be on the way toward disintegration. So between the rule of law at one end of a continuum and common decencies at its other end, there are the various conventional terms of cooperation that are necessary for the sustainability of American society. But they are not sufficient for it because terms of cooperation may be mistaken.

There are two ways in which they may be mistaken: the terms themselves may be fine, but they are misapplied; or they may be mistaken in some other way. Consider first the possibility of misapplication. It may happen if we follow a term of cooperation but are ignorant or mistaken about the relevant facts. An innocent person mistakenly accused of murder does not deserve to be punished for it. A student who cheats on an exam, does not deserve to pass. An enemy who pretends to be a friend does not deserve our loyalty. However, even if the facts are as they are assumed to be, they may be misapplied because those who apply them are mistaken about the appropriate proportion of what is deserved. A novel may deserve good reviews, but not the Nobel Prize. Thieves may deserve imprisonment, but not mutilation. Physicians may deserve to be compensated for their services, but not to be paid outrageous fees by their frightened and needy patients. Mistakes of fact and proportion lead to people getting good or bad things they do not deserve at all or to getting substantially more or less than what they deserve.

A less obviously detectable mistake is dogmatism about the goodness or badness of particular relationships, agreements, or actions. Moralists are mistaken if they suppose that telling a lie is always wrong, that contracts between employers and employees are always exploitative, or that suicide is murder. Their mistake is that they take to be always bad what may sometimes be right or excusable. Similarly mistaken are the assumptions that frugality is a sign of virtue, beating misbehaving children is good for their character, or that belief in God makes us all better than we would be without the belief.

Terms of cooperation include a wide array of relationships, agreements, and actions in the political system of American society. These terms are not invalidated if some of the evaluations that follow from them turn out to be mistaken about what is good or bad. The mistakes, if recognized, call for the correction of the evaluation of some conventional beliefs, practices, or actions, but they leave the large remaining part of a term of cooperation intact. It may happen, of course, that not merely a few but most evaluations that follow from a particular term of cooperation are mistaken. Then the term must be regarded as faulty in its entirety. This is just what happened to such terms of cooperation as medical treatment based on magic, relying on astrology to make predictions about future events, or seeking divine favor by human sacrifice.

Some terms of cooperation may come to be regarded as clearly mistaken, and then they gradually fall into desuetude and cease to be part of the political system of our society. Others continue to hold strong, are generally recognized, expected to be by and large followed, actions contrary to them are thought to require excuse, and if unexcused, then disapproved. Some terms of cooperation become widely accepted in the course of time and form part of common decencies. Some other terms are changing. This seem to be happening, for instance, to our prevailing evaluative attitudes toward aging, drugs, education, marriage, privacy, sexual practices, and suicide. Changes in the prevailing attitudes, conditions, and evaluations in American society lead to uncertainties and controversies about numerous conventional terms of cooperation. It is, therefore, not enough to rely on what has been and may continue to be a conventional term of cooperation. If we rely on it, we need to be able, if challenged, to provide reasons for it and reasons against revising or abandoning it. VUCA situations created by changing attitudes, conditions, uncertainties, and challenges can be reasonably met only if we have some standard we could rely on to evaluate the reasons that may be given for or against particular terms of cooperation. Moderate conservatives think that the standard is the test of time.

The Test of Time

The test of time is not the uncritical perpetuation of conventional terms of cooperation that happened to have endured in the history of American society. They may have endured for the wrong reasons. They may be deplorable, coercive, dogmatic, exploitative, ignorant, narrow-minded, unfair, or defective in some other way. The right reasons for adhering to them go beyond mere endurance and depend on several conditions.

First, they have become habitual and widely followed for a considerable length of time, measured in generations, not months. Second, we and others in our society have by and large been following them voluntarily, especially when we have considered and rejected the available alternatives. Following them, however, need not be an unconditional life-long commitment. We may come to doubt them after we have followed them for some time because they are inflexible in their responses to changing conditions or unresponsive to our growing dissatisfactions. Or new information or comparisons with other societies may acquaint us with new alternatives, and we may find them preferable to some of the prevailing terms of cooperation. We may then have the option to advocate revisions of the existing terms or even to abandon them in favor of others we find more ready to accommodate our dissatisfactions. Or, if our dissatisfactions with them have grown serious, we may opt to abandon them altogether and move to another society and follow its terms of cooperation which we believe may be better than what we have left behind. Part of the voluntary acceptance of the prevailing terms of cooperation is to leave room for the option of abandoning them. If, however, we continue to follow them because we prefer them to the available alternatives, and if our dissatisfactions with them are not so great as to lead us to reject them altogether, then our terms of cooperation meet the second condition of the test of time. The reasons we have for continuing to follow them are then stronger than the reasons we have for rejecting them.

The third condition is that the prevailing terms should be sufficiently flexible so that they could respond to changing conditions, cope with emergencies, and remain open to the expression of disagreements about the relative importance of the reasons for or against particular terms of cooperation. On that basis we evaluate what particular relationships are acceptable, questionable, or toxic. Whether we should continue to follow the conventional forms of agreements, contracts, and promises, or whether we think that they should be revised or abandoned. And we evaluate as well whether the existing requirements of security, law enforcement, and military preparedness should be strengthened, weakened, extended, or narrowed.

This flexibility and openness to changes in the prevailing terms of cooperation are attitudes toward particular, contextual details and evaluations that may be rightly or wrongly challenged. If the challenges concern only the reasons for changing or abandoning in some respect the details of the contents of these terms, then the health of a society depends on leaving ample room for them. But if the challenges are widespread and directed against the existence of all acceptable conventional terms of relationships, agreements, and the protection of security, then the society is threatened with dissolution. Without the general acceptance of some terms of cooperation, American society, or indeed any society, cannot endure.

Terms of cooperation that conform to these conditions meet the test of time. This would be no small thing. We then would not merely follow them, we would also depend on them for meeting our expectation that the requirements of justice are more likely to be met in our ordered society in which the terms of cooperation are generally followed than in a random society in which the consequences of following them are unpredictable. In an ordered society, we would be more likely to get what we deserve and not what we do not deserve than in a random society. Practical reason should guide all of us who live in our society to make it better ordered and less random than it is in some unfortunate respects. We rely on practical reason to make our society more just and less unjust; to follow the terms of cooperation; and expect that others will be inclined to do by and large the same.

The test of time does not guarantee that justice will always be done, nor that all of us in our society will always get what we deserve and never what we do not deserve. Particular terms of cooperation may be faulty and need to corrected. The beliefs, emotions, desires, and interpretations of our experiences that motivate us may be mistaken. Subverters in our society and its enemies outside of it may be motivated by ill will and act on it to our detriment. Adverse contingencies, conflicting evaluations, and the need to make compromises may frustrate even the faultless operation of practical reason. We do not live in the best possible world. Nevertheless, I agree with John Dunn's fine words[7] that

> human beings have done many more fetching and elegant things than invent and routinize the modern democratic republic, But in the face of endlessly importunate ... inherently chaotic and always potentially murderous onrush of needs and longing, they have, even now, done few things as solidly to their advantage.

The account I have been giving of justice as desert from the point of view of moderate conservatism is not—*it is not!*—meant to be a self-congratulatory celebration of the prevailing conditions of American society. It is meant to be a description of a consensus

---

[7] Dunn, John. *The Cunning of Unreason*. New York: Basic Books, 2000, 363.

shared by a large majority of the members of our society of why and how justice as desert ought to be improved. The political conditions of American society are not as they ought to be because many painfully familiar problems stand in its way.

We know that crime, poverty, and the debilitating drug trade are everywhere. The educational system fails on all levels. Many high school graduates are virtually illiterate, innumerate, and ignorant of elementary facts of history, geography, and the benefits and requirements of citizenship. The criminal justice system has become a marketplace for plea bargaining conducted by lawyers who know how to manipulate the system and by overwhelmed prosecutors and judges whose position requires them to participate in the malfunctioning system. The inhuman conditions of imprisonment guarantee to corrupt inmates even more than they have already been. There are vast differences between the poor who do not have enough of what they need for a decent life and the super-rich whose wealth surpasses the legendary historical fortunes of kings and princes. The murder rate is higher than in most civilized societies. Accusations of racism, sexism, exploitation, discrimination, police brutality, corruption in high places create a climate of reciprocal vituperation by immoderate moral and political activists on the left who favor one side, and on the right who favor the opposite side. Enormous sums need to be spent for the protection of peace and order against their external and internal subverters of them, for maintaining the rule of law, and for protecting law-abiding people from often armed criminals. All these and other problems threaten American society and the protection of the primary political good of justice as desert.

Defenders of moderate conservatism must acknowledge the serious threat these problems present to the protection of our political system. No reasonable person can deny that our political system is not as it should be. Nevertheless, I think that the center still holds, although it is besieged, mere anarchy is not yet loosed upon the world, everyday life goes on, and common decency still exists in face to face encounters.

Relationships continue to be formed and maintained, even as many of them are changing. The many familiar forms of love—and I do mean more than sex—between married couples, parents and children, lovers, friends, teachers and students, trainers and trainees, masters and disciples go on unabated. We continue to make efforts to protect children and the old; feel gratitude for good actions; remain loyal to persons, causes, and to our society; and to raise our children well. By and large, we endeavor to meet our responsibilities, and try in small and sometimes big ways to make our own, our family's, and our country's life better. There are failures, and they rightly stand out and are deplored. But they stand out against the continued flow of ordinary life in which we aim to maintain our relationships, honor the agreements we make, respect the security of others, and, generally speaking, observe the common decencies.

Agreements continue to be negotiated and routinely kept. If broken, redress is often available. Professionals practice their expertise. A great variety of commercial, financial, and trade negotiations go on, ultimately reach agreements, and in most of them some degree of reciprocal trust is involved. Debts are paid, hospitals do what they can, some well and others not so well, but they do them. Workers work, services are provided, shops sell and customers buy. Countless informal contacts between neighbors, colleagues, co-workers, and business people are maintained. Officials in state and local governments keep going the immense unwieldy bureaucratic system which they find as frustrating as do their clients, cars are repaired, electricity is delivered, shops are kept open, and so on and on with the innumerable details of the ordinary business of everyday life.

All this can go on only because the various security forces protect our society from internal and external threats. I repeat: life goes on, even though it is threatened. It goes on because it is in the interest of the great majority of Americans that it should go on, even though there are countless ways in which it could and should be improved. The rule of law is by and large enforced, terms of cooperation are being maintained, common decencies are observed by family members, friends, neighbors, acquaintances, and often extended to casual acquaintances and strangers as a matter of course. Continued efforts are being made to protect justice and make it more likely that we get what we deserve and not what we do not deserve. Life goes on, but not as well as it should. It requires much improvement.

The improvements, however, will not be made by the immoderate sloganeering of political activists who demonize those who disagree with them. We continue to be guided by the manifold economic, legal, medical, moral, political, prudential, and religious modes of evaluations some of which continue from the past to the present, while others are changing to keep up with the changing conditions of life in our society. The political system of our society is on the whole sustained and the test of time is being met. We cast our vote for it every day by our continued participation in it, even though we are dissatisfied with it in various respects, and support efforts to reform what we regard as its failures.

A constructive aim of moderate conservatism is to protect justice as desert, make gradual and careful piecemeal efforts to increase the likelihood that we all in our society get the good things we deserve and not the bad things we do not deserve. The pursuit of that aim is a requirement of practical reason, of trying maintain and improve the prevailing terms of cooperation by patiently building a consensus, because it is in everyone's interest in our society to make the necessary improvements.

Moderate conservatism also has the critical aim of resisting the dogmatic pursuit of what is mistakenly taken to be an unconditional, or overriding, or highest ideal that supposedly takes precedence over any consideration that may conflict with it. The following criticisms of it are not directed against any of the various primary political goods, but against the misguided pursuit of a supposed ideal political good that should always override any other good or any consideration that may conflict with or stand in its way.

Justice as Desert: For and Against

The best-known case against justice as desert is in Rawls's *Theory of Justice*.[8] He writes:

> There is a tendency for common sense to suppose that income and wealth, and the good things in life generally, should be distributed according to moral desert. Justice is happiness according to virtue. . . . Justice as fairness [i.e., Rawls's theory] rejects this conception. (313)

According to moderate conservatives, justice is desert, but it has no closer connection with happiness or virtue than has justice as fairness. As we have seen—but Rawls has not—justice as desert has to do with getting what we deserve and not getting what we do not deserve on the basis of the rule of law and our participation in the terms of cooperation of our society. What we deserve depends on what we are entitled to on the basis of our relationships, agreements, and how our actions affect the security of others. Our participation and our actions may contribute to or detract from our happiness or virtue, but that is not why we do or do not deserve what the rule of law or the terms of cooperation specify. What Rawls takes to be the conception of justice as desert is not the one that moderate conservatives regard as one of the primary political goods.

The root of his misunderstanding is the mistaken supposition that defenders of the conception of justice as desert fail to realize

---

[8] Rawls, John. *A Theory of Justice*. Cambridge, MA: Harvard University Press, 1971. Page references are to this edition.

that what people deserve depends on their innate capacities and the conditions of their lives. Rawls rightly rejects this conception:

> the initial endowments of natural assets are and the contingencies of their growth and nurture in early life are arbitrary from the moral point of view . . . no one deserves his place in the distribution of natural assets any more than he deserves his initial starting place in society. (311)

Rawls presents this truism as if it were a reason for rejecting the conception of justice as desert. But what he rejects is *not* the conception of justice as desert that moderate conservatives defend.

It is obviously true that we have no control over our native capacities and early conditions in life. But it is just as obviously true that as functioning adults we do have control over what we do with our capacities and how we respond to the conditions of our life. This is a plain fact of life testified to by our daily experience of contacts with others. The overwhelming majority of adults living in our society share that experience. We take that control for granted in countless the economic, legal, moral, political, prudential, and religious evaluations we and others make and rely on many times every day. This is the common-sense view of the context in which justice as desert is a primary political good. And this is not the extraordinary view that justice is happiness according to virtue that Rawls mistakenly attributes to those who simply follow the millennia-old old view that justice is desert.

The conception of justice accepted by moderate conservatives is that we should do what we can to make our society such that we get the good things we deserve and not the bad things we do not deserve. We may or may not be virtuous or vicious, happy or unhappy, lucky or unlucky in our early or later life, but, according to the moderate conservative conception of justice as desert, what we deserve does not depend on that. It depends on what we are entitled to on the basis of our relationships, agreements, and actions.

Rawls writes that "the idea of rewarding desert is impracticable" (312). Yet this supposedly impracticable idea we all generally and routinely follow and act on every day. We recognize and accept that we should treat others and they should treat us on the basis of what we and they think we deserve. When we violate the terms of cooperation in which we participate, we accept or should accept blame for it. This is as much part of our life as is talking to each other, even though we sometimes say what we should not. There is nothing impracticable about this. Of course we make mistakes. But they can be identified, blamed, corrected, or stubbornly denied to have been made.

It is natural to ask what could have led Rawls to reject the common-sense view and the daily practice of everyone in our society, namely that we hold each other responsible for the nature of our participation in the relationships we form, in the agreements we make, and in our actions that affect the security of others? What could have led Rawls to question the belief we all hold that how we deserve to be treated depends in part on how we treat others? I think that the answer is that he and his many followers are held captive by the untenable theory that gives the title of his celebrated book. I now turn to that theory. I cite again the claim made on the first page of Rawls's *Theory of Justice* that

> Justice is the first virtue of social institutions . . . laws and institutions no matter how efficient and well-arranged must be reformed or abolished if they are unjust. Each person possesses an inviolability founded on justice that even the welfare of society as a whole cannot override.

The rest of this long book is concerned with developing a theory of justice as fairness.

In what follows, I question some of the fundamental assumptions on which this theory of justice rests. First, Rawls asserts but gives no reason for supposing that social institutions have a first virtue. Why could they not have several virtues? Certainly, social institutions should be just. No one denies that. But social institutions should also have other virtues. They should maintain peace and order; protect security and public health; produce sufficient resources; provide employment and education; adjudicate conflicts between those who are subject to the social institutions; conduct negotiations with other societies; and so on. Why single out justice and call it *the* first virtue, rather than recognize it as one among others? I looked, and looked, but I have found no answer to this obvious question in Rawls' book.

Furthermore, it is an obvious and undeniable fact of life that highly desirable political goods routinely conflict. Resolving their conflicts depends on the evaluations of their relative importance in a particular context and conditions and on giving priority to the more important one. Rawls thinks that justice should always be regarded as more important than any political good that may conflict with it. Why should it? Why should not the requirements of public health, or resisting aggression, or suppressing religious intolerance be more important in some situations than following the arcane principles of justice that took Rawls 600+ pages to explain? Why should doing justice to a single person be always more important than protecting the society from foreign attacks, civil war, economic collapse, or an epidemic? Why should not the need for scarce resources vital to the welfare of a society override in some cases the just claim of someone to those resources?

Those who have political experience know that the political realities of a society unavoidably involve conflicts between important political goods. They know that the conflicts must be resolved because leaving them to fester would make matters much worse. And they know as well that however the conflicts are resolved, the highly desirable and reasonable claims, for instance, of the primary political good of justice, or liberty, or equality will have to be sacrificed in some conditions for the welfare of the society. Rawls denies this. He thinks that in all such conflicts, justice, being the first virtue of social institutions, should override whatever conflicts with its claims, regardless of its cost in the welfare of the society or the welfare of those who live in it. He is explicit about this:

> Each person possesses an inviolability founded on justice that even the welfare of society as a whole cannot override. (3)

What is the basis for this claim? This question brings us to what I believe is the deepest assumption in Rawls's theory. Its basis is what he calls an ideal theory.

> The reason for beginning with ideal theory is that it provides... the only basis for the systematic grasp of... more pressing problems. I shall assume that a deeper understanding can be gained in no other way, and that the nature and aims of a perfectly just society is the fundamental part of the theory of justice. (9)

And the ideal theory

> presents a conception of a just society that we are to achieve if we can. Existing institutions are to be judged in the light of this conception and held to be unjust to the extent that they depart from it without sufficient reason. (246)

Rawls's conception of justice is then that there are "pressing problems," we need an ideal theory which is "the only basis of the systematic grasp" of these problems, and for that we need an ideal theory that "presents a conception of a just society." Now moderate conservatives certainly agree that we have pressing problems, but they firmly reject the claims that without an ideal theory we cannot grasp the problems, and that existing institutions are unjust to the extent to which they depart from Rawls's ideal theory.

Let us then descend from the heights of the academic enterprise of theory construction, and consider one of our pressing problems, say the high murder rate. The problem is that people in our society are being murdered. Why do we need a theory, let alone and ideal one, to grasp that? Why do we need a conception of a just society to cope with that problem? Why should that conception be of a perfectly just society? The problem is the high murder rate. What we need to do is to reduce the number of murders. We do not need a theory to know that murders violate the rule of law, unjustly deprive their victims of their lives, violate the terms of cooperation that protect the security of those who live in our society, and that murder victims get what they do not deserve. It is absurd to suppose that the police, the prosecutors, and the courts need an ideal theory to justify the responses needed to reduce the high murder rate. Why do we need 600+ pages of *The Theory of Justice* to grasp that problem and other similar problems and to do what we can to cope with them? Why do we need an ideal theory to recognize what is unjust? Did we fail to cope with murder before we had the benefit of Rawls's ideal theory? Have no social problems been coped with in the history of humanity before the benefits of Rawls' ideal theory have become available?

Murder, of course, is just one the many regrettably familiar problems we have to cope with. Many who live in our society are treated unjustly: they get what they do not deserve and do not get what they do deserve. That is the problem with injustice. And the primary political good of justice requires us to enforce the rule of law and protect the terms of cooperation that meet the test of time and enable us to maintain our relationships, agreements, and security. We have ways of doing that. Sometimes we fail, and then we should endeavor to identify the reasons for our failure and to correct them. For that we do not need a theory, even less an ideal theory, and we most certainly do not need to settle the question of what a perfectly just society would be.

We do not need to persevere in continuing the futile effort of thousands of years of trying construct a universal, impersonal ideal theory that applies to everyone, always, in all contexts. According to moderate conservatives, what we need is to rely on practical reason informed by the political system of our society, on what we can learn from our historical experience, and on responding with flexibility and understanding to the changing contexts and conditions of our lives and to the unavoidable conflicts between the primary political goods that we have learned to value.

> The nature of man is intricate; the objects of society are of the greatest possible complexity; and therefore no simple disposition or direction of power can be suitable either to man's nature, or to the quality of his affairs. . . . The pretended rights of these theories are all extremes; and in proportion as they are metaphysically true, they are morally and politically false. . . . The rights of men . . . are often in balances between differences of good; in compromises between good and evil; and sometimes, between evil and evil. Political reason is a computing principle; adding, subtracting, multiplying, and dividing, morally, and not metaphysically or mathematically, true moral denominations.[9]

---

[9] Burke, Edmund. *Reflections on the Revolution in France*. Indianapolis: Liberty Fund, 1790/1999, 153–54.

7
Legal and Political Equality

The Aim

In the preceding chapter, I distinguished between the moderate conservative and the ideal theorist approaches to understanding and coping with our political problems and conflicts between primary political goods. Moderate conservatives rely on the rule of law, justice, legal and political equality, liberty, and private property, as they have been understood in the course of the history of American society and its political system. These primary goods are now among our guides to how we should understand and cope with the problems and conflicts we face.

Ideal theorists rely on what they regard as the ideal political good whose importance should override any consideration that may conflict with it and guide our responses to our political problems and conflicts. They differ about whether the overriding ideal is justice, liberty, equality, God's law, a classless society, happiness, or something else. I refer to those who think that the ideal is equality as egalitarians and discuss them in this chapter.[1]

The aim of this chapter is both constructive and critical. It is to give reasons for the moderate conservative conception of legal and political equality in the context of our political system, and reasons against the egalitarian conception of equality as the ideal political

---

[1] For a survey of the vast literature and a bibliography of the relevant works, see Richard Arneson, "Egalitarianism." https://plato.stanford.edu/archives/sum2013/entries/egalitarianism/.

good that should in all contexts and conditions override any consideration that may conflict with it.

I begin with the eloquent statement of the constructive aim from the second paragraph of *The Declaration of Independence*:

> WE hold these Truths to be self-evident, that all Men are created equal, that they are endowed by their Creator with certain inalienable Rights, that among these are Life, Liberty, and the Pursuit of Happiness—That to secure these Rights, Governments are instituted among Men, deriving their power from the Consent of the Governed.

Libraries have been and continue to be filled with volumes that interpret, justify, criticize, and explore the implications of Jefferson's rousing sentences. They are the first words on equality in the American political system, but very far indeed from the last. I am concerned with the moderate conservative interpretation and justification of these fine words.

It has been generally agreed in the American political system, even when it has not been consistently followed, that equality is one of the primary political goods. Beyond that, however, its interpretation and extent have become one of our most controversial political problems. We may approach it by way of the ancient and abstract Aristotelian formula: treat like cases alike and different cases differently. The application of this formula to particular cases in our context and conditions requires specifying what the relevant cases in fact are and in what respects should they be treated alike or differently. It has also been generally agreed that the relevant cases are those in which it has to be decided whether particular human beings should be treated alike or differently on the basis of their likeness or differences.

Obvious questions then immediately arise: Who are the particular human beings who should be treated in these ways? What are the ways are in which they should or should not be treated alike or differently? Who should treat them in the way equality requires? How should conflicts between equality and other primary political goods be resolved? And what is the justification of this moderate conservative conception of equality?

The moderate conservative answers to these questions are as follows. The human beings in question are all and only American citizens. The ways in which they should be treated alike or differently are specified by the Constitution, the primary political goods, and the prevailing terms of cooperation. One particular way in which they should be treated alike is their equal legal and political standing as citizens. This should be recognized and followed in our political system, by those who act on its behalf in various official capacities, and also by those in our society who act on their own behalf as private persons.

This approach to our political problems and to conflicts between legal and political equality and other primary political goods depends on the conditions of the context in which the problems and conflicts occur, on what the conflicting political goods are, and on the political experience of those whose responsibility it is to cope with the unavoidable conflicts between the primary political goods. The justification of this moderate conservative conception of legal and political equality is that it has met the test of time as shown by the voluntary acceptance and participation of Americans in the political system, as we discussed in the preceding chapter.

The moderate conservative conception of legal and political equality, being dependent on the American political system, leaves open the question of what the conception of equality is or should be in other societies. The histories and experiences of other societies are very different from ours. We may or may not share with them some or many of the primary political goods. It is likely, however, that even if we do share them, we evaluate differently their relative importance in complex conditions when they conflict. Our understanding of the complexities of the history and political system of other societies is likely to be as imperfect as theirs is of ours. That is why moderate conservatives are reluctant to try to justify or criticize the political systems of other societies. Apart from the simple, awful, and unfortunately many cases of humanitarian atrocities, moderate conservatives advise restraint in moralizing about other societies.

Egalitarians do not share this reluctance. They claim that equality is a context-independent, unconditional, overriding ideal and that morality and politics require that it should be pursued by all societies regardless of differences between them. According to them, equality is not merely an American legal and political ideal. It includes as well the context-independent moral and political requirements of equal respect for all human beings in all contexts, which includes the equalization of economic resources both across and within all societies. The egalitarian conception of equality, then, is an all-inclusive ideal. Societies that fail to pursue this ideal are morally and politically reprehensible. Just so that there should be no doubt that egalitarians really hold this conception of equality as the overriding political ideal, here are some well-known statements of this view. I will continue to refer to them in what follows.

> All humans have an equal basic moral status. They possess the same fundamental rights, and the comparable interests of each person should count the same in calculations that determine social policy.[2]
>
> Equal concern is the sovereign virtue of political community—without it government is only tyranny.[3]
>
> Every plausible political theory has the same ultimate source, which is equality.... A theory is egalitarian ... if it accepts that

---

[2] Arneson, Richard. "What, if Anything, Renders All Humans Morally Equal?" in *Singer and His Critics*. Edited by Dale Jamieson. Oxford: Blackwell, 1999, 103.
[3] Dworkin, Ronald. *Sovereign Virtue*. Cambridge, MA: Harvard University Press, 2000, 1.

the interests of each member of the community matter, and matter equally.[4]

Everyone matters just as much as everyone else. [I]t is appalling that the most effective social system we have been able to devise permits ... material inequalities.[5]

Being egalitarian in some significant way relates to the need to have equal concern, at some level, for all persons involved.[6]

The essence of the principle of equal consideration of interests is that we give equal weight in our moral deliberations to the like interests of all those affected by our actions.[7]

Here is a representation of the differences between the moderate conservative and the egalitarian conceptions of equality, followed by an explanation of what they are and what consequences follow from them.

LEGAL AND POLITICAL EQUALITY AS A POLITICAL GOOD

MODERATE CONSERVATIVE	EGALITARIAN
primary good	overriding ideal
contextual	context-independent
conditional	unconditional
practical	theoretical
tested by time	morally required

The simplest disagreement from which the other disagreements indicated above follow is whether equality is only one of the important

---

[4] Kymlicka, Will. *Contemporary Political Philosophy*. Oxford: Clarendon Press, 1990, 4.
[5] Nagel, Thomas. *Equality and Partiality*. New York: Oxford University Press, 1991, 20.
[6] Sen, Amartya. *Inequality Reexamined*. Cambridge, MA: Harvard University Press, 1992, ix
[7] Singer, Peter. *Practical Ethics*. 2nd ed. Cambridge: Cambridge University Press, 1993, 21.

primary political goods that may conflict with other no less important primary political goods, or whether it is the ideal political good whose importance always in all contexts and conditions overrides whatever may conflict with it. If equality is such an overriding political ideal, then its pursuit should be the context-independent and unconditional aim of all societies, in all conditions. If it is only one of the primary political goods, then in our political system there may be contexts and practical conditions in which the protection of the rule of law, justice, liberty, or private property may be more important for sustaining the entire political system than the protection of equality.

This is not merely a verbal difference between the moderate conservative and the egalitarian conceptions of equality. It is a difference that makes a vital difference to those who live in our context. Upholding the Constitution, the continuity of our political system, evaluative framework, terms of cooperation, and our conception of how we think we should live all depend on it. Egalitarians claim and moderate conservatives deny that the ideal of equality should take precedence over all these considerations and that its pursuit should be recognized as an overriding, context-independent, unconditional moral and political requirements that all societies should aim to meet. Let us now consider some reasons for and against these claims.

Contextuality

I start with an agreement between moderate conservatives and egalitarians about a context-independent evaluation: basic human needs ought to be satisfied and human beings ought not to be harmed in ways that would make it impossible for anyone to live afterward a normal human life. Enslavement, mutilation, physical or psychological torture, being blinded or driven insane are examples of such harms. Morality requires that basic needs ought to be satisfied and no one ought to be deprived of their satisfaction. I refer to this as the humane requirement. It is an unfortunate fact of life that it is often violated, sometimes intentionally and sometimes because serious practical obstacles prevent meeting it.

A reasonable claim that something ought or ought not to be done requires that it should be morally, politically, and practically possible to do or not to do it. In some cases, what ought to be done cannot be done, because it is prevented by natural disasters, emergencies, scarcity of resources, serious social unrest, war, conflicts of legitimate interests, and the like. And in some other cases what normally ought not to be done nevertheless ought be done in order to avoid even worse violations of the humane requirement, as in sacrificing some innocent lives in order to save many more no less innocent lives, or if meeting the humane requirement in one case has the unacceptable consequence of violating it in another case. It is a disservice to morality and politics to require doing what is practically impossible or very difficult to do, or if doing it has just as bad or even worse consequences than not doing it.

Moderate conservatives and egalitarians may generally agree that there is a strong presumption in favor of meeting the humane requirement, even if they disagree about particular cases in which there are serious practical obstacles to meeting it. Be that as it may, even in the case of the humane requirement, the very strong moral, political, and practical presumption in favor of meeting it is contextual and conditional. The conflict between the moderate conservative and egalitarian conceptions of equality occurs at points *beyond* (!) their shared agreement that if there are no prohibitive moral, political, or practical obstacles to meeting the humane requirement, then it ought to be met. The political good of equality is a response to what should happen beyond the point of this shared agreement.

The moderate conservative conception is that the primary political good of legal and political equality requires that members of our society should be treated equally in respect to their legal and political rights and responsibilities, provided they meet certain elementary conditions that apply equally to everyone, such as citizenship, sanity, and minimum age and intelligence. It is difficult to be more specific about these conditions because some of them are matters of degree, and that makes individual cases disputable. Perhaps these disputes can be avoided by specifying that the presumption is that members of our society actually meet these elementary conditions, and the burden of proof lies with those who in some cases deny it.

Those who meet these conditions have equal right to political participation and protection by laws. Their particular rights are specified by the rule of law, the laws of justice, and the customary widely followed terms of cooperation that have met the test of time. With the rights go responsibilities that are specified in the same ways. If the responsibilities are not met by some people, then their rights are jeopardized. What the particular rights and responsibilities are, and whether or not they have been met, are, as we all know, subject to endless disputes. It is the task of the legal system to adjudicate these disputes by following the appropriate laws and procedures. If all goes as it should, everyone in our society has equal political and legal rights and responsibilities provided he or she meets the relevant conditions.

Egalitarians accept these commonplaces, but they go beyond them and claim that it is a moral and political requirement that all human beings should be treated with equal respect. And they claim as well that equal respect involves equalizing the economic resources of members of our society and to extend the effort to equalize the economic resources of all human beings in all societies. Egalitarians then claim that this extension of all-inclusive respect and the equalization of economic resources to all human beings is an overriding, context-independent, and unconditional moral and political requirement that all societies ought to meet. Moderate conservatives think that this egalitarian claim elevates what they wish into an unattainable moral and political ideal.

To avoid misunderstanding, I stress that the deep disagreement between egalitarians and moderate conservatives is not about meeting the humane requirement, but about the equalization of respect and economic resources beyond the level of the humane requirement. The moderate conservative view is *not* that those living in a moderately well-off society may be justifiably indifferent to whether the humane requirement of people in other societies is met. Morally and politically committed people should not be indifferent to the starvation, enslavement, mutilation, murder, torture, and to other all too familiar horrors inflicted on people in any society. The disagreement between moderate conservatives and egalitarians is about the question of whether equalization of economic resources both across and within societies is a moral and political requirement. Egalitarians claim that it is an overriding, unconditional, context-independent moral and political requirement. The earlier citations leave no doubt that egalitarians really do make this claim. Moderate conservatives deny it. In this denial they are supported by Aristotle:[8]

> [if we] inquire what is the best constitution for most states, and the best life for me, neither assuming a standard of excellence which is above ordinary persons, nor an education which is exceptionally favored by nature and circumstances, nor yet an ideal state which is an aspiration only, but having regard to the life in which the majority are able to share, and to a government which states in general can attain.

Turning now to reasons against this egalitarian conception of equality, I note that, as far as I know, none of the works cited earlier discuss the following centrally relevant practical obstacles to doing what egalitarians claim ought to be done. First, the egalitarian moral

---

[8] Aristotle. *Politics*, 1295a25-31. Translated by Benjamin Jowett in *The Complete Works of Aristotle*. Edited by Jonathan Barnes. Princeton, NJ: Princeton University Press, 1984.

and political requirement in some cases should not be met because the conditions in the receiving society make it probable that the resources will be used in a civil war, or in massacring segments of its own people, or in waging an aggressive war against another political system, or in enriching thieving oligarchs, or in the brutal repression of its citizens. It cannot be a context-independent moral or political requirement to equalize resources that would be used to make matters worse than they already are in a society. This is one reason why contexts matter, contrary to the egalitarian denial of it.

Another reason is that it may be that a society could not benefit from the equalization of economic resources because it would endanger its way of life. The consequences of meeting the supposed egalitarian political and moral requirement in such a case would be far worse than doing nothing. The long-standing equilibrium of many traditional African, Indian, and tribal societies in various parts of the world have been disrupted by bestowing on them benevolently intended economic resources, like insecticides that increase the yield of their crops but poison their domestic animals, teaching them hygiene that lowered their resistance, introducing new crops that disrupted their traditional diet and caused new diseases, or contraception that resulted in fewer children who could learn from their elders traditional and necessary skills on which they have relied since time immemorial and who would later look after the aged in their family. This is a second reason why contexts matter, and ignoring it has morally and politically unacceptable consequences.

A third reason is that egalitarians do not consider the possibility that some societies may be responsible for their impoverished economic condition. The impoverishment of their economic resources may be caused by corruption, nepotism, theft, bribery, or extortion by organized banditry. The practices of a society may be responsible for its economic hardships. Is that not a relevant consideration in considering the supposed egalitarian moral requirement to transfer additional resources to them, which will then strengthen their native exploiters? Are societies not responsible for the consequences of their practices? Would it have been an overriding, context-independent, unconditional political and moral requirement to equalize American, German, and Japanese economic resources in WWII? or American, Iranian, and Chinese economic resources now? or Shiite and Sunni economic resources at any time in history? This is another reason why contexts matter, and why egalitarians are wrong to ignore it.[9]

It might be thought that egalitarians could not possibly make claims from which such obviously unacceptable consequences follow. But they do:[10]

Arneson: "All humans have an equal basic moral status. They possess the same fundamental rights, and the comparable interests of each person should count the same in calculations that determine social policy."

Dworkin: "Equal concern is the sovereign virtue of political community—without it government is only tyranny."

---

[9] "Their very way of living led these writers to indulge in abstract theories and generalizations regarding the nature of government, and to place blind confidence in these. For living as they did, quite out of touch with practical politics, they lacked the experience which might have tempered their enthusiasms. Thus they completely failed to perceive the very real obstacles in the way of even the most praiseworthy reforms, and to gauge the perils involved in even the most salutary revolutions. That they should not have had the least presentiment of these dangers was only to be expected, since ... they had little acquaintance with the realities of public life, what, indeed, was *terra incognita* to them. ... As a result, our literary men became much bolder in their speculations, more addicted to general ideas and systems, more contemptuous of the wisdom of the ages, and even more inclined to trust their individual reason than most of those who have written books on politics from a philosophic angle." Alexis de Tocqueville, *The Old Regime and the French Revolution*. Translated by Stuart Gilbert. New York: Doubleday, 1858/1955, 140–41.

[10] Arneson, Richard J. "Equality" in *A Companion to Contemporary Political Philosophy*. Edited by Robert Goodin and Phillip Pettit. Oxford: Blackwell, 1993, 489. Dworkin, Ronald. *Sovereign Virtue*. Cambridge, MA: Harvard University Press, 2000, 1. Nagel, Thomas. *Equality and Partiality*. New York: Oxford University Press, 1991, 20. Rawls, John. *A Theory of Justice*. Cambridge, MA: Harvard University Press, 1971, 100–101. Sen, Amartya. *Inequality Reexamined*. Cambridge, MA: Harvard University Press, 1992, ix. Singer, Peter. *Practical Ethics*. 2nd ed. Cambridge: Cambridge University Press, 1993, 21.

Nagel: "Everyone has reasons deriving from an impersonal standpoint to want the world arranged in a way that accords better with impartiality."

Rawls: "The idea is to redress the bias of contingencies in the direction of equality."

Sen: "Being egalitarian in some significant way relates to the need to have equal concern, at some level, for all persons involved."

Singer: "The essence of the principle of equal consideration of interests is that we give equal weight in our moral deliberations to the like interests of all those affected by our actions."

Egalitarians claim that the equalization of economic resources is an overriding, context-independent, unconditional, moral and political requirement regardless of who are the givers and the receivers, what the conditions are in the contexts in which resources are unequal, and why the conditions are as they are. It is a waste of words and economic resources to urge acting on a moral and political requirement that is practically impossible to meet. Helping others depends on familiarity with their plight and their context. Yet egalitarian ideal theorists are indifferent to what the facts are. They focus on the ideal of equality which they claim holds in all contexts regardless of what the facts are. And this, I have tried to show, has unacceptable consequences.

I think that what egalitarians really have in mind is that America should aid poor countries in need of it. This is a plausible claim, provided we forget about the implausible ideal theory in which it comes packaged. In point of fact, meeting that claim has been a longstanding American policy whose justification does not depend on the egalitarian ideal theory. The policy is called Foreign Aid. It has been routinely provided since the middle of WWII. It does not depend on urging policy-makers to follow the egalitarians' rhetoric and nor does it ignore the contextual facts. Nor does it pursue a supposedly overriding, unconditional, context-independent political and moral requirement to disregard how the recipients of the aid are likely to use the gifted resources, what effect it may have on the recipients' form of life, and whether or not there may be corrupt practices in the receiving context that make it likely that the transferred resources will enrich the very people who are responsible for the economic hardships of their people.

Conditionality

Moderate conservatives think that legal and political equality is a conditional primary political good. It may conflict with other conditional primary political goods and in some conditions one, in other conditions another should override the conflicting one. If anarchy threatens, protecting the rule of law is more important than equality. If liberty is endangered by religious or ideological fanatics, then its defense should take precedence over treating its friends and enemies with equal respect. If felonies are widespread, then the enforcement of the laws of justice overrides the felons' claim to equality and liberty. Being a primary political good, there is always a presumption in favor of legal and political equality, but the presumption can be defeated in certain conditions. This is true of all primary political goods. Political life is full of cases in which they conflict. All the primary political goods are dependent on the prevailing conditions, especially when in adverse conditions the evaluations that follow from them conflict. Such conflicts are natural and expected parts of the American political system. They call for flexibility and the willingness to respond non-dogmatically to changing conditions.

If equality were an unconditional political good, as egalitarians claim that it is, it would have unacceptable consequences. In order to fix this point, consider yet another example close to home. In the Covid epidemic, especially early on, the supply of vaccines was limited. No reasonable American could suppose that it is a moral and political requirement of American society to equalize the distribution of the vaccines by making fewer of them available to Americans so that more could be sent, say, to Brazil or India. If equality were an unconditional political good, American policymakers would be morally and politically required to do this. If they did it, they would betray their elementary obligation to the people whose interests they were supposed to protect.

It is easy to talk in abstractions about the moral and political requirements of equal respect and the equalization of economic resources. When, however, we face concrete situations in which not everyone can be equally respected and the much-needed economic resources are scarce, then fine words must be replaced by making hard choices that take into account the prevailing conditions and contextual considerations. In such situations, which are routine in our society, insisting that the ideal of equality is overriding, unconditional, and context-independent would make matters much more difficult than they already are. Why then do egalitarians insist that all human beings in all contexts and conditions have a right to equal respect and an equal share of economic resources?

In considering this question, it is crucial to remember that the dispute between egalitarians and moderate conservatives is not about meeting the humane requirement. They agree that it should be met, provided it is practically possible and its moral and political consequences are acceptable. The question is about the egalitarian claim and the moderate conservative denial of it that it is a context-independent and unconditional moral and political requirement that all human beings should be equally respected and have an equal share of economic resources beyond the humane requirement. In this respect, moderate conservatives have the unlikely support of both Locke and Kant. According to Locke:

> Though I have said above, *Chap. II that all men by nature are equal*, I cannot be supposed to understand all sorts of equality: *age* or *virtue* may give men a just precedency: *excellency of parts and merit* may place others above the common level: *birth* may

subject some, and *alliance* or *benefits* others, to pay observance to those to whom nature, gratitude, or other respects, may have made their due.[11]

Kant agrees:

This thoroughgoing equality of individuals within a state, as its subjects, is quite consistent with the greatest inequality in terms of the quantity and degree of their possessions, whether in physical or mental superiority over others in external goods.... Every member of a commonwealth must be allowed to attain any level of rank within it ... to which his talent, his industry and his luck can take him; and his fellow subjects may not stand in his way.... He may bequeath ... whatever ... can be acquired as property and also alienated by him, and so in a series of generations produce a considerable inequality of financial circumstances among the members of a commonwealth.[12]

According to moderate conservatives, human beings have not only rights but also responsibilities. In our society the rights are defined by the Constitution, the rule of law, the laws of justice, and by the less formal terms of cooperation. Some rights are written down and whether an action violates them is decided by the courts, judges, or referees. Other rights are informal, conventional, and merely understood. Their violation is a lesser breach of a relationship, a verbal agreement, a custom, or of the more or less informal rules of some practical activity, like respecting privacy, being polite or hospitable, and customary ways of expressing

---

[11] Locke, John. *Second Treatise of Government*. Edited by C.B. Macpherson. Indianapolis: Hackett, 1690/1980, Chapter VI, par. 54.
[12] Kant, Immanuel. "On the common saying: That may be correct in theory, but it is of no use in practice" in *Practical Philosophy* in *The Cambridge Edition of the Works of Immanuel Kant*. Translated and edited by Mary J. Gregor. Cambridge: Cambridge University Press, 1996, 292–93.

disagreement, regret, or gratitude, or treating dogs or cats, and so forth. Responsibilities are to honoring rights and avoiding violations of them. Thus rights and responsibilities are intimately connected. Rights can be taken away, given up, lost, or fall into disuse, and then responsibilities fade with them. But if the rights hold, then so do the responsibilities.

If rights and responsibilities are understood in this way, then they are obviously contextual, conditional, and practical because they are parts of some formal or informal social practice. There are no overriding, context-independent, and unconditional rights and responsibilities. Both are conventional social arrangements. Human rights are rights human beings have in the context of a particular society. There are no rights outside of human societies. It makes very good sense to say that there are things human beings should have in all societies, or things that should not be done to human beings in any society. But saying that is no more than expressing the wish that human beings will not be treated in inhuman ways. That wish is surely shared by all decent people regardless of their moral and political differences. Making that wish more than a wish, however, depends on the context and the conditions of a human society.

Now egalitarians once again go beyond this and claim that it is an overriding, context-independent, and unconditional right of all human beings to be equally respected and to have an equal share of humanity's economic resources. What in practical terms does this mean? Respect is a way in which human beings should treat one another. Who should treat whom with respect? Some egalitarians say that it should be the representatives of the society who treat individuals with equal respect and provide an equal share of economic resources to those who are and those who are not part of the society? Now why should the representatives of our society treat in these ways the armed forces who defend it and those who attack it? those who sustain it and those who betray it? or its homegrown criminals and their victims?

Perhaps the supposed overriding, context-independent, and unconditional requirement is that equal respect and equal economic resources are owed to all human beings on some basic universally human level to which all human beings have a right simply because they are human. I ask: what does this basic respect involve? It cannot be simply that the humane requirement of every human being should be met. As we have already seen, there are conditions in which it could not be met, and other conditions in which it should not be met even if it were possible. These conditions are, for instance, when the humane requirements of different people conflict; or when crises, natural disasters, war, the scarcity of resources, or emergencies prevent meeting them for everyone. In such conditions hard choices have to be made, and not everyone's humane requirement could be met. Meeting the humane requirement cannot then be the overriding, context-independent, and unconditional moral and political requirement that egalitarians claim that it is. And, in any case, the egalitarian claim goes far beyond meeting the humane requirement of treating everyone equally.

The additional egalitarians claim is that it is an overriding, context-independent, and unconditional moral and political requirement of all societies to equalize the economic resources of all human beings. Now consider how exactly that could be done? Egalitarians might say that the way to proceed is to put a monetary value on all the economic resources of all societies and then aim to equalize the amount held by each and every society. What then would count as an economic resource? Only gold deposits, cash, income, future tax revenues, and investments? How about patents, agricultural, engineering, medical expertise? Are buildings, mineral deposits, roads, trains, tourist attractions economic resources? And could they be equalized?

Even if, unlikely as that is, reasonable answers were found to these and many similarly difficult questions, the monetary value of economic resources constantly fluctuates as needs, production costs, supplies, demands, and conditions change. Making sense of the egalitarian requirement of equalizing everyone's economic resources depends on specifying how the requirement could be met. Moderate conservatives doubt that this could be done. Giving aid to the needy does not equalize economic resources. It uses the surplus of one society to help the needy in another society. That is certainly a good thing to do. But it could no more be described as the equalization of everyone's economic resources than giving a dollar to a beggar could be.

I think that what egalitarians find objectionable is that some people are well-off while others live on the subsistence level and sometimes fall below it. Certainly, those who have much should help those who have less than enough. But for that we do not need an ideal theory that makes it an overriding, context-independent, unconditional moral and political requirement that all governments should respect all human beings equally and set up a perpetual world-wide redistributive system that has the impossible aim of equalizing the economic resources of all human beings in all societies. If we look beyond the fine words of egalitarian ideal theorists, what we find are difficult practical questions that stand in need of practical answers. Moderate conservatives certainly agree that answers are needed. But finding them depends on moral, political, and practical considerations that differ with contexts and conditions.

Let us then pass over the egalitarian ideal theory of what representatives of governments are morally and politically required to do, and concentrate instead on their claim that individual human beings who are acting in a private capacity are morally required to respect equally all other individual human beings. Respecting them involves acting or refraining from acting toward them in particular ways. Egalitarians are not forthcoming about what particular respectful treatments they have in mind. I assume, however, that in normal conditions it involves treating others in ordinary encounters with consideration, taking care not to injure their interests or to offend them, be friendly rather than hostile to them, in short, treating them with common decency and good will. This is clearly possible, but it raises the question of why reasonable people would do it. It is not an adequate answer that they should because they are responding to human beings.

Being human is indeed a necessary condition of being treated with equal respect, but it is not sufficient for it. Respect depends not just on being human but also on actions and on how they affect others. Why should we treat with equal respect friends and enemies of humanity? those who protect and those who violate the humane requirements of others? or victimizers and their victims? We have not only rights, but also responsibilities. We are not responsible for the capacities we are born with, but we are responsible for what we make of them. If we are unable to foresee the obvious consequences of our actions, then we are not responsible for them. Our responsibility is for the consequences we can be reasonably expected to foresee and evaluate in the situations in which we can decide how we should act. They include respecting the rights of others. If we violate them, we damage both them and our right to equal respect.

From the point of view of moderate conservatism, this seems to be in the great majority of cases the plain common sense connection between rights and responsibilities. Sometimes complexities make it difficult to decide whether or not rights in particular cases have been respected and responsibilities met. But most cases in everyday life are straightforward. We do not have rights and responsibilities because we are human. We have them because of what we make of our humanity. And the respect we are owed and the responsibilities we have unavoidably vary with who we are, in what context we have to act, what possibilities are open to us, and especially on what we do. The egalitarian view of equal rights ignores the facts of life.

Practicality

This brings us to another crucial difference between moderate conservatism and egalitarianism: the approach of the first is practical, the approach of the other is theoretical.[13]

The first acknowledges that we have to face and cope with perennial problems in VUCA situations; the second assumes that we can rely on an ideal theory from which we can infer what reason requires us to do.

In order to understand better the implications of this difference between them, start with the fact that our society presently faces exceptionally serious problems that affect our entire way of life. Among them are the Covid epidemic; the deep divisions during President Trump's term in office and the contested outcome of the election at the end of it; the assault on the Capitol; the increasing power and militancy of China; waves of illegal immigration; racial conflicts; episodes of police brutality; spreading insecurity and reciprocal hatreds; the rise of armed militant antigovernment organizations; unacceptably high and increasing rate of murder; and numerous other problems that could be added to this list.

Each of these problems in its own way challenges our political system, the rule of law, justice, and the existing terms of cooperation. Our political system routinely yields conflicting economic, legal, moral, political, and religious evaluations of how we should cope with the problems we face. We need to understand the complexities involved in them and find reasonable ways of responding to them.

---

[13] "Historians, and even common sense, may inform us, that, however specious these ideas of *perfect* equality may seem, they are really, at bottom, *impracticable*; and were they not so, would be extremely *pernicious* to human society. Render possessions ever so equal, men's different degrees of art, care, and industry will immediately break that equality. Or if you check these virtues, you reduce society to the most extreme indigence; and instead of preventing want and beggary in a few, render it unavoidable to the whole community." Hume, David. *Enquiry concerning the Principles of Morals*. Edited by Tom L. Beauchamp. Oxford: Oxford University Press, 1777/1998, 91.

The problems are complex because what we do about them affects our national interest, security, standard of living, welfare programs, procedures for conflict-resolution, public health, law enforcement, educational system, reform of obsolete practices, international negotiations about the resolution of conflicting interests; and so on and on. The complexities of these problems increase manifold because the on-going changes in foreign and domestic conditions require the continuous evaluation and re-evaluation of the relative urgency of these already pressing complex problems. And that, in turn, depends on the practical political experience and the general grasp of the possibilities and limits of our policies of those who have to make the difficult decisions. It does not depend on ideal theorists who deliberately construct their theories in abstract terms as far removed as possible from the political realities of the particularities of the contexts and conditions to which they apply their theories. One political thinker who saw this clearly was Hume.[14]

Even if egalitarians were right, and we should be guided by an ideal theory, it would still have to be applied to the complex problems we face. And that can be reasonably done only if we focus on the relevant contexts, the prevailing conditions, the available alternatives, their likely consequences, and the acceptability of the various possible policies to Americans in general. These complex practical problems call for practical responses to concrete problems in particular conditions within the acceptable limits of economic, legal, moral, political, and religious modes of evaluation. The very nature of ideal theories—their commitment to an overriding, context-independent, unconditional ideal—prescinds

---

[14] "[Hume was] a particularly fine representative of one strand in conservative thinking, whose main characteristics are a cautious and moderate approach to politics (which does not exclude progressive change, provided this is gradual), backed up by a sceptical attitude towards all grandiose schemes for social or political reconstruction erected on rationalist foundations. This has at most times been the dominant element within British conservatism, and Hume might with justice be awarded pride of place in an account of that tradition." Miller, David. *Philosophy and Ideology in Hume's Political Thought.* Oxford: Clarendon Press, 1981, 15

from the complexities of practical considerations that are unavoidably particular and cannot be general. The more we concentrate on coping with complex practical problems, the less help we can get from any ideal theory, whatever may be the overriding ideal its defenders favor. This was very clear to William James,[15] but not to ideal theorists:

> The philosopher, then, *qua* philosopher, is not better able to determine the best universe in concrete emergency than other men.... He sees ... not a question of this good or that good simply taken, but of two total universes with which these goods respectively belong. He knows that he must vote always for the richer universe but which particular universe this is he cannot know for certain in advance.

Why then do egalitarians rely on their ideal theory in seeking politically feasible responses to complex practical problems? In the words of Rawls,[16] who introduced the term into egalitarian thought,

> The reason for beginning with ideal theory is that it provides ... the only basis for the systematic grasp of ... more pressing problems.... I shall assume that a deeper understanding can be gained in no other way, and that the nature and aims of a perfectly just society is the fundamental part of the theory of justice.

These words and the idea they express have become exceptionally influential in egalitarian thought.

---

[15] James, William. "The Moral Philosopher and the Moral Life" in *Writings: 1878–1899*, New York: The Library of America, 1992, 595–617/614.
[16] Rawls, John. *A Theory of Justice*. Cambridge, MA: Harvard University Press, 1971, 9, 8.

Moderate conservatives deny that an ideal theory is the only basis we have for coping with complex practical problems. What we need for coping with the Covid epidemic depends on having and administering the vaccine. Responding to the challenges presented by China depends on skillful diplomacy, reducing our dependence on their manufacturing capacities, countering their unfair trading policies, and strengthening our military capacities. Coping with illegal immigration depends on finding ways of stemming the tide of those who seek a better life here than what they have in their own country. Reducing the threat of militant anti-government organizations and the murder rate depends on making assault weapons unavailable to would-be murderers. And so on for finding practical ways of coping with our practical problems. It cannot be reasonably supposed that the ideal theory of equality is, as Rawls and his followers suppose, "the only basis for systematic grasp of . . . pressing problems," that "a deeper understanding can be gained in no other way," and that we must rely on it to cope with our problems.

The moderate conservative view is that finding reasonable ways of coping with complex practical problems depends on relying on the political experience of those who have been elected or appointed to do what needs to be done within the possibilities and limits of our present conditions. They need to be flexible enough to respond to the contingencies that beset us, to changing conditions, and to conflicts between primary political goods. And we need to accept that if we resolve our political conflicts in favor of one of our primary political goods at one time, then we must shortchange the other; and that changes in our conditions require continuous adjustments of parts of our political system in order to be able to continue to rely on the temporarily unchallenged and unproblematic parts of it.

This, then, is the moderate conservative practical approach to our complex political problems. Part of it is to recognize that in our political system legal and political equality is one, but only one, of the primary political goods. It may conflict with other primary political goods, such as the rule of law, justice, liberty, and private property. How their conflicts should be resolved depends on finding reasonable ways of responding to the complexities, conflicts, and to foreign and domestic threats.

Egalitarians, by contrast, are ideal theorists. Their approach to our complex and difficult problems is theoretical and it is guided by regarding equality as the unconditional, and context-independent ideal that overrides any consideration that may conflict with it. So consider how egalitarians might respond to the complex problems we, in our society, now face and have to cope with. If consistent, they will be guided, as we have seen in Note 3, by their belief that "each person should count the same in calculations that determine social policy"; "everyone matters just as much as everyone else"; "the need to have equal concern ... for all persons involved"; and give "equal weight in our moral deliberations to the like interests of all those affected by our actions."

The egalitarian approach then requires, among other things, that we should have equal concern, say, for Chinese, North Korean, Iranian, and American interests in the protection of national security, standard of living, humane responses to suffering, law enforcement, public health, system of education, and so forth. And we should distribute equally between us, them, and the rest of the world the economic resources needed for the satisfaction of these interests.

Any government that proceeded in this way would violate the basic interests that they have been elected to protect. It would treat our enemies as if they were friends, and our friends in the same way as we treat our enemies. It would require us to set up a system of world-wide re-distribution of our resources regardless of how that might affect the lives of those who provide and those who receive the resources. It would involve using the taxes collected from us to benefit those in other, often hostile, societies. And if egalitarians were consistent in their commitment to their ideal theory, they would follow such destructive policies since they regard equality as the overriding ideal according to which morality and politics require the equal treatment of all those who may be affected by our actions. No reasonable person who realized the practical complexities, difficulties, and implications involved in following the egalitarian ideal theory would accept it. Yet egalitarians are committed to it.

Perhaps they do so because they are appalled by the inequalities in our society and the disadvantage of some of our fellow citizens when compared with the advantages of others. This is understandable, humane, and calls for ameliorative policies. Such policies, however, are already in place. This is what the many and various welfare program are designed to do and this is what graduated tax rates are intended to finance.

Furthermore, the proposed policy that follows from the egalitarian ideal theory is to equalize the resources of all human beings in all societies, not just those of our fellow citizens. The proposed policy is that "each person should count the same in calculations that determine social policy"; "everyone matters just as much as everyone else"; and we should "have equal concern . . . for all persons involved." Since our resources are limited, the more of them are directed toward people in other societies, the less remains for our disadvantaged fellow citizens. The egalitarian policy would worsen the situation of those in our society whose predicament prompted the policy in the first place.

This is one small part of the complexities involved in applying the egalitarian moral and political requirement of how we should cope with the problems our society faces. Before issuing moral and political imperatives, egalitarians should understand that all of our policies have costs; we can do something we should only if we do not do something else we should also do; our resources are limited; and we cannot do all that we should like to do. It is practically impossible for us to follow the egalitarian ideal theory. We have to know the contexts and the conditions of the recipient societies, weigh the relative costs and benefits, the complexities of the various societies history and form of life. And we have to make hard choices, rather than try to follow practically impossible moral and political requirements that follow from an ideal theory.

Egalitarians should understand as well that the reasonable response to the complexities of our problems and the limitations of our resources is not to construct an ideal theory that has destructive consequences for our society and doubtful ones for other societies. And should not issue moral and political imperatives without taking account of the relevant facts, evaluating the relative importance of the various costs and benefits of incompatible policies, and form a realistic, fact-based view of the short- and long-range consequences of following one among the various available policies. But this is not what they do. Although unelected, self-appointed, and politically inexperienced, they construct an ideal theory about how the world could, would, and should be if only it conformed to their ideal theory.

Moderate conservatives think that the reasonable alternative to egalitarianism is to face our complex problems and be guided by politically experienced people who have been elected to do just that. It is the responsibility of such people to follow the Constitution, the rule of law and the other primary political goods, to take into account the relevant facts, weigh the costs and consequences of various policies, and be flexible enough to change them if conditions require it. That is what our political system has been doing for over 300 years. It has not always done it well. With more political experience and hindsight we can now see how it could and should have done it better, more prudently, more fairly. But it has sustained our society that, with all its many faults and past and present problems, has met and continues to meet the test of time and it is voluntarily supported by the great majority of those who live in it.

The upshot of these considerations is that egalitarians face a dilemma. If they remain committed to equality as an overriding political ideal, then the policies that follow from their commitment are destructive of American society and have practically impossible aims. If they allow that equality is only a primary political good, then they must renounce their ideal theory, accept that equality is not an overriding political good, that it may conflict with other primary political goods, that coping with conflicts between political goods depends on contextual and changing facts and conditions. They should not, then, appoint themselves as legislators for all of humanity and moralize about the political systems of other societies. In effect, they should regard equality as do moderate conservatives.

Justification

The justification of the moderate conservative conception of legal and political equality is that it is a time-honored part of our political system that has been meeting the test of time for 300 years. It is sustained by the voluntary participation of the great majority of Americans who live conventional lives, do what they can to observe common decencies, raise a family, earn a living, pay taxes, follow and benefit from the primary political goods of the rule of law, justice, legal and political equality, liberty, and private property. They form the solid middle that sustains American society. They are unaffected by the polemics of theoreticians, moralists, and by the scurrilous, truth-twisting, sensationalism of the media. They sustain the political system that holds the country together. The protection of it is the aim and the justification of moderate conservatism. And that is what egalitarians aim to change.

Moderate conservatives ask: what is the justification of the egalitarian conception of equality as the ideal political good that morality and politics supposedly require all societies to follow? Here are some answers well-known egalitarians give:[17]

---

[17] Berlin, Isaiah. "Equality" in *Concepts and Categories*. Edited by Henry Hardy. London: Hogarth Press, 1978, 102 Feinberg, Joel. *Social Philosophy*. Englewood Cliffs, NJ: Prentice-Hall, 1990, 4.

Berlin: "Equality is one of the oldest and deepest elements in liberal thought . . . Like all human ends it cannot be defended or justified."
Feinberg: Equality "is not grounded on anything more ultimate than itself, and it is not demonstrably justifiable."
Nagel: seeks "a moral basis for the kind of liberal egalitarianism that seems to me plausible. I do not have such an argument."
Rawls writes in concluding his discussion of "The Basis of Equality": "essential equality is . . . equality of consideration. . . . Of course, none of this is literally an argument. I have not set out the premises from which this conclusion follows."
Williams: "We believe . . . that in some sense every citizen, indeed every human being . . . deserves equal consideration. . . . There is nothing more basic in terms of which to justify it. . . . But for us, it is simply there."

Imagine the howl of outrage with which egalitarians would treat libertarians, Christian, Jewish, or Moslem fundamentalists, communists, or indeed conservatives if they responded to egalitarian challenges of their moral conviction with the same complacent confidence as these egalitarians respond to challenges of their own certainties. These egalitarian "justifications" simply re-affirm what is in question, and that can satisfy only those who already accept the views that are being questioned. And then they go on to condemn all those who do not accept their views for being:[18]

Nagel, Thomas. "Equality" in *Mortal Questions*. Cambridge: Cambridge University Press, 1979, 108.
Rawls, John. *A Theory of Justice*. Cambridge, MA: Harvard University Press, 1971, 507, 509.
Williams, Bernard. "Philosophy as a Humanistic Discipline" in *Philosophy as a Humanistic Discipline*. Princeton, NJ: Princeton University Press, 2006, 194–95.

[18] Arneson, Richard. "What, if Anything, Renders All Humans Morally Equal?" in *Singer and His Critics*. Edited by Dale Jamieson. Oxford: Blackwell, 1999, 103.
Dworkin, Ronald. *Sovereign Virtue*. Cambridge, MA: Harvard University Press, 2000, 103.
Kymlicka, Will. *Liberalism, Community, and Culture*. Oxford: Clarendon Press, 1989, 40.

"white supremacist or admirer of Adolf Hitler . . . [and] rightly regarded as beyond the pale of civilized dialogue"; for their "neglect of equality in contemporary politics is therefore shameful"; for holding "theories, like Nazism [that] deny that each person matters equally. But such theories do not merit serious consideration."

Instead of abusing their critics and offering dogmatic restatements of their views, egalitarians should give sorely needed reasons for them that would justify the far-reaching implications of the egalitarian commitment to equality as an overriding, context-independent, unconditional, and morally and politically required ideal. In the name of that admittedly unjustifiable ideal, egalitarians condemn all societies as morally and politically unacceptable because they fail to treat with equal respect violators and defenders of the humane requirement and protectors and subverters of the society that sustains them. Egalitarians ignore the fact that no society in human history has ever come even close to meeting what they claim to be moral and political requirements. It follows from their claims that all human societies known to us, including our own, are beyond the pale of civilized dialogue, shameful, and like Nazis. Yet, when their claims are challenged, egalitarians respond by the dogmatic assertion that their challenged and unjustified faith is the foundation on which morality and politics rest.

Egalitarians reject these criticisms. They will say, I think, that on a fundamental level that underlies human differences, the humane requirement of all human beings should be met at all times, in all societies, contexts, and conditions. If this were all that egalitarians claimed, there would be no difference between moderate conservatives and egalitarians. But they claim much more. They claim that beyond meeting the humane requirement there is the moral and political requirement of the equal distribution of economic resources and equal respect of every human being in all contexts and conditions, regardless of the rationality, morality, and practical consequences of their intended beneficiaries' actions. And they claim that this is a moral and political requirement that all societies should meet.

This untenable claim goes far beyond the humane requirement. It ignores the elementary fact of moral and political life that no past or present society would be willing to distribute its economic resources equally to all human beings in the entire world and treat all human beings with equal respect, regardless of their actions. No society could, should, or would accept doing that as an overriding, context-independent, unconditional moral requirement. Yet this is what egalitarians claim is a moral and political requirement that all societies, in all conditions, in all contexts should meet.

A particularly vexatious egalitarian stratagem is that when their claims are challenged, they accuse their critics of advocating the violation of the humane requirement, which moderate conservatives in fact accept. And then egalitarians go on to claim far beyond the humane requirement that it is an overriding, context-independent, unconditional moral and political requirement that all societies should distribute economic resources equally to everyone, without explaining how that could possibly be done. And they claim as well that it is a moral and political requirement to treat all human beings with equal respect, regardless of the consequences of their actions for the well-being of their society and for the human beings who are affected by their actions. These are the claims beyond the humane requirement that moderate conservatives find unacceptable.

In closing, I stress that the moderate conservatives conception of legal and political equality is that it is a primary political good. It has been recognized and valued as such in the history of American society and our political system. According to it, it is a moral and political requirement that Americans should be treated equally by the laws and have equal right to participate in the political system by voting, running for office, and expressing approval or disapproval of laws and elected officials. Legal and political equality understood in this way is a right that all adult American citizens are presumed to have unless disqualified by mental incapacity or criminality.

It is a lamentable fact that this right has often been violated. This ought not to have happened. American society can continue to meet the test of time only if the legal and political equality of Americans is better protected in the future than it has been in the past. This is one of the practically realizable aims of moderate conservatism.

8
Liberty

The Concept and Its Complexities

A great deal of theoretical work has been done to clarify the concept of liberty,[1] but no consensus has so far emerged from it. It is generally agreed that liberty is to be able to live and act as we want. But this must be immediately qualified by the acknowledgment that how we live and act must in some ways and for some reasons be limited. And then the complexities begin: what should the limits be; should they be economic, legal, moral, personal, political, religious, or something else? is everyone constrained by the same limits? do and should the limits hold only in some societies but not in others? are the limits natural or social? are they enforced? by whom and how? are the limits personal we impose on ourselves, or social imposed by authorities? and what authorities, if any, are entitled to impose them? are violations of the limits punishable by law? morality? social disapproval? private conscience? is the mere threat of punishment a limit? are limits justified? how? what are the particular choices, opportunities, actions, customs, ways of life that are, may be, or should be limited? All these questions and the various answers given to them are complex and often conflicting.

The concept is even more complex and contested than this because the disagreements about it persist even if, unlikely as that is, agreement is reached about what particular components

---

[1] For two among numerous other surveys and bibliography, see Flickschuh, Katrin. "Freedom" in *The Routledge Companion to Social and Political Philosophy*. Edited by Gerald Gaus and Fred D'Agostino. New York: Routledge, 2013, 562–72, and Carter, Ian. "Liberty." https://plato.stanford.edu/entries/liberty-positive-negative/.

the concept includes and excludes. For there will be further disagreements about the relative importance of the agreed upon components. Some limits, opportunities, the losses of some liberties, and some violations of the limits are more important than others. Some conflicts between the components of liberty, and between liberty and the other political goods—the rule of law, justice, legal and political equality, and private property—are more wrenching than others, and have much-disputed importance from the point of view of the society and the individuals whose liberty is limited.

Liberty, as all the other primary political goods, are subject to the perennial problems of adverse contingencies, conflicts between it and other political and non-political goods, and to compromises we have to make when we must limit liberty in order to protect other goods that are just as important in some contexts and conditions as liberty is. These complexities lead to VUCA situations, and we have to find reasonable ways of dealing with them.

Moderate conservatives do not think that these VUCA situations can be resolved once and for all. There cannot be a general theory of the concept of liberty that all reasonable and knowledgeable people will upon reflection accept because its importance depends on the context and the conditions of the society in which the VUCA situations have to be faced and contend with. Liberty is a primary political good, but how the perennial problems affecting it are reasonably answered depends on the political system of the society in which the questions arise, the relative importance of the answers given to them from an economic, legal, moral, personal, political, or religious point of view, and the variety of the external and internal conditions of the society in which the questions arise and the answers need to be given.

It makes a great difference to where the limits of liberty are drawn and how conflicts between liberty and other primary political goods are resolved whether the society is at peace or war, whether it is affluent or impoverished, law-abiding or crime-ridden, whether it is surrounded with trading partners or hostile enemies, whether its educational system, healthcare, and productivity are good, middling, or bad, whether common decencies are generally observed, whether there are respected and followed moral, political, and religious authorities, whether there is widespread religious and racial harmony or hostility, and so on and on. There are reasonable questions and answers about liberty and its limits in most contexts and conditions, but they are unavoidably particular and vary with contexts and conditions.

Burke rightly advises caution about unqualified commitments to liberty:

> When I see the spirit of liberty in action . . . I must be tolerably sure, before I venture to publicly to congratulate men upon a blessing, that they have really received one. . . . I should therefore suspend my congratulations . . . until I was informed how it had been combined with government; with public force; with the discipline and obedience of armies; with the collection of an effective and well-distributed revenue; with morality and religion; with the solidity of property; with peace and order; with civil and social manners. All these (in their way) are good things too; and, without them, liberty is not a benefit.[2]

This chapter is not intended to be a contribution to a general theory of liberty, not even if one were possible. It is meant to be an account of one of the various conceptions of liberty, namely the moderate conservative one of liberty as a primary political good in the context and conditions of the American political system. It is a conception that is particular (not general), practical (not theoretical), and conditional (not universal). It is a limited conception that has a stable center defined by the Constitution, and

---

[2] Burke, Edmund. *Reflections on the Revolution in France* in *Select Works of Edmund Burke*. Vol. 2. Indianapolis: Liberty Fund, 1790/1999, 93–94.

more flexible components that are responsive to the often conflicting requirements of the other primary political goods and to the changing external and internal conditions of American society. It is not concerned with the psychological processes involved in the uses we make of liberty. Psychological processes are always involved in our exercise of liberty, but I will avoid discussing them as much as possible.

I consider three conceptions of liberty. Following Isaiah Berlin's much discussed distinction,[3] I call the first conception *negative* liberty, which is freedom *from* interference. It leaves it up to each one of us to decide how we live. Whatever it is, we are responsible for it. The second conception is of *positive* liberty, which is the freedom *to* live by pursuing some ideal, which may be aesthetic, historical, moral, personal, political, religious, or something else. A basic difference between negative and positive conceptions of liberty is that the first leaves it up to each one of us to decide what use we make of our liberty, whereas the second regards liberty as the pursuit of some specific ideal of how we should live. The ideal may be our own or one that we have chosen or been taught to follow from among the ideals available in our society. The third conception is of *limited* liberty. It combines in a yet to be specified way the defensible components of both negative and positive conceptions of liberty in the context set by the Constitution and the American political system.

Each of these conceptions regards liberty as a primary political good and any account of them that fails to recognize their pivotal importance is faulty. These conceptions overlap in some ways, but they also differ in how they respond to the perennial problems affecting the conception they favor. I will be critical of both the negative and the positive conceptions. I discuss them in order to learn from their mistakes how the conception of limited liberty can avoid

---

[3] Berlin, Isaiah. "Two Concepts of Liberty" in *Four Essays on Liberty*. London: Oxford University Press, 1969, 118–72.

their mistakes and how the complex questions about liberty can be reasonably answered by moderate conservative defenders of limited liberty.

Negative Liberty

I begin with John Stuart Mill's impassioned declamation in his classic *On Liberty*.[4]

> The object of this essay is to assert one very simple principle, as entitled to govern absolutely the dealings of society with the individual in the way of compulsion and control, whether the means used be physical force in the form of legal penalties or the moral coercion of public opinion. That principle is that the sole end for which mankind are warranted, individually or collectively, in interfering with the liberty of action of any of their number is self-protection. That the only purpose for which power can be rightfully exercised over any member of a civilized community, against his will, is to prevent harm to others. His own good, either physical or moral is not a sufficient warrant [9] [And he writes a few pages later:] The only freedom which deserves the name is that of pursuing our own good in our own way, so long as we do not attempt to deprive others or impede their efforts to obtain it. Each is his proper guardian of his own health, whether bodily *or* mental and spiritual. (12)

After these inspirational words, we get the qualifications in which Mill takes back much of what his earlier rhetoric misleadingly implies.

---

[4] Mill, John Stuart. *On Liberty*. It has numerous editions. Page references are to the Indianapolis: Hackett, 1859/1978 edition.

This doctrine is meant to apply only to human beings in the maturity of their faculties. We are not speaking of children and young persons.... For the same reason we may leave out of consideration those backward states of society in which the race itself may be considered in its nonage. Despotism is a legitimate mode of government in dealing with barbarians. Liberty, as a principle, has no application to any state anterior to the time when mankind have become capable of being improved by free and equal discussion. (9–10)

It does not apply to the Popes, Emperors, and their followers who have for centuries struggled with each other (58); nor to Calvinists and all others who think that human nature is radically corrupt (59); nor to the entire Byzantine Empire that has endured for a thousand year (62); nor to all those living in the vast areas in the world where

the despotism of Custom is complete [which is] over the whole East (67); we have a warning example in China... they have become stationary—have remained so for thousand years. (69)

And Mill adds to the hundreds of millions of those who are undeserving of liberty

the average man whose honor and glory... is that he is capable of following the initiative [of the] gifted and instructed *one* or *few*... [so] that he can respond internally to wise and noble things, and be led to them with his eyes open. (63–64)

Who then we might ask are deserving of liberty? And Mill answers: they are the

few persons... whose experiments [in living], if adopted by others, would be likely to be any improvement on established practice. But these few are the salt of the earth; without them, human life would become a stagnant pool. Not only is it they who introduce good things which did not before exist; it is they who keep the life in those which already existed. (61)

But what about those who are not setting the example that the multitude of those undeserving of liberty should merely follow? He addresses that question in *Utilitarianism*.[5] He writes that they should be taught as a religion that

> as between his own happiness and that of others, utilitarianism requires him to be as strictly impartial as a disinterested and benevolent spectator ... utility would enjoin, first, that laws and social arrangements should place the happiness, or ... the interest, or every individual, as nearly as possible in harmony with the interest of the whole; and secondly, that education and opinion ... should ... establish in the mind of every individual an indissoluble association between his own happiness and the good of the whole ... so that not only he may be unable to conceive the possibility of happiness to himself, consistently with conduct opposed to the general good, but also that the impulse to promote the general good may be every individual one of the habitual motives of action. (218)

So the "simple principle" applies only to a few people and the rest should be taught what Mill calls a religion that requires the multitudes to place the happiness of others before their own. This shift from *On Liberty* to *Utilitarianism* is justified by the need for the paternalistic indoctrination of vast numbers of Mill's fellow citizens that is done, according to Mill, for their own good. In his

---

[5] Mill, John Stuart. *Utilitarianism* (1861) in *Collected Works of John Stuart Mill*. Edited by John M. Robson & Jack Stillinger. Indianapolis: Liberty Fund, 1981/2006.

Autobiography,[6] published 15 years after *On Liberty*, having had time to reflect on what he had written, he writes that

> he saw clearly that to render [this] social transformation either possible or desirable, an equivalent change of character must take place both in the uncultivated herd who now compose the labouring masses, and the immense majority of their employers [who] dreaded the selfishness and brutality of the masses [239]; [and] the working classes, though differing from those in some other countries in being ashamed of lying, are yet generally liars. (274)

Thus wrote John Stuart Mill the celebrated defender of liberty. His conception began as freedom from interference, and then it gradually changed into a paternalistic interference with the lives of the working class who have "no need of any other faculty than the ape-like one of imitation" (56). They should be taught by the enlightened few that it is their moral obligation to sacrifice their well-being in order to follow the ideal prescribed by the few who are the salt of world. And this Mill calls a religion and the ideal of liberty.

With some relief I leave Mill and go on to consider Friedrich A. Hayek's defense of negative liberty in *The Constitution of Liberty*.[7] Hayek is concerned with

> the ideal of freedom which inspired modern Western civilization [1] [and he claims that] liberty is not merely one particular value but that it is the source and condition of most moral values [6] in which coercion of some by others is reduced as much as is

---

[6] Mill, John Stuart. *Autobiography* (1873) in *Collected Works*.

[7] Hayek, Friedrich A. *The Constitution of Liberty*. Chicago: Regnery, 1960/1972. For an excellent interpretation and criticism of it, see Kukathas, Chandran. *Hayek and Modern Liberalism*. Oxford: Clarendon Press, 1989. Page references are to this edition.

possible in society. This state we shall describe throughout as a state of liberty or freedom . . . in which a man is not subject to coercion by the arbitrary will of another or others. (11)

Hayek is clear that

> our definition of liberty depends upon the meaning of the concept of coercion [and] by "coercion" we mean such control of the environment or circumstances of a person by another that, in order to avoid greater evil, he is forced to act not according to the coherent plan of his own but to serve the ends of another. . . . Coercion is evil precisely because it eliminates an individual as a thinking and valuing person and makes him a bare tool in the achievement of the ends of another [20–21]. In free action . . . a person pursues his own aims by the means indicated by his own knowledge. . . . It presupposes the existence of a known sphere in which the circumstances cannot be so shaped by another person as to leave one only the choice prescribed by the other. (21)

Unlike Mill, Hayek rightly recognizes that some coercion is unavoidable

> because the only way to prevent it [i.e., coercion] is by the threat of coercion. The coercion which a government must still use is reduced to a minimum and made as innocuous as possible by restraining it through known general rules. . . . Coercion according to known rules . . . becomes an instrument assisting the individuals in the pursuit of their own ends. (21)

Hayek, then, makes the following strong claims about his conception of liberty. Liberty is an overriding political good because it is the source of nearly all moral values. It is a condition in which we are not subject to arbitrary coercion by others. Coercion is not arbitrary if it is the monopoly of the state, not of individuals, and it functions according to known general rules.

The reason why liberty—freedom from arbitrary coercion—is an overriding political good is that it releases through our agency

> the creative power of civilization (22) [it involves] successful striving for what is at each moment attainable ... [and that] progress is movement for movement's sake. (41)

Progress is through

> the growth of knowledge [which] is of such special importance because ... once achieved becomes gratuitously available for the benefit of all (43).

But what if the knowledge gained by liberty is misused? Hayek replies:

> it is ... no argument against individual freedom that it is frequently abused. Freedom necessarily means that many things will be done which we do not like. Our faith in freedom [rests] on the belief that it will, on balance, release more forces for the good than for the bad. (31)

I call this the secular faith, discuss it shortly, and return to it once more later.

Reasons against Negative Liberty

The moderate conservative response to this more than a little upbeat assessment of the human condition is to question some assumptions on which it rests: the generality of the laws through which state uses its monopoly of coercion; the secular faith that liberty releases creative forces from which we all benefit; and that liberty is the ideal political good on which most moral values depend.

Consider the state's monopoly of coercion. Hayek writes:

> The conception of freedom under the law is the chief concern of this book.... When we obey laws, in the sense of general abstract rules laid down irrespective of their application to us, we are not subject to another man's will and are therefore free.... This, however, is true only if by "law" we mean the general rules that apply equally to everybody. (153)

This is indefensible for two reasons. One is the supposed generality and abstractness of the laws. Laws are the laws of a society and apply only to those who live in that society. It is, for instance, a law in our society that those whose income is above a certain level must pay income tax. This law is not general and abstract because it does not apply to everyone. Excluded from it is the income earned by non-citizens who live in other societies and by those in our society whose income is below a certain level. A reasonable interpretation of a law must recognize that its content needs to be specified. When that is done, the law ceases to be abstract and general, and applies only to those who meet the particular conditions specified by the law.

Now the requirement to pay income tax meets the conditions Hayek specifies: it is laid down irrespective of its application to any particular person, it does not subject us to another person's will, and it is in everyone's interest in a society that income tax be paid. But it cannot be reasonably claimed that paying income tax makes us free or freer. It coerces us to use the moneys we have earned in the way the government sees fit. This coercion may or may not be justified, but it certainly limits our liberty. And this remains true of all the many laws to which we are subject. The limits placed on our liberty is a price we pay for living in our society. And that means that there are other political goods we value apart from liberty, goods that make it reasonable for us to give up some of our liberty. Such political goods may be security from foreign attacks, the reduction of violent crimes, the protection of public health, the prevention of monopolies from charging exorbitant prices, making false advertising criminal offense, regulating immigration, and so on. The unavoidable consequence of any law is to limit the liberty of those who are subject to it. Contrary to Hayek's claim, then, it is not true that

> liberty is not merely one particular value but that it is the source and condition of most moral values. (6)

Liberty is certainly a political good, but it is one among others. Political goods often conflict, and liberty does not and should not always override any political good that may conflict with it.

Another reason against Hayek's claim about the generality of laws has to do with the content of laws. As far as I know, he does not acknowledge that there can be and in fact often have been and are bad laws that are not just contrary to liberty but also to human well-being. China now, Russia when it was the Soviet Union, Nazi Germany, and many of the other unconscionable dictatorships were scrupulous about making laws that legalized the persecution of those who were deemed by the legislators to be enemies of the state. In other contexts, there were general laws that applied to all slaves, to all wives whose husbands had control over the wives' property, laws that condemned people to forced labor in concentration camps, and so on. These laws were made by the state, they applied to everyone who came under their jurisdiction, and they did not depend on the arbitrary authority of any particular person, but on the authority of the state. They met the conditions Hayek specified.

He would recognize, indeed insist, that such laws are bad. But his discussion of the rule of law and the nature of laws does not consider the possibility that laws may be bad, nor does he explain how good and bad laws can be distinguished, and what makes laws good or bad. This is a very serious problem with

> defending the conception of freedom under the law [which Hayek writes] is the chief concern of this book. (153)

Hayek was familiar with the ghastly episodes of human history, in fact he lived through some of the horrors that were purported to be justified by bad laws, and I think, although he does not say so, that knowledge of the awful facts was part of his reason for writing *The Constitution of Liberty*.

In the light of these consideration, it demands an explanation of how in his defense of liberty and the rule of law he could have failed to take into account that laws enacted by following procedures that were themselves enacted by impersonal legislation could be not just bad, but very bad indeed. I think the answer is his commitment to what he himself calls his faith, and what I call the secular faith to avoid confusion with religious faith:

> our faith in freedom does not rest on the foreseeable results in particular circumstances but on the belief that it will, on balance, release more forces for the good than for the bad. (31)

Now consider some facts, those spoilers of theories, about the nature of the lives and actions of millions of people in the present context and conditions of the American political system. I searched Google in May 2021 and got the following information. The population in America is 331+ million. Of that number:

- 30+ million did not graduate from high school
- 13+ million cannot hold a permanent job because of mental illness
- 19+ million cannot hold a permanent job because of drug addiction

46+ million are below the basic level of literacy
1.8 million are in jail
16+ million have at least one major depressive episode each year
6+ million are incapacitated by Alzheimer disease
40+ million believe that aliens in UFOs have visited Earth
100+ million believe that God created everything between 6,000 and 10,000 years ago
100+ million believe in ghosts

Bearing in mind these disheartening numbers, consider whether the exercise of negative liberty by these people would "on balance, release more forces for the good than for the bad"? whether their actions are "likely to release the creative power of civilization"? or "contribute to the growth of knowledge"? or involve "successful striving for what is at each moment attainable"? or contribute to progress, to "the growth of knowledge," or eventually "become gratuitously available for the benefit of all"?

Consider what would happen if we accepted and acted on the secular faith in the beneficial outcome of the uses these millions of people might make of negative liberty in our affluent society. And then consider further what would be likely to happen if, guided by the secular faith, our society abandoned paternalistic welfare programs, such as school lunches and food stamps; stopped enforcing public health regulations; abolished the entire welfare system; no longer paid unemployment insurance, maintained emergency rooms in hospitals that tend to the medical needs of indigent or imprudent people, and so on for countless other government financed services that cater to the needs of those who are unable to benefit from or misuse the blessings of negative liberty.

The predictable consequences of such policies would outrage the common decency of most Americans. It would be destructive of our society if the government failed to use its monopoly to make coercive laws that curtail the negative liberty of those who cannot make reasonable use of it and of those who did not accept the dire need of paying for policies that help those who cannot help themselves. If our society adhered to negative liberty in either Mill's or Hayek's version, if it left to the discretion of individuals what they should do with their negative liberty, then we would make life in our society unlivable. We need to remember Madison's wise words[8] that

> If men were angels, no government would be necessary. If angels were to govern men, neither external nor internal controls on government would be necessary. In framing a government which is to be administered by men over men, the great difficulty lies in this: you must first enable the government to control the governed; and in the next place oblige it to control itself.

Hayek has not asked or considered whether human beings are angels who could enjoy the benefits of negative liberty within the rule of law, or who must be coerced for their own good.

Moderate conservatives do not share this secular faith. This is not because they hold the opposite faith that negative liberty left free of coercion would release more bad than good. It is rather that the forces that are released by negative liberty are the forces of human motivation that is neither basically good nor bad, but ambivalent. And whether the good or the bad dominates our motives depends on the prevailing conditions, the context, the available possibilities, and the experiences of those who are influential in forming the policies that governments and legislators follow. These matters are varied, complex, and do not lend themselves to overall generalizations that would support Hayek's or indeed any other faith about human motivation, laws, governments, and the results that follow from them.

---

[8] Madison, James. *The Federalist*, No. 51. Edited by George W. Carey and James McClellan. Indianapolis: Liberty Fund, 1788/2001, 269

Positive Liberty as Autonomy

Positive liberty is the freedom to have and to follow an ideal that gives meaning and purpose to the lives of those who have it. It is their guide in life, and its importance overrides any consideration that may conflict with it. There is a great variety of moral, political, and religious ideals: of artistic or literary creativity; historical or scientific research; commitment to the pursuit of beauty, career, fame, goodness, power, reform, respect, status, success, truth, understanding, or wealth; or those that cherish participating in and continuing the traditional way of life of a craft, family, farming, profession, religion, scholarship, teaching, trade, and so on and on. As far as I know, the first explicit formulation of the conception of autonomy as one of the ideals of positive liberty is by Isaiah Berlin:[9]

> The "positive" sense of the word "liberty'" derives from the wish on the part of the individual to be his own master. I wish my life and decisions to depend on myself, not on external forces of whatever kind. I wish to be an instrument of my own, not of other men's acts of will. I wish to be a subject, not an object; to be moved by reasons, by conscious purposes, which are my own, not by causes which affect me, as it were, from outside ... a doer—deciding ... self-directed.

Berlin thus conceives of autonomy as individualistic and anti-authoritarian. We can make ourselves autonomous by acts of will. We ourselves, no authority external to us, give us conscious purposes.

The justly celebrated essay from which I cite has led to an avalanche of publications.[10] Autonomy is now at the center of

---

[9] Belin, Isaiah. "Two Concepts of Liberty" in *Four Essays on Liberty*. Oxford: Oxford University Press, 1969, 1990, 131.
[10] For a survey and bibliography, see Christman, John. "Autonomy." https://plato.stanford.edu/archives/spr2018/entries/autonomy-moral/.

contemporary moral and political discussions. The influence of Kant is ever-present in them. Numerous interpretations of it have referred to autonomy by a variety of names, such as reflective self-evaluation; second-order self-evaluation; self-constitution; self-determination; self-direction; self-governance; strong evaluation; and so on. These interpretations, and no doubt there are others, differ in detail, and stress different components of positive liberty as autonomy. But the key conception of the ideal of autonomy is expressed by John Rawls as:[11]

> A person is acting autonomously when the principles of his action are chosen by him as the most adequate possible expressions of his nature as a free and equal rational being.

By Gerald Dworkin as:[12]

> Autonomy is conceived of as a second-order capacity of persons to reflect critically upon their first-order preferences, desires, wishes, and so forth and the capacity to accept or attempt to change these in the light of higher order preferences and values. By exercising such a capacity, persons define their nature, give meaning and coherence to their lives, and take responsibility for the kind of persons they are.

And by Christine Korsgaard as:[13]

> The appeal to autonomy... is found in Kant and contemporary Kantians constructivists, especially John Rawls. Kantians believe

---

[11] Rawls, John. *A Theory of Justice*. Cambridge, MA: Harvard University Press, 1971, 252.
[12] Dworkin, Gerald. *The Theory and Practice of Autonomy*. New York: Cambridge University Press, 1988, 20.
[13] Korsgaard, Christine. *The Sources of Normativity*. New York: Cambridge University Press, 1996, 19.

that the source of the normativity of moral claims must be found in the agent's own will.... The capacity for self-conscious reflection about our own action confers on us a kind of authority over ourselves and it is this authority which gives normativity to moral claims.

Notice how strong are these claims for autonomy. It is said to express our nature; give meaning and coherence to our life; and guides our self-conscious moral reflection on how we should live and act. The ideal of autonomy is then to create conditions in which we can choose freely between alternative ways of living and acting, based on our understanding of the available alternatives and following the one we personally regard as more worthy of choice than any of the others. Autonomy includes making choices about how we should live and act, but it requires that our choices be based on self-conscious, moral, and critical reflection. To do this is to be fully autonomous. In fact, autonomy is usually only partial because our will is often curtailed by legal, moral, personal, and political limits; by the infirmity and the ambivalence of our will; and by our understanding, intentions, and evaluations, which are often partial, conflicting, and based on faulty beliefs, emotions, desires, and misinterpreted experiences.

Defenders of autonomy ("autonomist" from now on) claim that we should aim at autonomy as our overriding moral and political ideal and do what we can to increase our own and others' autonomy by overcoming obstacles to living as we personally think we should.[14] Autonomists then have a *life-enhancing* and a *protective* aim. Their *life-enhancing* aim is to create and maintain the conditions in which we can all live autonomously and thereby

---

[14] The historical development of autonomy is traced by Schneewind, J.B. *The Invention of Autonomy*. New York: Cambridge University Press, 1998. For a recent survey and bibliography, see Christman, John. "Autonomy." http://plato.stanford.edu/entries/autonomy-moral/, and Dworkin, Gerald. "Autonomy" in *A Companion to Contemporary Political Philosophy*. Edited by Robert Goodin E. and Phillip Pettit. Oxford: Blackwell, 1993.

make lives better. Their *protective* aim is to remove obstacles from the way of increasing everyone's autonomy.

Moderate conservatives think that this interpretation of autonomy as the positive ideal of liberty is mistaken for two main reasons. One is that while autonomy is indeed a fine moral and political ideal, it is not an overriding one. There are many other, no less fine, moral, personal, political, and religious ideals. Autonomy is one, but no more than one, of them. None of them should always, at all times, and in all contexts override all the others. It is not true, as autonomists claim, that we can express our nature, live a meaningful and coherent life, and act morally only if we are autonomous. Autonomy is a good way of life, but there are also others. Denying this is the *exclusivist* mistake made by autonomists. The assumption underlying this mistake is that fully autonomous actions will be moral and immoral actions will be non-autonomous. I call this mistake the *secular faith*. I have earlier faulted Hayek for making it.

The Exclusivist Mistake

The source of this mistake is that, contrary to Rawls, acting autonomously is only one of several possible expressions of our nature, and it need not be the most adequate one. Contrary to Dworkin, critical reflection on our first-order preferences is not the only way of living a coherent, meaningful, and responsible life. And contrary to Korsgaard, we can live morally and responsibly, even if we are not autonomous. Autonomy is a fine way of living. It is good if a society creates and maintains conditions in which people can, if they wish, reflect critically and live autonomous lives. But it is not true that we can live a meaningful life and make reasonable choices between the different possibilities we might try to realize only if we reflect critically in the way autonomists say we should if we are to act morally and responsibly. Our ideal of how we should live may be to accept and follow the authority of an impersonal moral, political, religious, or social mode of evaluation even if it is contrary to our will. We may realize that our will is selfish, some of our desires are unworthy, and we are divided by conflicts between our beliefs, hopes, fears, incompatible desires. Our will is just as mistake-prone as are all components of our inner life.

The obvious fact is that millions of people in our society who have been born into a traditional way of life that is followed by their family members, friends, neighbors, schoolmates, and co-religionists. They earn a living by following the conventions of an art, a business, a trade, a profession, or some form of public service. They derive their ideals of how they should live from the traditions of their community, neighborhood, ethnic group, occupation, or religion. They by and large observe the common decencies, earn a living, get married, and raise a family. They assume as they are growing up that they will live in one of the familiar ways they were born into, just as their relatives, neighbors, and most other people they know have done. They are familiar with that context, know its conventions, and live their lives by participating in it. They could abandon it, leave their community, experiment with other ways of life, but they are reluctant to do so. They like their circumstances and feel secure in it. Such people form the backbone of American society.

Conventional lives need not be idyllic. They may disrupted by ill health, accidents, economic crises, marital strife, troublesome children, financial difficulties, unwelcome changes in their community, and the like. Then those who live conventional lives try to cope as well as they can. They know how they want to live and by and large live that way. Habit, custom, and routine are their guides in life. If the even temper of their lives is disrupted by difficulties, they do what they can to cope with them and return their lives to an even keel. Only when it is difficult to do so might they be in need of self-conscious reflection. But they feel that need only in exceptional circumstances. Normally they do not have to seek a way of expressing their nature, or reflecting critically on their first-order preferences, or developing higher order preferences, or formulating a principle of their actions. They would not dream of evaluating the reasons for and against their action by pondering whether its principle could or should be made into a universal law.

The exclusivist mistake autonomists make is to evaluate non-autonomous ways of life by the same standard as they think autonomous lives should be evaluated. They want everyone to live in the way autonomists aim to live. They fail to understand the millions of people who live by following the authority of a traditional, conventional, social, familial, or religious way of life whose authority they accept and by and large follow. This is how the great majority of human beings have always lived and continue to live now.

The life autonomists regard as ideal is aimed at largely by intellectuals who talk to, write for, and socialize with each other. They fail to recognize that their ideal of life is only one ideal among many and that they should not evaluate the non-autonomous lives of others by the standards they use for evaluating autonomous lives. Autonomists become dogmatic moralists who condemn those who do not live as autonomists think they should for moral failure. But the failure is by autonomists. A case in point is Korsgaard's specification of the conditions of moral deliberation that they claim should be followed by everyone:[15]

> To deliberate is to formulate a maxim, stating the complete package of considerations that together favor the performance of a certain action.... Your maxim, once formulated, embodies your proposed reason. You then test it by the categorical imperative, that is, you ask whether you can will it to be a universal law, in order to see whether it really is a reason. Universalizability is a condition on the form of reason, and if a consideration does not meet this condition, then it is not merely outweighed—rather, it is not a reason at all.

---

[15] Korsgaard, Christine. *Self-Constitution*. Oxford: Clarendon Press, 2009, 51.

I ask readers to consider whether they themselves or anyone they know have gone through this mind-blogging universalizing procedure when they keep a promise, express their love, admonish their children, pay the bill for what they bought, or signal before turning their car at an intersection. As for myself, I have never done anything remotely like this. Given the claims of Rawls, Dworkin, and Korsgaard, we could act autonomously, morally, and express our nature only if we go through this extraordinary procedure. This seems to me an utterly implausible requirement of deliberate and morally right actions.

Perhaps I am wrong about this, and some of us actually follow this deliberative procedure before they act. Autonomists assume that if we follow this procedure, it will make us more autonomous and moral than we were before we embarked on it. Suppose then that I formulate a maxim, test it by this procedure, ask whether I would wish the principle of my action to become a universal law, and conclude that my intended action fails these tests. What would then happen?

It need not change my intended action. I may still act as I want and say to myself that if autonomy and morality require me not to act the way I want, then there is something wrong, not with me, but with autonomy and morality. I say to myself that I really want to express my ill will toward some people, pursue my ambition, make a profit, prevail over my competitors, lie if I must in order to get my way. I do not much care whether my action would be condemned as morally wrong by others, because. I care more about acting as I want than about other people's opinion of it. That, I say to myself, is what acting autonomously is. Acting autonomously and reflecting critically does not mean that I will even try to act morally. I see no reason why autonomous actions could not be amoral or immoral, nor why non-autonomous action could not be based on careful deliberation and critical reflections on possible gains and losses. Autonomists assume that autonomous actions will in some sense be good rather than bad, or at least better than non-autonomous actions. In making this assumption they ignore the endlessly familiar facts of life and, being led by the secular faith, they deny them.

The Secular Faith and Its Problems

The secular faith is a deep and pervasive assumption widely held in much of historical and contemporary moral and political thought, as the passages I cite below make clear.[16] And it is this assumption that underlies the defense of autonomy as the overriding moral and political ideal and the aim of positive liberty. I turn now to considering the reasons against it.

---

[16] Hume, David: "It requires but very little knowledge of human affairs to perceive that a sense of morals is a principle inherent in the soul, and one of the most powerful that enters into its composition." *A Treatise of Human Nature*. Oxford: Clarendon Press, 1939/1960.

Rousseau, Jean-Jacques: "Man is a naturally good creature, who loves justice and order . . . there is no original perversity in the human heart." "Letter to Beaumont." Translated by Timothy O'Hagan in *Rousseau*. London: Routledge, 1999, 15.

Kant, Immanuel: "[man is] *not basically* corrupt (even as regard his original predisposition to good) . . . and does not . . . repudiate the moral law. . . . The law, rather, forces itself upon him irresistibly by virtue of his moral predisposition." *Religion within the Bounds of Reason Alone*. Translated by Theodore M. Green and Hoyt H. Hudson. New York: Harper & Row, 1794/1960, 31.

Mill, John Stuart: "the social feeling of mankind—the desire to be in unity with our fellow creatures, which is already a powerful principle in human nature, and happily one of those which tend to become stronger, even without inculcation." *Utilitarianism*. Indianapolis: Hackett, 1861/1979, 31–32.

Rawls, John: "[man] is a subject with ends he has chosen, and his fundamental preference is for conditions that enable him to frame a mode of life that expresses his nature as a free and rational being." *A Theory of Justice*. Cambridge, MA: Harvard University Press, 1971, 561.

Raz, Joseph: "the ideal of personal autonomy . . . holds the free choice of goals and relations as an essential ingredient of individual well-being." *The Morality of Freedom*. Oxford: Clarendon Press, 1986, 369.

Foot, Philippa: "acting morally is part of practical rationality . . . no one can act with full practical rationality in pursuit of a bad end." *Natural Goodness*. Oxford: Clarendon Press 2001, 9, 14.

Korsgaard, Christine: "it is human nature to be governed by morality. . . . Human nature, moral government included, is therefore normative, and has authority for us." *The Sources of Normativity*. Cambridge: Cambridge University Press, 1966, 66.

The secular faith is held even though it is undeniable that the same aggressive, cruel, greedy, intolerant, prejudice-driven, selfish, or unjust actions have been frequent and recurrent in all known societies, including our own, regardless of great differences in political conditions, and moral and religious creeds. Autonomists attribute this to the insufficient autonomy of the wrongdoers. Its insufficiency, however, is not taken to indicate anything adverse about human beings. Wrongdoing is supposed to be frequent because societies fail to foster autonomy and create political conditions that corrupt people and make them into wrongdoers.

The conviction at the core of this secular faith is, as the passages just cited show, that human beings are by nature disposed to act morally. When they act that way, they express their nature. When they are corrupted by bad political conditions, they act non-autonomously, contrary to their nature, and become wrongdoers. It is, therefore, the bad political conditions that have corrupted wrongdoers that should be held responsible for the wrongdoers' non-autonomous wrong actions, not the wrongdoers themselves. If the political conditions were not bad, people would not become wrongdoers and act contrary to their natural disposition to act morally.

Moderate conservatives think that the secular faith is mistaken. The belief that most wrongdoing is caused by bad political conditions ignores the obvious question of how political conditions have become bad. Political conditions are created and maintained by human beings who could change them. And they have done so again and again as is obvious from history. If human beings were basically disposed to act morally, then how could they create and maintain bad political conditions? The inexperience or incompetence of basically moral human beings may explain why they create some bad political conditions. But once they realize that there is widespread insecurity, crime, and social unrest as a result of bad social conditions, then they cannot fail to realize that the political conditions they have created are bad. And then inexperience and incompetence can no longer explain why they maintain the bad conditions.

If human beings were as much at the mercy of bad political conditions as defenders of the secular faith suppose, then how could autonomists have escaped being corrupted by them to an extent sufficient to become critical of them? If, contrary to the assumption held by defenders of the secular faith, it were possible to escape the bad political conditions, then how could continued adherence to the bad conditions not have something to do with the pre-existing dispositions of wrongdoers to act in morally wrong ways? Were their pre-existing dispositions also the products of bad political conditions? If so, how did those political conditions become bad? And how do defenders of the secular faith explain that many of those who have been subject to the same bad political conditions did not become wrongdoers? Does not the difference between those who do and those who do not become wrongdoers show that human beings are not as much at the mercy of bad political conditions as defenders of the secular faith suppose?

The secular faith, however, is not merely unsupported by the facts, but inconsistent with them. The facts are that the same familiar vices and the wrong actions that follow from them are as frequent in all societies, as are the same familiar virtues and the right actions that follow from them, regardless of what their political conditions are. We know from history, literature, morality, politics, and religion that courage and cowardice, wisdom and folly, restraint and excess, honesty and dishonesty, benevolence and malevolence have existed and continue to exist in all societies and political conditions. They are often expressed in slightly different ways in response to different conditions, but we readily understand and praise or deplore the recorded actions of human beings who lived in societies and conditions very different from our own.

There certainly are great differences between how human beings live in different societies at different times, places, and political conditions. But there also are similarities. If there were not, we could not understand the lives, motives, and actions of human beings who have responded to very different economic, legal, moral, political, and religious conditions in the contexts of different societies, times, and places. Nor could we applaud or deplore the actions of iconic historical benefactors and scourges who have benefited or harmed human beings in the past. We can and do benefit from reflection on the lives and actions of people in contexts very different from our own. This is what the Humanities used to enable us to do before ideologues perverted it in pursuit of their deplorable aims.

Autonomists may deny that they are committed to the secular faith. They may concede that some of their much too optimistic predecessors in the early days of the Enlightenment have held the faith, but deny that they hold it now. They claim that they can be as hard-headed about wrongdoing as anyone else. In that case, however, they owe a justification for supposing that by increasing autonomy they will make wrongdoing less frequent. If wrong actions were mainly autonomous, then increasing the autonomy of wrongdoers would make wrongdoing more frequent, so that cannot be the justification autonomists need to give. If, on the other hand, wrong actions were mainly non-autonomous, then non-naïve autonomists still need to explain why increasing autonomy would make wrong actions less frequent. If they disavow the secular faith in the basic human disposition toward morality, if they believe that human beings are often ambivalent and that virtues and vices may both be natural and basic, then they cannot justifiably suppose that increasing autonomy will give greater scope to virtues and lesser scope to vices.

The reasons for and against increasing autonomy depend on the prevailing and changing historical, moral, political, and religious conditions of our society, on the extent to which our modes of evaluation meet the test of time, and the satisfactions and dissatisfaction of those who live in our society. In some contexts and conditions, increasing autonomy may have good consequences.

In different ones, it may have bad consequences. If this is so, then it cannot be reasonably supposed that autonomy is an overriding ideal. Autonomy is an important political good, but it is only one among other important political goods. It may conflict with the rule of law, justice, legal and political equality, and private property. And there is no universal, or theoretical, or context-independent answer to the question of what the reasonable resolution of such conflicts is.

Limited Liberty

The Preamble to the *Constitution* makes clear that securing the "Blessings of Liberty to ourselves and our Posterity" is one of the important political goods of the American political system. It makes clear as well that liberty is only one of the important political goods. "Justice," "domestic Tranquility," "common defense," "the promotion of general Welfare" are some of the others. And *Amendment XIV* adds the no less important ones of "life," "property," "the due process of law," and the "equal protection" of American citizens by the laws.

One implication of these words is that in the American political system liberty cannot be an overriding political good because there are several other equally important political goods. They may conflict, and the protection of one of them often requires having less of one or the other primary political goods in order to secure more of another. Another implication is that no conception of any of the important political goods can be acceptable in the American political system if it is elevated above all the other political goods and claimed always to override them in all conflicts, contexts, and conditions. The conflicting claims of these political goods need to be weighed, balanced, and then priority be given to one of the conflicting ones in some contexts and conditions and to another in other contexts and conditions. The relative importance of these political goods must be continually balanced and re-balanced in response to changing contexts and conditions. This is the difficult and typically controversial business of politics.

Defenders of the negative and positive conceptions of liberty, claim that their favored one is overriding. Mill claimed this for his "simple principle," Hayek for liberty within the rule of law, and many political and moral theorists claim it now for autonomy. Each claims that all the other political goods presuppose and depend on the one to which they attach overriding importance. Moderate conservatives think that they are all mistaken, although in different ways and for different reasons. I have discussed these conceptions of liberty in this chapter in order to learn from their mistakes how a defensible conception of limited liberty can avoid them.

Consider first the claim made by defenders of the negative and positive conceptions of liberty that the one they favor is presupposed by all the other primary political goods because they can be pursued only by those who have the liberty to pursue them. This is true. But it is also true that the other political goods, including liberty, can be pursued only if the rule of law, rather than anarchy or tyranny prevails; only if the laws of justice protect the security and adjudicate disagreements among the pursuers; only if the laws apply to every American equally, so that all citizens have an equal right to pursue their conception of liberty; and only if all the pursuers have sufficient property that enables them to pursue their conception of liberty. Liberty is presupposed by the other political goods, but so are the rule of law, justice, legal and political equality, and private property. That is why these political goods are primary. No primary political good is always more important than any of the others. None of them should always, in all contexts, and in all conditions override the others when they conflict.

Consider next the disheartening facts I have cited earlier in this chapter that millions of Americans are unable to enjoy the blessings of liberty because they are uneducated, illiterate, innumerate, mentally ill, disabled by addiction to drugs or alcohol, suffer from

Alzheimer disease, and are ignorant of the most basic facts of the world around them. They cannot pursue liberty because they are unable to do so. And then the government needs to step in, paternalistically interfere with the lives of those who are unable to enjoy its blessings, and protect them from the destructive consequences of their loss of the small amount of liberty they may once have had. Such interference is contrary to both the negative and positive conception of liberty I have discussed. The consequences of non-interference would outrage the common decency of most Americans and be unacceptable to them.

A further reason against regarding liberty as the overriding political good is that there are and always have been people in American society who have consciously and deliberately given up much of their liberty and accepted the authority of a moral, personal, political, religious, or some other tradition from which they derive their conception of the possibilities and the limits of how they should live. They do not want to construct an experiment in living, as Mill thought everyone should. They willingly subject themselves to the constraining and restraining authority of a tradition and do what Hayek calls evil because he mistakenly supposes that curtailing one's liberty by the acceptance of authority of a tradition "eliminates an individual as a thinking and valuing person." But he does not say why the acceptance of some traditional conception of how one should live is incompatible with being a thinking and valuing person and why it would be contrary to the "creative power of civilization."

And then there is the supposedly overriding contemporary ideal of autonomy that is claimed to give meaning and purpose to one's life. There is no doubt that autonomy is an attractive and reasonable ideal. Many intellectuals in American society try to follow it. However, the acceptance of autonomy as a guide in life does not make it an overriding guide even for oneself, and certainly not for everyone. Yet this is how autonomists often regard it. They say, as does Rawls, that autonomy expresses our "nature as a free and equal rational being." He thereby implies that those who are not autonomous act contrary to their nature. Autonomy may express the nature of some people. But others may express their nature by following a moral, personal, political, or religious authority on which they rely for guidance to how they should live when it is difficult to do so. Or they may adventurously experiment with following one way of life for a while and then they opt to follow another, and thus live by exploring as many possibilities of life as they can, without regarding any of them as overriding. Or they say to God as some Christians do in their daily prayer: Thy will be done.

Lastly, moderate conservatives are critical of the negative and the positive conceptions of liberty, but not because they are mistaken about its moral and political importance. Defenders of both conceptions are right about that. Their mistake is to go beyond recognizing the importance of liberty, and claim that it is always, in all contexts and conditions more important than any consideration that may conflict with it. This commits them to condemning all those who fail to live and act in accordance with their supposedly overriding ideal of a serious moral and political failure. Thus they are committed to condemning for this failure all those who give up much their liberty to serve in the military; or become priests, nuns, or monks in a strict religious order; or dedicate themselves to following the example and authority of the life and work of a teacher, an artist, a scientist, a politician, or the master of a craft. Defenders of negative and positive liberty condemn for these alleged failure all those who live in a way that is incompatible with the supposedly overriding requirement of liberty. And defenders of these conceptions of liberty maintain their intolerant dogmatic view in the name of liberty.

The moderate conservative conception of liberty is limited because it rejects the claim that liberty is an overriding political good. It acknowledges liberty as one of the primary political goods. And it insists that in the context of the American political system there is always a presumption in favor of liberty. But the presumption can be defeated in contexts and conditions in which there are good reasons to suppose that one or another of the rule of law, the laws of justice, the equal legal and political status of American citizens, or the yet to be discussed primary political good of private property should take precedence over it. Such reasons are good if they show that the protection of the American political system as a whole depends on giving precedence to one of the primary political goods over liberty.

This may happen in war, crime waves, natural disasters, economic crises, shortage of essential resources, seriously threatening social unrest, and the like. And then the reasons for and against resolving conflicts between the primary political goods in favor of one or another must be weighed and balanced. There is no blueprint for doing that. Finding the most reasonable way of coping with such conflicts is always difficult and contestable. But the contests are about finding the best means to protecting an agreed upon end. That end is the protection of the American political system. And the ultimate justification of that political system is that it has met the test of time for over 300 years and has continued to be supported by most of those who voluntarily accept and by and large follow it. They do so partly because by participating in that system they can enjoy the blessings of limited liberty, as well as of the rule of law, justice, legal and political equality, and private property.

9
Private Property

The Reason for It

Hume succinctly states the reason for private property:

> When men . . . have observ'd, that the principal disturbance in society arises from those goods, which we call external, and from their looseness and easy transition from one person to another; they must seek remedy . . . This can be done after no other manner than by a convention enter'd into by all members of the society to bestow stability on the possession of those external goods, and leave every one in the peaceable enjoyment of what he may acquire by his fortune and industry. By this means every one knows what he may safely possess . . . which is so necessary to their well-being . . . as well to our own.[1]

This is the basic reason why private property is one of the primary political goods in our political system. It is because the material resources we call property enable us to live a civilized life in which, being freed from brute necessities, enjoying the benefits of the rule of law, justice, legal and political equality, and liberty, we can pursue our well-being. This is one main reason why our political system has continued to meet the test of time for over 300 years. In this chapter I consider the moderate conservative conception of private

---

[1] Hume, David. *A Treatise of Human Nature.* 2nd ed. Edited by P.H. Niditch. Oxford: Clarendon Press, 1739/1999, 489.

property and propose a new way of thinking about its justification. It builds on old and familiar ways, but goes beyond them.[2]

I begin with where we now are. The "we" are members of American society, as it is with all its achievements, problems, conflicts, and dissatisfactions. A convincing justification of private property must explain why it is reasonable to value it both in itself and in relation to the other political goods. This may seem too obvious a starting point to need mention, but it is routinely spurned by political thinkers situated all along the left-right spectrum.

Some of them start with a pseudo-historical speculation about the origin of private property in the mist of pre-history.[3] One reason against this approach is that these accounts are so many "just so" stories unsupported by anthropological or historical evidence. There is no credible evidence that any form of social contract, tacit or otherwise, has ever taken place. And, even if it had occurred, it would have no more bearing on the justification of private property now than an account of the origin of cannibalism would now have on its justification.

Another starting point is a theory about what an ideal society would be like, and then justify or criticize private property from its point of view. The problem with this is that the theorists are led by their political predilections—I do not say prejudices—to choose one of the many political goods they value, ascribe overriding importance to it, and then make the justification of private property depend on its importance for the pursuit of the supposedly overriding political good. I will return to the pseudo-historical and the

---

[2] For surveys and bibliographies see, Becker, Lawrence C. "Property" in *Encyclopedia of Ethics*, 2nd ed. Edited by Lawrence C. Becker & Charlotte B. Becker. New York: Routledge, 2001; Munser, Stephen R. "Property" in *Routledge Encyclopedia of Philosophy*. Edited by Edward Craig. London: Routledge, 1998; Pennock, J. Roland and John W. Chapman, eds. *Property*. Nomos XXII. New York: New York University Press, 1980. Waldron, Jeremy. "Property" in the *Stanford Encyclopedia of Philosophy*: http://plato.stanford.edu/entries/property/.

[3] This is the approach of Hobbes, Thomas. *Leviathan*, John Locke, *Second Treatise of Government*, Rousseau, Jean-Jacques. *Social Contract*, and their many contemporary followers.

ideal-theorizing approaches later, but only to reinforce my claim that both are vitiated by arbitrariness.

Another possibility is to start with the idea of self-ownership and then gradually extend it to include private property as it is usually understood. The reason against this strategy is that the sense in which we have a self is very different from the sense in which we have, for instance, a house. We and the properties we own are contingently connected: we can sell, loan, bequeath, give away, or forfeit our property, but we cannot do this with our self. We are connected to it necessarily, not contingently. And this is radically different from what is normally meant by owning a property. The self we have cannot be nationalized or expropriated, and there is no law needed to guarantee that no one will steal the self we have. We have many things we may have but do not own, such as a good marriage, a bad temper, or a passion for Bach. Our self is another. Of course, political theorists are free to stipulate any meaning they like, but it is highly misleading to claim that having a self is like owning a house, not even if it is our beloved home.

Yet a further approach is to begin with the claim that we have a natural right to our property. The idea of natural right to anything is as problematic as the idea of self-ownership. What seems to be meant by natural right is that we have some basic needs and their satisfaction is a minimum condition of our well-being. Natural rights, then, are supposed to be our rights to pursue such satisfactions. And then the rights are supposed to impose a corresponding obligation on others not to prevent us from trying to satisfy our basic needs.

I agree that the satisfaction of basic needs is a minimum condition of our well-being, that it is good to satisfy them, and that it is normally bad to prevent others from satisfying them. I also agree that basic needs derive from our nature which we share with other members of our species. If this were all that is meant by natural rights, then the idea of it would not be problematic. But its defenders claim more. They claim that we are entitled at least to non-interference with our natural rights. I can make sense of this only on the assumption that we live in a society whose laws, conventions, or customs create our entitlement. I fail to see how anyone could be entitled to anything outside of one society or another. Nothing entitles a chimpanzee to his food. There are rights, of course, but they are conventional, not natural in the sense that defenders of natural rights intend.

It makes matters worse that even if there were natural rights, the right to private property would not be one of them. Having private property is not a basic need whose satisfaction is a minimum condition of well-being. Basic needs could be satisfied even if all property were owned by the state, or by benevolent people, or jointly by a community. Beggars, spongers, mendicant friars, and ascetic hermits have been enabled by others to satisfy their basic needs even though they owned no private property. Owning private property is conditional on legal, moral, and political conventions about how we may acquire, use, or dispose of it. These conventions are historically conditioned and changeable.[4]

Instead of these dubious starting points, I begin with where we are, with the plurality of political goods we value. Private property is one among them. The right to it is conventional because it is defined by changeable laws and customs. It is conditional because it changes as conditions change. And it is defeasible because it may conflict with other political goods we value and the conflicts may be reasonably resolved in favor of a political good other than private property.

The core idea of private property is the ownership of some material object, such as a car or a violin. But the idea is often extended to include money, patents, undeveloped resources, shares, future payments, options, inventions, reputation, and so forth. I will

---

[4] I follow Hart, H.L.A. "Are There Any Natural Rights?" *Philosophical Review* 64(1955): 175–91 and "Utilitarianism and Natural Rights" in *Essays in Jurisprudence and Philosophy*. Oxford: Clarendon Press, 1983.

discuss private property only in a narrow sense to include only material objects and money. The issue of justification is complex enough, and I want to avoid complications that follow from intangible possessions. If the justification works, it may be extended beyond the narrow sense. The mere possession of an object, however, does not make it my property. I may possess a car, because I stole it or bought it from someone who stole it. It is in my possession, but it is not my property, because I came to possess it illegally. Property is legal possession. Furthermore, property need not be owned by a single person. It may be owned jointly by several people; or by a cooperative, a church, or a labor union; or by the state, as are roads or parks.

The justification of private property—the property of a single person—must do more than justify owning property in general. It may be that a collectivity or a state owns some property, but no individual does. My concern is with the justification of the legal possession of private property.[5] What needs to be justified is its possession and use within legally defined limits. Each constituent of this right—possession, use, and limits—is in turn limited by law. The right to private property, therefore, is a bundle of rights, not a single one.[6] And the specific rights that constitute the bundle typically vary with societies, legal systems, and changes in specific laws. Reference to private property, then, is nothing more than a convenient shorthand that is a place-holder awaiting specifications. Two societies may each be committed to the right to private property and yet interpret it quite differently.

The right to private property in our society includes having exclusive physical control of it; deriving income from it; holding it

---

[5] For an excellent discussion of the complexities of how property should be understood, see Waldron, Jeremy. *The Right to Private Property*. Oxford: Clarendon Press, 1988. Part One.

[6] This way of understanding the right to private property is indebted to A.M. Honoore's now classic now classic "Ownership" in *Oxford Essays in Jurisprudence*. Edited by A.G. Guest. Oxford: Oxford University Press, 1961.

without time limit; having legal protection against its expropriation, theft, or unwanted destruction; and so forth. It includes deciding whether, how, or when to use it; permitting others to use it; consuming, modifying, or destroying it; selling, exchanging, bequeathing it, or donating it as a gift; and so forth. And the limits exclude having acquired it illegitimately. Given this understanding of private property, I turn to the question of why we regard it as important.

Its Importance

Private property is important because it enables us to pursue our well-being and have some control over how we live. By control I mean directing how we live, not dominating others, imposing our will on them, or being obsessed with the minute details of daily life. To be in control of our life is to be our own master, not to be at the mercy of the will or kindness of others, not to depend on them to provide the resources we need, to make decisions for ourselves, and to live with the consequences. Private property is a means to this kind of control. Acting on the intentions we form, the opportunities we seek, and the activities we engage in depend on it. We use the control we have to satisfy our needs. Some of them are the basic needs of subsistence. Their satisfaction is a minimum condition of our well-being. We also have many needs beyond the basic ones. Some of them are psychological and financial security; relief from drudgery; interesting and rewarding work; lasting intimate relationships; possessing the material objects we need, such as instruments for musicians, books for a scholar, a well-lit studio for a painter, or reliable equipment for a rock climber; we also need some privacy and distraction from drudgery; a car for travel, decent housing to live in, a computer to keep records and communicate with others; and so forth. I refer to these needs jointly as secondary.

Basic and secondary needs are alike in that their satisfaction is a requirement of our well-being. They also differ because we all have the same primary needs, but different secondary ones. Prolonged deprivation of the satisfaction of our basic needs makes our well-being impossible. But this is not so with secondary needs. Only the frustration of many of the important ones makes our life not worth living. By calling these needs basic and secondary I do not intend to suggest that the former are always more important than the latter. Soul-destroying work, being incapacitated to follow our chosen profession, unhappy lifelong relationships, and persistent insecurity are as incompatible with well-being as starvation. The satisfaction of both basic and some important secondary needs is essential for our well-being, but we can satisfy them only if we have the required resources, and that is why private property is indispensable for having control of how we live. If we understand this about private property, then doubts about its importance as a primary political good will be seen as groundless.

As to the charge that the importance we attribute to it is a symptom of greed, it is so only for those who are obsessed with possessions. But it is not so for numerous others who want no more private property than they need for controlling how they live, with some extra perhaps as a margin of safety. Nor need the importance we attribute to private property be a symptom of selfishness. We may use our private property to acquire skills that will benefit others, or to improve the life of our family, support a worthy cause, and, of course, to pay taxes, much of which funds welfare programs. Recognizing the importance of private property, therefore, may be a symptom of public spirit, love, or business acumen, not just of selfishness.

There are ascetics who are satisfied with their well-being, even though they have no private property. But not even they can live without resources. They depend on others who provide the resources at least for the satisfaction of their basic needs. The ascetics' refusal to own private property no more calls into question its importance than the renunciation of sex by celibates casts doubt on its importance for those who are otherwise inclined.

There still remains the point that recognizing the importance of property for well-being is not the same as recognizing the importance of private property for it. Property may be owned by a collectivity or by the state. The private ownership of property is important because it allows us to control how we live, whereas collective or state ownership could take control from us. Our use of property would then be subject to the approval or disapproval of some impersonal authority. This would be an unacceptable interference with the rule of law, justice, legal and political equality, and liberty in our political system. It would also endanger our well-being, since no one acting on behalf of an impersonal entity could possibly know nearly as well as we ourselves do what secondary needs we have and what would be an adequate satisfaction of them. No society committed to the well-being of its members could be in favor of depriving them of the control of how they live. Since that control depends on private property, collective or state ownership is not a workable option, as we know from the dismal failure of all state owned economies.

The reasons against collective or state ownership are not reasons against a society limiting in various ways the possession and uses of private property. There is obvious need for such limits, because a society must coordinate the endeavors of its members to control how they live. Appropriate limits make it illegitimate to possess and use private property in ways that prevent others from doing the same. The scarcity of resources necessitates additional limits. It has the unavoidable consequence that the scarce private property one person has prevents others from having it. The terms of legitimate competition for scarce private property must therefore be set, and this further limits what we can do to obtain and use the private property we need for having adequate control of how we live. We inevitably chafe under such limits, but if they are reasonable and no more extensive than what is needed to make the possession and use of private property secure, then we should recognize their necessity and put up with them.

This explanation of the importance of private property is not an adequate justification of it. The explanation tacitly presupposes one or another problematic justification of private property, as I will now proceed to show. I will not examine these justifications in detail, because what I find problematic with them are not the details, but their overall strategy. These problematic justifications are based on interest, entitlement, and utility.

Interest-Based Justification

The basic idea is that we have needs and it is in our interest to satisfy them.[7] Doing so depends on having the necessary resources and on being able to use them as our interests prompt us to do. Private property enables us to have, control, and use as we see fit the resources for satisfying our needs. Since a good society must protect the conditions in which its members can pursue their well-being, and since private property is essential for that, a good society will provide that protection by means of the primary political goods of the rule of law, justice, legal and political equality, and liberty. These political goods must themselves be protected, and that depends on having the resources needed for the complex apparatus of protection. Thus the primary political goods are interdependent. Their relative importance varies depending on the contingencies of the changing contexts and conditions of our society.

There are two serious problems with this interest-based justification. The first is that we are prone to make mistakes about having a need we think we have, for instance for fame or revenge; or feel a

---

[7] See, e.g., Dworkin, Ronald M. *Taking Rights Seriously*. Cambridge, MA: Harvard University Press, 1977, and MacCormick, Neil. *Legal Rights and Social Democracy*. Oxford: Clarendon Press, 1982.

need we in fact do not have, as hypochondriacs may do for medical treatment; or not to feel a need we should feel, such as for correcting our ignorance. Well-being, therefore, does not depend merely on satisfying the needs we feel we have, but on satisfying needs we really have. If the justification of private property is that it serves our interest, then a good society will not leave it to our often faulty discretion to control the uses we make of our private property, since the uses we make of it may be contrary to our interests. Why should a good society enable its members to waste scarce resources, for instance in frivolous lawsuits or buying and destroying works of art we dislike?

Much more needs to be said, therefore, to justify private property than merely that it serves our interests by enabling us to satisfy our needs. But the more is said, the less control will be left to individuals, and the more qualified the right to private property will become. A good society, therefore, may well conclude that the collective or state ownership of property better serves the interests of its members than private ownership, or that there are often good reasons for interfering with the use individuals make of their private property. And this conclusion shows the inadequacy of the interest-based justification. We certainly have and want to protect our interests, but only within reasonable limits. And the interest-based justification is silent about what the limits are and how to tell whether they are reasonable.

A second problem with this attempted justification is that it assumes that the required private properties are available and the only problem is to decide who should control them. But this is not so. Properties have to be produced before they could be owned by anyone. If their control is left to the discretion of the producers, then, given the scarcity of resources and the partiality of the producers to their own interests, many of us will lack the resources we need. The protection of the private property of the producers will be contrary to the interests of many people who need the scarce resources the producers will not produce. If, however, the control of their private property is taken from the producers, why would reasonable producers produce them?

Neither problem is unsolvable. The reason for calling attention to them is to make clear that much more is required than a simple appeal to our needs and interests. Reasonable limits must be set to the satisfaction of needs and interests, and that unavoidably appeals to considerations other than our possibly mistaken personal opinion about which of our needs and interests should be satisfied. Complex often conflicting economic, legal, moral, and political evaluations must be considered and evaluated in order to decide what limits are reasonable. The interest-based justification founders on the problem of limits.

Entitlement-Based Justification

The entitlement-based justification of private property has several versions, distinguished mainly by what the entitlement is based on. According to the earliest version, individuals are entitled to private property if they mixed their labor with generally available resources and after they have done so enough is left of the resource for others to do likewise if they wish.[8] Those who acquire property in this way can sell, exchange, or bequeath it. Others may acquire a right to it if they receive it from the original owner by legitimate means.

This justification has great intuitive appeal. It appeals to the well-deserved rewards of hard work and skill. If out of driftwood I found lying on a beach I build a beautiful table, who but I would have a right to it? And if I decide to give it as a birthday present to my daughter, then who but she could claim to have a right to it? There is no doubt that this justification holds good in some cases, but it does not hold in many others. To begin with, it is virtually impossible

---

[8] See, e.g., Locke, John. "Property" in *Second Treatise of Government*. Indianapolis: Hackett, 1690/1980.

to trace the chain of ownership back to the original acquisition of, say, a piece of land. And if it is traced back as far as we are likely to be able to go in the undocumented past, we frequently find that it was acquired by dispossessing its earlier owner by force. Virtually all nations presently in existence began by killing or enslaving the native population. No one, then, could claim legitimate possession of any land presently owned in these nations.

Suppose next that I contract with a person to build a house for me, and he does. He mixes his labor with it and he may build it very well, but he certainly does not acquire the right to the house. The house is mine, even though I have neither mixed my labor with it nor have I acquired it from someone who did so. The builder is entitled to payment for his labor, but not to anything more. Take another case. I buy a lottery ticket, win a sum of money, invest it, and the money grows. I am clearly entitled to the proceeds, but I have done nothing remotely resembling mixing my labor with the money I won. For these reasons, among others, contemporary defenders of the entitlement-based justification tend to ignore the past and concentrate on present possession.[9]

They also begin with intuitively appealing cases, as does Robert Nozick with his not quite fictional Wilt Chamberlain. He is a great basketball player and people willingly pay again and again a lot of money to see him practice his artistry. He becomes wealthy and he is entitled to his wealth. He cheated no one, he delivered what people expected, everyone was better off, and no one was worse off. He has a right to do what he pleases with the money he has earned: he can spend it, invest it, give it away, leave it to his children, use it to support a cause he believes in, and so forth. Who could reasonably doubt that he has the right to possess and use the private property he has acquired in this way? A critic could.

A critic might say, to begin with, that the case has intuitive appeal only to those who share the conventions on which the case rests. But

---

[9] See, e.g., Nozick, Robert. *Anarchy, State, and Utopia.* New York: Basic Books, 1974

these conventions are deplorable, says the critic, sharing them is a sign of corruption, and a society would be better off without them. One of these conventions is the commercialization of sports. It is a bad thing for a society that a great athlete, like Wilt Chamberlain, sells his talent for money. He does with basketball what prostitutes do with sex. People should be allowed to pay money for either, but surely a society should not encourage it and it should not base the right to private property on such dubious cases. And it is not just Wilt Chamberlain who demeans himself, critics may say. Those who pay to watch him also do so, because by finding enjoyment in the passive observation of an endlessly repetitive activity of bouncing an inflated ball, they betray a vacuum in their inner lives.

The moderate conservative point is not that these critics are right to condemn commercial sports. The point is that they are right to claim that the Wilt Chamberlain case rests on conventions it presupposes, but does not justify. This entitlement-based justification takes for granted the conventions involved in the acquisition of private property, but its acquisition in conformity to prevailing conventions does not by itself entitle people to what they possess.

Consider an ordinary person without any great talent. He earns a living doing a low-paying job and supports his wife and three young children. On his way home from work he is killed in a freak accident for which no one could be blamed. His family is now destitute. Would a good society not be remiss in failing to protect the well-being of its members if it did not tax the earnings of the talented Wilt Chamberlain and used the funds to support those who through no fault of their own are destitute? The reason for doing so may be pity, fellow-feeling, or charity, but it need not be. It may simply be prudence, for destitution that follows from misfortune creates needs that should be satisfied in some way. Crime is a natural option, and if there is a lot of it, the society will be destabilized, and private property will be endangered. Once again, no reasonable person could say that the talented Wilt Chamberlain should not be taxed so as to avoid these consequences.

The problem with the entitlement-based justification is that the conventions that entitle us to possess private property need to be examined and justified. They cannot be justified on the basis of entitlement. That would simply assume that the conventions appealed to have been justified, and that, of course, is precisely what is in question. The justification of the conventions, therefore, must proceed in some other way. Regardless of what that way is, the need for it shows the insufficiency of the entitlement-based justification. We are not entitled to private property we acquire by extortion, theft, fraud, and so forth. But to draw a reasonable distinction between private property to which we are and those to which we are not entitled is a complex question that cannot be settled by appealing to prevailing conventions. Perhaps the prevailing conventions are mistaken. The entitlement-based justification, therefore, is too simple to solve the problem of how to tell whether or not private property is justifiably held.

Utility-Based Justification

Defenders of utility-based justifications focus on some good they take to be essential for human well-being and then argue that private property is a necessary condition of the efficient pursuit of that good. Versions of this justification differ, because they postulate different goods. The version I will discuss has liberty as the important good aimed at.[10] The argument for this version has a constructive and a critical component.

The constructive one claims to show that liberty is necessary for our well-being, because it enables us to decide how we want to live and allows us to choose without interference between the available

---

[10] There are numerous defenders of this version. Perhaps the best-known representative is Hayek, Friedrich A. *The Constitution of Liberty*. Chicago: University of Chicago Press, 1960, and *The Mirage of Social Justice*. Vol. 2 of *Law, Legislation and Liberty*. Chicago: University of Chicago Press, 1976.

alternatives. Liberty should be curtailed only to prevent interference with the liberty of others. By protecting private property, a society enables its members to create prosperity and produce the resources needed for the meaningful use of liberty. The critical component of the argument shows that collective or state ownership of property will not create the needed prosperity and that it leads to an unjustifiable restriction of liberty.

Moderate conservatives agree that the utility-based justification is correct in both its constructive and critical claims, but claim that it nevertheless falls short of providing an adequate justification of private property. The fundamental reason for this is that, although it is true that liberty and prosperity are necessary for our well-being, it is also true that there are other goods necessary for it. The rule of law, justice, and legal and political equality often conflict with private property, and there may be strong reasons for curtailing liberty and private property in order to secure the other primary political goods.

It is an obvious fact of contemporary politics that liberty and private property can be pursued by unacceptable means, such as crime, monopoly, false advertising, or selling shoddy goods. It is similarly obvious that protecting the other primary political goods may require curtailing both liberty and the right to private property. Goods that are necessary for our well-being often conflict. The reasonable resolution of these conflicts is to balance the conflicting goods so as to have as much as possible of all the goods we need. It cannot be reasonably supposed that when liberty and private property conflict with one or more of these primary political goods, then liberty and private property should always in all contexts and conditions override whatever conflicts with them.

Some of the conditions in which this may be reasonable are for instance those in which private property is used in ways that endanger public health, such as the discharge of industrial waste into rivers, advertising cigarettes to adolescents, or selling unsafe cars. Or when it threatens security, such as selling sophisticated weapon systems to terrorists, or using scarce resources needed for defense to produce more profitable luxury goods. Or when it undermines the rule of law and justice by paying lawyers who specialize in securing the acquittal of criminals on technicalities, or publishing newspapers that malign public officials by spreading innuendos about their private lives that skirt but skillfully avoid libel. Or when it puts stability at risk by allowing great inequalities between the wealthy and the indigent.

Defenders of the utility-based justification may respond by acknowledging the necessity of these other political goods in our political system, but arguing that the protection of liberty and private property should still take precedence over them because these other primary political goods can be pursued only by those who can make choices freely and who have the necessary resources. And these are the conditions that liberty and private property provide. I think this response is correct, but it still fails to show that liberty and private property should take precedence over the other goods when they conflict. For just as the pursuit of other political goods presupposes liberty and private property, so the pursuit of liberty and private property presupposes, among other things, the rule of law, justice, and legal and political equality, not to mention education, order, peace, public health, security, or stability.

In the complex contemporary conditions of our society, liberty and private property cannot be reasonably pursued unless there is a general understanding of the alternatives among which we can choose. This presupposes adequate education. In an unstable society, everyone is at risk, liberty is severely curtailed by the necessity of self-protection, and private property cannot be put to its intended uses, because no one's private property is safe. The liberty and private property we value are possible because the rule of law, justice, and legal and political equality prevail in our society. When we use our liberty to make choices, we make predictions about how the various alternatives open to us would be likely to affect us in the future. In seeking private property we assume that what we acquire now we can continue to hold in the future. These predictions and assumptions presuppose stability. In the midst of war and epidemic, everyone's well-being depends on commandeering resources and severely restricting the liberty of choices about medical care, travel, and the uses of necessary services. Our present enjoyment of liberty and private property is possible only because public health is protected and peace is maintained.

The preceding remarks are intended to make clear that the goods necessary for our well-being are interdependent and mutually presuppose and strengthen one another. The utility-based justification is correct to insist that private property must be protected if we are to have a free society. But it is mistaken in forgetting that the pursuit of these important goods conflicts with the pursuit of other important goods, that the reasonable resolution of such conflicts requires balancing all the important political and non-political goods, and that achieving a reasonable balance is possible only if we resign ourselves to having less liberty and private property than we would like in order to secure other important goods, although they too to a lesser extent than we would like. This is the problem of balancing goods, and the utility-based justification of the right to private property is too simple to cope with it.

I conclude that the attempted justifications of the right to private property based on interest, entitlement, and utility are inadequate. I say inadequate, not wrong, because they rightly stress the importance of the interest we all have in satisfying our needs, in having resources to which we are entitled, and in enjoying liberty. Nevertheless, they fail to justify private property, because they have not faced the problem of how to set reasonable limits to legitimately owned property, and how to balance important goods. We need a complex justification for that. The moderate conservative one I will now propose and try to defend combines what I take to be right in the three simple justifications, overcomes their inadequacies, and replaces the assumptions that lead them astray with a more realistic one. The upshot is that private property can be justified, but only in a way that is much less philosophical, general, and theoretical and much more practical, concrete, and political than it has been supposed by defenders of the simple justifications.

Complex Justification

The basic reason why the interest, entitlement, and utility-based justifications of private property are too simple is that they assume that there is an indisputable standard—a principle, a theory, or a highest good—conformity to which makes the justification adequate. These attempted justifications disagree about what the standard is, but they agree that an adequate justification must be based on it. Moderate conservatives propose a complex justification that rejects this assumption. The right to private property is a bundle of rights and the components of the bundle need to be justified separately and differently. The complex justification must set reasonable limits, distinguish between rightly and wrongly held private property, and balance conflicting political goods.

The complex justification accepts much of the entitlement-based justification. The possession of private property is justified if its acquisition and uses conform to the terms of cooperation as described in Chapter 5. The problem with the entitlement-based justification is that it presupposes, but neither identifies nor justifies these terms of cooperation. The complex justification, therefore, must do what the entitlement-based one fails to do. How, then, can the terms of cooperation guiding the acquisition and uses of private property be justified?

The first step is to remind ourselves of how plausible are these terms of cooperation. Two parties make a formal or informal agreement that one will do a job, lease an apartment, or sell a car and the other will pay wages, rent, or the purchase price. The first party to the agreement does what creates an entitlement to the private property that the second party should transfer to the first. Or consider terms of cooperation involved in relationships. Parents should be financially responsible for the upbringing of their children, investors should get a share of the profit, executives should not run companies mainly for their own benefit. Such terms of cooperation create entitlements to what their explicit or implicit terms specify. A large part of these entitlements is constituted of the terms of cooperation in the background. They need not be actually spoken because in our political system they are generally understood. You said you would do it, so do it. You bought it, so pay for it. He is a friend, so be loyal to him. Adhering to them is part of what I called in Chapter 2 common decencies. These terms of cooperation are obvious and well-known to normally intelligent members of our society. Their obviousness, however, may just show that they are customary and prevalent, but not that they are justified.

The second step is to show what would justify them. Moderate conservatives think that they are justified if members of our society rely on and follow them voluntarily because they regard them as important for their well-being. They meet the test of time. They have endured for a considerable length of time, measured in decades rather than months. They are widely known and taken for granted by a great majority of us in our context. In the appropriate situations, we are naturally and spontaneously guided by and rely on the terms of cooperation and reasonably expect others in our society to do the same. If this expectation is not met, and it may not be, then its violation is widely regarded as blameworthy or requiring an excuse.

Terms of cooperation may endure as a result of coercion that makes the failure to follow them too costly for most of us. One indication of the voluntary acceptance of the terms of cooperation is that we, as members of our society, need not be coerced to follow them. Another indication is that although there are acceptable legal, moral, and political ways of challenging and trying to change the terms of cooperation, we by and large habitually follow them. A further indication is that even though we could leave our society, we do not, and we continue to follow the terms of cooperation in appropriate circumstances. None of this requires our conscious and articulate approval of the terms of cooperation. Most of us in our society follow them voluntarily without needing or wanting to give the matter serious thought.

Voluntary conformity, however, may just indicate habit, indoctrination, or that it is easier to go with the current than to swim against it. There may be a good reason for it, however, even if this reason is not uppermost in our minds when we follow the terms of cooperation. The good reason is that by conforming to them we can acquire, control, and use the resources we need for satisfying our basic and secondary needs. The reason, then, why the terms of cooperation have become generally accepted and why they are uncoerced and generally followed is that our well-being depends on it. We do not question or feel the need to justify the terms of cooperation, because we willingly take them for granted.

There is no society in which all terms of cooperation about the ownership of private property are in this happy state. Some of the terms of cooperation are routinely questioned and then they need to be justified, reformed, or abandoned. This is what happened to primogeniture, to the control husbands have of their wives' property, or to the imprisonment of debtors. And this is what is happening in our society now about the inequities of taxation. It may also happen that most of the terms of cooperation are being questioned and their justifications are found wanting. Then the society in which this happens is on the brink of revolution, as England was 1642, France in 1789, Russia in 1917, and the Soviet Union in 1989.

The essential point in our present context is that according to the complex justification, the possession of private property is justified if it has been acquired in accordance with the terms of cooperation that continues to meet the test of time and are generally followed because it is rightly assumed to be a condition of well-being in our society. This justification resolves the problem of what justifies the possession of private property. This is the problem on which the entitlement-based justification foundered. But it is nowhere near the end of the matter, because it says nothing about the justified uses and limits of rightfully possessed private property.

I turn next to how the complex justification resolves a problem that arises in the context of the utility-based justification of private property. That justification, it will be remembered, is that our well-being depends on private property because we rely on it to provide the resources we need for living as we want. The problem with this justification is not with any of its claims, which I think are correct, but with its failure to take into account other claims that are no less correct. These claims are made on behalf of goods that are also necessary for our well-being. Some of them are the other primary political goods: the rule of law, justice, legal and political equality, and liberty. Some others are education, order, peace, public health, security, and stability. The problem is that the protection of these goods often requires limiting the right to private property. We need to have some non-arbitrary way of deciding what limits are reasonable and how to balance the conflicting claims of the various goods we need for our well-being. In this way, the problems of coping with conflicting goods and setting reasonable limits to the claim of each good are closely connected.

I have stressed again and again the moderate conservative view that primary political goods will conflict and their conflicts cannot be reasonably resolved by claiming that one of them is always, in all contexts and conditions, more important for our well-being than any of the others. All of them are important, and sometimes one, sometimes another is more important than the others. There are and have been numerous contexts and conditions in which the claims of the rule of law, justice, legal and political equality, or liberty are strong enough to justify interference with private property, for instance by raising taxes, prohibiting monopolies, or outlawing fraudulent business practices. But if the problems cannot be reasonably resolved by attributing overriding importance to one of the goods we obviously need for our well-being, then how can they be resolved?

The complex justification is a reasonable approach to coping with this problem that the utility-based justification could not handle. Three considerations are crucial to it. First, the reasonable resolution of conflicts among important goods rarely involves an all-or-none decision. Usually it is a matter of deciding how much of each we can have, so we will typically have to find a way in which we can have as much as possible of both. For instance, the protection of security or public health requires increased taxation and that unavoidably interferes with private property. A reasonable decision, then, is not to choose one or the other, but finding the greatest possible protection at the least increase in taxation. And that calls for a political decision based on understanding the context and the conditions.

Such decisions cannot be deduced from a theory. They require careful attention to the facts and politically experienced judgments about evaluating how serious are the threats to security and public health, how burdensome the level of taxation already is, and what are the long-term economic and social consequences of whatever decision might be made, and so forth. These are complex decisions and they need complex justifications. Calculations of utility will be part of them, but the morality of the decision, the likelihood of compliance with it, resistance to its enforcement will need to be some of the other considerations that must be weighed. Utility by itself is too simple for making such complex decisions.

Second, a reasonable choice cannot be to decide once and for all which of the conflicting important goods should always override the others. The choice between them almost always depends on the context and the conditions in which we have to decide which is more important than the other. It may be that coping with the threat to security is more important than interfering with private property by increased taxation. If in another context and conditions the threat to security is not great, or private property is already over-taxed, then their priority should be reversed. Reasonable conflict-resolutions vary with contexts and conditions. And that excludes once and for all context-independent conflict-resolutions. Even if consideration of utility were our most important concern, what is utile varies with contexts and conditions.

Third, at any given time in our society there are many goods whose necessity for well-being is generally recognized. These goods are embedded in the political system of our society that has met the test of time. The protection of the political system itself is always more important than any of the particular goods that jointly constitute it. Reasonable conflict-resolutions, therefore, have a standard to which they can appeal: the relative importance of the conflicting goods for the protection of the political system as a whole. Whether a particular conflict-resolution is reasonable depends on which of the conflicting goods is more important for sustaining the political system in that context and in those conditions.

An approach to conflict-resolution that takes into account only the respective importance of the particular conflicting goods is bound to go wrong because it fails to consider the effect of the conflict-resolution on the entire political system. This is just what the utility-based justification fails to do, and the complex justification does do. This complex justification is just as concerned with well-being as the utility-based one, but it recognizes that in any context and conditions well-being depends on the protection of many goods, not just on one or two of them.

The complex justification, therefore, provides an approach to finding a reasonable balance of goods and setting reasonable limits to the pursuit of goods in the same way: by appealing to the standard constituted by the entire political system. Reasonable balance is the one that best protects the political system in a particular context. And a reasonable limit is one that restricts one, or perhaps both, of the conflicting goods in order to protect the entire political system. The right to private property then may be reasonably limited if it is necessary for protecting the rule of law, justice, legal and political equality, and liberty on which our well-being also depends.

It may be objected to the complex justification that it does precisely what it criticizes the utility-based justification for doing: arbitrarily assigning priority to a particular good and resolving conflicts in its favor. But this objection rests on a misunderstanding of the standard to which the complex justification appeals. The standard is not a particular good, but all the goods forming the political system. And the appeal to it is not arbitrary, because the goods that form the political system are recognized as necessary for the well-being of everyone in the context and conditions of our society. No one can reasonably suppose that the primary political goods and other goods like education, order, peace, prosperity, public health, security, and stability are arbitrarily regarded as goods. The serious question about them is not whether they are really good, but which of them should have priority when they conflict. And it is that question that is answered by the complex justification.

It may also be objected to the complex justification that politicians competing for scarce resources cannot be expected to consider the wider consequences of the outcome of their competition. They need to make important and necessary decisions then and there in order to serve the interests of the people who elected them and to remain in power. It is much too demanding that they should take a wider view, which may actually require them to go against the interests, including their own, they are expected to represent. This is unfortunately true of many politicians, but it is not an objection to the complex justification. For what that justification aims to provide is a reasonable approach to conflict-resolution. That many politicians are shortsighted and insufficiently reasonable is not exactly news, nor is it an objection to the complex justification moderate conservatives propose.

We have now seen how the complex justification goes about justifying private property and, when warranted, interference with it. From this it is but a small step to providing a justification for the remaining component of the right to private property: its actual use. Private property provides resources we need for the satisfaction of our needs. As the interest-based justification rightly claims, it is in our vital interest to be able to use our private property as we see fit. However, the interest-based justification fails to note that we may misuse it by satisfying needs that should not be satisfied, or by not satisfying needs that should be satisfied.

The number of ways in which we can and have misused private property is large and depressing. We may be led to it by addiction, fanaticism, ignorance, neurosis, self-deception, stupidity, unreasonable risk-taking, vindictiveness, and so on and on. Legal, moral, and political strictures against misuse cannot possibly take into account the countless ways in which we may waste our resources by using them contrary to our own interests. Protection of private property must proceed, therefore, by thinking of interests in impersonal terms, that is, as interests that any normal adult in a particular context is going to have. The misuse of private property, then, may be understood as using it in ways contrary to interests impersonally conceived.

We can go a step further in specifying the ways in which the interests of others may be violated by the misuse of private property. We can rely on what has already been said about justified possessions and limits. The misuse of private property is to use it in ways that prevent others from acquiring or using their legitimately acquired private property. The reasonable use of private property, then, is within limits that strengthen rather than weaken the system of goods on which everyone's well-being in our society depends. Legitimate acquisition and reasonable limits of how private property may be used define an area of discretion within which we should be able to use our private property as we see fit. We may still misuse it of course, but we can blame only ourselves if thereby our interests suffer. One of the proper tasks of our political system is to protect private property and to protect us from interference by others. Its task is not to protect us from acting contrary to our own interests by misusing our private property.

In conclusion, the moderate conservative justification of private property depends on justifying its possession, use, and limits. Possession is justified if it has been acquired legitimately in accordance with the prevailing terms of cooperation that have met the test of time, are voluntarily adhered to, and serve our well-being. Limits are justified if they are set by the political system on which the well-being of all of us depends in the context and conditions of American society. This justification explains the importance of private property by interpreting it as the means of controlling resources we need for our well-being. It avoids the problems that beset the entitlement, utility, and interest-based justifications. And it offers a justification of the possession, uses, and limits of private property.

10
Last Words

One of the maxims inscribed on the pediment of the ancient sanctuary at Delphi was "Nothing in Excess." It expressed the virtue of *sophrosyne*, which we translate as moderation or restraint. And that is the attitude that guides moderate conservatives in our present political context and conditions. It does not tell us what we should do as we face perennial problems. It tells us how we should go about defending the primary political goods of the rule of law, justice, liberty, legal and political equality, and private property. And it tells us as well what we should not do. We should avoid excess because whatever we may gain by having more of any of the primary political goods, we are going to have less of other equally important political goods. If we recognize that all the primary political goods are essential to maintaining our political system, we will want always to avoid excess and balance their claims, especially when we face adverse contingencies and conflicts between the goods we value. We will try to find a compromise that allows us to have as much of all the primary political goods as the context and conditions allow. Doing that well is the art of politics—the art!—not the science of politics. It is an art that is practical, not theoretical; pluralistic, not dedicated to the pursuit of some absolute GOOD; it is limited to our context and conditions, and does not aspire to universal and unconditional applicability to all societies, conditions, and times. This is the art to which moderate conservatives have apprenticed themselves. They practice it, but they have no illusion about possessing the key to its perfection. There is no blueprint for that. There is only trial and error, and the commitment to learning from them. The background against which the perennial problem of contingencies, conflicts, and compromises occur is formed of the external and internal conditions of our lives. They change in ways we have not sought and to which we must willy-nilly adjust. We have a great plurality of political and non-political evaluative commitments that should guide our responses to the contingencies that follow from these changes, but the possible responses often conflict. We have to choose between them, opt to be guided by one of them, and act contrary to the conflicting ones. But the conflicting ones also follow from our evaluative commitments. So that no matter how successful is the response we choose to act on, it will unavoidably lead to the need to compromise some of our commitments. In this way and for these reasons, the satisfactions we enjoy come with dissatisfactions with what they exclude. By saying "yes," we have to say "no" to the other commitments we have made and could not honor. Our affirmations are inseparably connected with our denials of what we could or perhaps should have but did not affirm. We celebrate our life-enhancing affirmations, but tend to forget about the losses that unavoidably go with them. Contingencies, conflicts, and compromises are and will remain perennial problems and permanent adversities we have to face and struggle with forever because we are the kind of beings we are and the world is what it is.

This is the condition of life to which ideal theorists and moderate conservatives are both responses. I have inveighed throughout the book against ideal theories. I acknowledge that the pursuit of some ideal of the GOOD has been an enduring part of human history. It is true that it inspires, consoles, and gives hope to countless people. But all that is a way, one of many, of consoling ourselves along our life's way as we are again and again beset by contingencies, conflicts, and moral compromises. If all goes well we can cope with them one by one as they occur and endlessly recur, but we can never eliminate them because they are part of our condition: the human condition.

Perennial problems are akin to aging, sensory limits, and basic needs. We have to cope with them again and again. Contingencies, conflicts, and compromises are permanent and recurring problems that are unavoidable parts of our life. Only when we reach our end do we reach the end of the perennial problems we have to face. The promise of the ideal of the GOOD whose realization would free us from perennial problems is unfulfillable. It would remain so even if there really were a metaphysical, moral, personal, political, or religious ideal of the one and only GOOD, because perennial problems would make its realization impossible.

What, then, do moderate conservatives offer as a better response? First, to be prepared for contingencies by making the evaluation and re-evaluation of the relative importance of our evaluative commitments a lifelong habit. Second, to ameliorate conflicts between our evaluations by not treating them as absolute all-or-nothing choices, but as more-or-less ones, and thereby making our evaluations flexible and open to their changing relative importance as our contexts, conditions, and sometimes we ourselves change. And it is to tolerate our moral compromises by asking ourselves which of our incompatible evaluations is more and which less important to being the kind of person we want to be. We teach ourselves to evaluate, not what we might gain, but what we can give up and still remain the person we can respect.

The key to moderate conservative attitude is to combine a sense of what is important to us with a permanent readiness to revise what we care about. In Peter Winch's fine words:[1]

> A man's sense of importance of something to him shows itself in all sorts of ways: not merely in precautions to safeguard that thing. He may . . . contemplate it, to gain some sense of his life in relation to it. He may wish thereby, in a certain sense, to *free* himself from dependence on it. I do not mean by making sure that it does not let him down, because the point is that, *whatever* he does, he may still be let down. The important thing is that that

---

[1] Winch, Peter. "Understanding a Primitive Society" in *Ethics and Action*. London: Routledge, 1964/1972, 38–39.

he should understand *that* and come to terms with it.... He must see that he can still go on even if he is let down by what is vitally important to him; and he must so order his life that he still *can* go on in such circumstances.

These strategies for coping with perennial problems involve treating our evaluative commitments as conditional, rather than unconditional. This cannot be done by those who have made an unconditional commitment to a way of life, a cause, the pursuit of an ideal, or to the love of a person, family, tradition, or institution. One of the deep human differences is between those who have made an unconditional commitment to something and those who have not. There are reasons for and against both. Unconditional commitments are vulnerable to tragic conflicts, lack flexibility in responding to perennial problems, but they provide clarity and certainty about what is more and what less important. Conditional commitments are much less vulnerable to tragic conflicts, but they are also less clear and certain, and more ambivalent about the relative importance of evaluative commitments to how to live.

The choice between these contrary attitudes to life is personal. There are reasons for and against both. This book is not about the evaluation of that choice and those reasons. I merely note that the choice and the reasons lead to different responses to perennial problems. Moderate conservatism is an attitude to politics that is centrally concerned with how we should respond to perennial problems and be guided by balanced political evaluations. It seems clear, at least to me, that moderate conservatives will not make unconditional political commitments. I see no reason, however, why they could not make unconditional non-political commitments if they are prepared to take the risks that go with them.[2]

In politics, however, we

---

[2] I discuss this subject in *Hard Questions*. New York: Oxford University Press, 2019, and *Wisdom*. New York: Oxford University Press, 2020.

sail a boundless and bottomless sea; there is neither harbour for shelter nor floor for anchorage. The enterprise is to keep afloat on an even keel. . . . A depressing doctrine, it will be said. . . . But in the main the depression springs from the exclusion of hopes that were false and the discovery that guides reputed to be of superhuman wisdom and skill, are, in fact, of a somewhat different character. If it deprives us of a model laid up in heaven, at least it does not lead into a morass where every choice is equally good or equally to be deplored.[3]

---

[3] Oakeshott, Michael. "Political Education" in *Rationalism in Politics*. Indianapolis: LibertyPress, 1991, 60.

References

Allitt, Patrick. *The Conservatives*. New Haven, CT: Yale University Press, 2009.

Aristotle. *Politics*. Translated by Benjamin Jowett. *The Complete Works of Aristotle*. Vol. 2. Edited by Jonathan Barnes. Princeton, NJ: Princeton University Press, c.340 BC/1984.

Aristotle. *Nicomachean Ethics*, 1104a1-6. Translated by W.D. Ross. Revised by J.O. Urmson. In *The Complete Works of Aristotle*. Vol. 2. Edited by Jonathan Barnes. Princeton, NJ: Princeton University Press. c.340 BC/1984.

Arneson, Richard. "Egalitarianism." https://plato.stanford.edu/archives/sum2013/entries/egalitarianism/

Arneson, Richard. "What, if Anything, Renders All Humans Morally Equal?" In *Singer and His Critics*. Edited by Dale Jamieson. Oxford: Blackwell, 1999.

Arrowsmith, William, "Introduction" to *The Complete Greek Tragedies: Euripides III: Hecuba*. Chicago: University of Chicago Press, 1969.

Bacevich, Andrew J., ed. *American Conservatism*. New York: Library of America, 2020.

Bacon, Francis. "Of Studies." In *The Essayes or Counsels, Civil and Morall*. Edited by Richard Foster Jones. New York: Odyssey Press, 1597–1625/1937.

Bate, Walter Jackson. *John Keats*. Cambridge, MA: Harvard University Press, 1963.

Becker, Lawrence C. "Property." In *Encyclopedia of Ethics*. 2nd ed. Edited by Lawrence C. Becker and Charlotte B. Becker. New York: Routledge, 2001.

Berlin, Isaiah. "Equality." In *Concepts and Categories*. Edited by Henry Hardy. London: Hogarth Press, 1978.

Berlin, Isaiah. "Two Concepts of Liberty." In *Four Essays on Liberty*. Oxford: Oxford University Press, 1969.

Burke, Edmund. "An Appeal from the New to the Old Whigs." In *Further Reflections on the Revolution in France*. Edited by Daniel E. Ritchie. Indianapolis: Liberty Fund, 1791/1992.

Burke, Edmund. *Reflections on the Revolution in France*. Indianapolis: Liberty Fund, 1790/1999.

Carter, Ian. "Liberty." https://plato.stanford.edu/entries/liberty-positive-negative/

Cavell, Stanley. "The Availability of Wittgenstein's Later Philosophy." In *Must We Mean What We Say?* Cambridge, MA: Harvard University Press, 1969.

Christman, John. "Autonomy." https://plato.stanford.edu/archives/spr2018/entries/autonomy-moral/

REFERENCES

Cornford, F.M. *From Religion to Philosophy.* New York: Harper & Row, 1912/1957.

Davidson, Donald, ed. "How Is Weakness of Will Possible?" In *Essays on Actions and Events,* 21–42. Oxford: Clarendon Press, 1980.

Davidson, Donald. "Paradoxes of Irrationality." In *Philosophical Essays on Freud.* Edited by Richard Wollheim and James Hopkins, 289–305. Cambridge: Cambridge University Press, 1982.

Dunn, John. *The Cunning of Unreason.* New York: Basic Books, 2000.

Dworkin, Gerald. "Autonomy." In *A Companion to Contemporary Political Philosophy.* Edited by Robert E. Goodin and Phillip Pettit. Oxford: Blackwell, 1993.

Dworkin, Gerald. *The Theory and Practice of Autonomy.* New York: Cambridge University Press, 1988.

Dworkin, Ronald. *A Matter of Principle.* Cambridge, MA: Harvard University Press, 1985.

Dworkin, Ronald. *Sovereign Virtue.* Cambridge, MA: Harvard University Press, 2000.

Dworkin, Ronald. *Taking Rights Seriously.* Cambridge, MA: Harvard University Press, 1977.

Feinberg, Joel. *Social Philosophy.* Englewood Cliffs, NJ: Prentice-Hall, 1990.

Feldman, Fred, and Brad Skow. "Desert." https://www.rep.routledge.com/articles/thematic/desert-and-merit/v-1.

Finnis, John. *Natural Law and Natural Rights.* Oxford: Clarendon Press, 1980.

Flickschuh, Katrin. "Freedom." In *The Routledge Companion to Social and Political Philosophy.* Edited by Gerald Gaus and Fred D'Agostino. New York: Routledge, 2013.

Foot, Philippa. *Natural Goodness.* Oxford: Clarendon Press 2001.

Frankfurt, Harry G. *Taking Ourselves Seriously and Getting It Right.* Stanford, CA: Stanford University Press, 2006.

Frohnen, Bruce, et al. eds. *American Conservatism.* Wilmington, DE: ISI Books, 2006.

Hampshire, Stuart. *Innocence and Experience.* London: Allen Lane, 1989.

Hampshire, Stuart. *Justice Is Conflict.* Princeton: Princeton University Press, 2000.

Hart, H.L.A. "Are There Any Natural Rights?" *Philosophical Review* 64(1955): 175–91.

Hart, H.L.A. *The Concept of Law.* Oxford: Clarendon Press, 1961.

Hart, H.L.A. "Utilitarianism and Natural Rights." In *Essays in Jurisprudence and Philosophy.* Oxford: Clarendon Press, 1983.

Hartle, Ann. *What Happened to Civility.* Notre Dame, IN: University of Notre Dame Press, 2022.

Hayek, Friedrich A. *The Constitution of Liberty.* Chicago: Regnery, 1960.

Hayek, Friedrich A. *The Mirage of Social Justice*. In *Law, Legislation and Liberty*, Vol 2. Chicago: University of Chicago Press, 1976.

Hobbes, Thomas. *Leviathan*. Edited by Richard Tuck. Cambridge: Cambridge University Press, 1651/1996.

Honoré, A.M. "Ownership." In *Oxford Essays in Jurisprudence*. Edited by A.G. Guest. Oxford: Oxford University Press, 1961.

Hume, David. *A Treatise of Human Nature*. 2nd ed. Edited by P.H. Nidditch. Oxford: Clarendon Press, 1739/1978.

Hume, David. *Enquiry concerning the Principles of Morals*. Edited by Tom L. Beauchamp. Oxford: Oxford University Press, 1777/1998.

Hume, David. "Of the Protestant Succession." In *Essays Moral Political and Literary*. Edited by Eugene F. Miller. Indianapolis: Liberty Press, 1741/1999.

Hume, David. "The Rise of Arts and Sciences." In *Essays Moral Political and Literary*. Edited by Eugene F. Miller. Indianapolis: LibertyClassics, 1777/1985.

Hume, David. "The Sceptic." In *Essays Moral Political and Literary*. Edited by Eugene F. Miller. Indianapolis: LibertyClassics, 1777/1985.

Hume, David. *Dialogues Concerning Natural Religion*. Indianapolis: Hackett, 1779/1980.

Kant, Immanuel. "On the common saying: That may be correct in theory, but it is of no use in practice." In *Practical Philosophy* in *The Cambridge Edition of the Works of Immanuel Kant*. Translated by Mary J. Gregor. Cambridge: Cambridge University Press, 1996.

Keats, John. Letter to George and Thomas Keats, December 21, 1817. Cited in Walter Jackson Bate, *John Keats*. Cambridge, MA: Harvard University Press, 1963.

Kant, Immanuel. *Religion within the Bounds of Reason Alone*. Translated by Theodore M. Green & Hoyt H. Hudson. New York: Harper & Row, 1794/1960.

Kekes, John. *Against Liberalism*. Ithaca, NY: Cornell University Press, 1997.

Kekes, John. *A Case for Conservatism*. Ithaca, NY: Cornell University Press, 1998.

Kekes, John. *Hard Questions*. New York: Oxford University Press, 2019.

Kekes, John. "Justice." *Social Philosophy and Policy* 23(2006): 88–106.

Kekes, John. *Wisdom*. New York: Oxford University Press, 2020.

Kluckhohn, Clyde. "Culture and Behavior." In *The Collected Essays of Clyde Kluckhohn*. New York: Free Press, 1962.

Korsgaard, Christine. *Self-Constitution*. Oxford: Clarendon Press, 2009.

Korsgaard, Christine. *The Sources of Normativity*. New York: Cambridge University Press, 1996.

Kukathas, Chandran. *Hayek and Modern Liberalism*. Oxford: Clarendon Press, 1989.

Kymlicka, Will. *Contemporary Political Philosophy*. Oxford: Clarendon Press, 1990.

Kymlicka, Will. *Liberalism, Community, and Culture*. Oxford: Clarendon Press, 1989.

Lewis, R.W.B. *The American Adam*. Chicago: University of Chicago Press, 1955.

Locke, John. *Second Treatise of Government*. Edited by C.B. Macpherson. Indianapolis: Hackett, 1690/1980.

Lovejoy, Arthur O. *The Great Chain of Being*. New York: Harper & Row, 1960.

Madison, James. *The Federalist*, No. 51. Edited by George W. Carey & James McClellan. Indianapolis: Liberty Fund, 1788/2001.

MacCormick, Neil. *Legal Rights and Social Democracy*. Oxford: Clarendon Press, 1982.

McIntyre, Kenneth B. *Nomocratic Pluralism: Plural Values, Negative Liberty, and the Rule of Law*. Cham, Switzerland: Palgrave/Macmillan, 2021.

Mill, John Stuart. *Autobiography*. In *Collected Works of John Stuart Mill*. Edited by John M. Robson and Jack Stillinger. Indianapolis: Liberty Fund, 1981/2006.

Mill, John Stuart. *On Liberty*. Indianapolis: Hackett, 1859/1978.

Mill, John Stuart. *A System of Logic*, Book VI, Chapter X, par. 5. In *Collected Works of John Stuart Mill*. Edited by John M. Robson and Jack Stillinger, vol. 8. Indianapolis: Liberty Fund, 1898/2006.

Mill, John Stuart. *Utilitarianism* (1861). In *Collected Works of John Stuart Mill*. Edited by John M. Robson and Jack Stillinger. Indianapolis: Liberty Fund, 1981/2006.

Miller, David. "Desert and Merit." https://www-rep-routledge/articles/thematic/desert-and-merit/.

Miller, David. "Justice." https://plato.stanford.edu/entries/justice/.

Miller, David. *Philosophy and Ideology in Hume's Political Thought*. Oxford: Clarendon Press, 1981.

Montaigne, Michel. *The Complete Works of Montaigne*. Translated by Donald M. Frame. Stanford, CA: Stanford University Press, 1588/1943.

Munser, Stephen R. "Property." In *Routledge Encyclopedia of Philosophy*. Edited by Edward Craig. London: Routledge, 1998.

Nagel, Thomas. "Equality." In *Mortal Questions*. Cambridge: Cambridge University Press, 1979.

Nagel, Thomas. *Equality and Partiality*. New York: Oxford University Press, 1991.

Nozick, Robert. *Anarchy, State, and Utopia*. New York: Basic Books, 1974.

Oakeshott, Michael. *On Human Conduct*. Oxford: Clarendon Press, 1975.

Oakeshott, Michael. "Political Education." In *Rationalism in Politics*. Indianapolis: Liberty Press, 1991.

Oakeshott, Michael. *The Politics of Faith and the Politics of Scepticism*. Edited by Timothy Fuller. New Haven, CT: Yale University Press, 1996.

Oakeshott, Michael. "The Rule of Law." In *On History and Other Essays*. Oxford: Blackwell, 1983.

O'Hagen, Timothy. *Rousseau*. London: Routledge, 1999.
Pennock, J. Roland, and John W. Chapman, eds. *Property*. Nomos XXII. New York: New York University Press, 1980.
Rawls, John. *A Theory of Justice*. Cambridge, MA: Harvard University Press, 1971.
Raz, Joseph. *The Morality of Freedom*. Oxford: Clarendon Press, 1986.
Raz, Joseph. "The Rule of Law and Its Virtue." In *The Authority of Law*. Oxford: Oxford University Press, 1977.
Rousseau, Jean-Jacques. *The Social Contract*. Translated by John T. Scott. Chicago: University of Chicago Press, 1762/2012.
Rousseau, Jean-Jacques. "Letter to Beaumont." Translated by Timothy O'Hagan in *Rousseau*. London: Routledge, 1999.
Schneewind, J.B. *The Invention of Autonomy*. New York: Cambridge University Press, 1998.
Sen, Amartya. *Inequality Reexamined*. Cambridge, MA: Harvard University Press, 1992.
Sher, George. *Desert*. Princeton: Princeton University Press, 1987.
Singer, Peter. *Practical Ethics*. 2nd ed. Cambridge: Cambridge University Press, 1993.
Smith, Adam. *The Theory of Moral Sentiments*. Indianapolis: Liberty Classics, 1853/1969.
Solomon, Robert C., and Mark C. Murphy, eds. *What Is Justice?* New York: Oxford University Press, 2000.
Strawson, P.F. "Freedom and Resentment." In *Freedom and Resentment*. London: Methuen, 1974.
Strawson, P.F. "Social Morality and Individual Ideal." In *Freedom and Resentment*. London: Methuen, 1974.
Tocqueville, Alexis de. *Democracy in America*. Translated by Henry Reeve. New York: Knopf, 1848/1985.
Waldron, Jeremy. *The Right to Private Property*. Oxford: Clarendon Press, 1988.
Waldron, Jeremy. "Property." http:/plato.stanford.edu/entries/property/.
Waldron, Jeremy. "The Rule of Law." http://https//plato.stanford.edu/archives/sum2020/entries/rule-of-law/
Williams, Bernard. "Philosophy as a Humanistic Discipline." In *Philosophy as a Humanistic Discipline*. Edited by A.W. Moore. Princeton: Princeton University Press, 2006.
Winch, Peter. "Understanding a Primitive Society." In *Ethics and Action*. London: Routledge, 1964/1972.
Wollheim, Richard, and James Hopkins, eds. *Philosophical Essays on Freud*. Cambridge: Cambridge University Press, 1982.

Index

For the benefit of digital users, indexed terms that span two pages (e.g., 52–53) may, on occasion, appear on only one of those pages.

Aristotle, 31, 68, 88–89, 150
Arneson, 142, 145, 152
autonomy, 188–203

Berlin, 29, 62, 69, 101, 168–169, 176, 188
Burke, 31, 118, 141, 175

Cavell, 22
common decencies, 15–21
complexities, 27–33, 68–75
compromises, 17, 56–62, 69–75
conditionality, 154–160
conflicts, 17, 48–56
constitution, 1, 4, 199–203
contextuality, 147–154
contingencies, 17, 39–48
conventional lives, 11–15
Cornford, 22
Cottingham, 40, 43

Davidson, 84–87
desert, 114–124, 135–141
Dunn, 76, 131
Dworkin, Gerald, 189
Dworkin, Ronald, 101–102, 145, 152, 169, 212

egalitarianism, 142–172
equality, 142–172
Euripides, 40
extremism, 2–3, 111–113

Feinberg, 169

Finnis, 59, 98, 109
Foot, 195
Frankfurt, 73

Good, The, 4, 10, 18–26, 28–33, 36–37

Hampshire, 50–51, 68, 70
Hart, 92, 98–99, 208
Hayek, 97, 102, 180–186, 200, 217
Hobbes, 205
Honore, 208
humaine requirement, 34–36
Hume, 12–13, 36–37, 65, 77, 82–84, 115, 161, 193, 204

James, 163
justice, 114–141

Kant, 155–156, 195
Keats, 82–83
Kierkegaard, 59
Kluckhohn, 22
Korsgaard, 189–191, 193–195
Kymlicka, 146, 169

Lewis, 24
liberty, 173–203
Locke, 155–156, 205, 214–216

Madison, 167
McIntyre, 98
Mill, 25, 123, 177–180, 195, 200–201
Miller, 162

242 INDEX

modes of evaluation, 21–26
Montaigne, 71, 80

Nagel, 146, 153, 169
negative capability, 82–87
negative liberty, 177–182
Nozick, 215–216

Oakes family, 11–12
Oakeshott, 74, 97, 234

perennial problems, 9–10, 34–62
personal attitudes, 75–82
Popper, 53
positive liberty, 188–194
practicality, 161–168
private property, 204–229
    complex justification, 221–229
    entitlement-based justification, 214–217
    interest-based justification, 212–214
    utility-based justification, 217–229
procedural and substantive laws, 96–101, 108–113

Rawls, 29, 36, 102, 114–115, 135–140, 153, 163–164, 169, 189, 195
Raz, 29, 195
Rousseau, 195, 205
rule of law, 90–109

secular faith, 195–203
Sen, 146, 153
Singer, 146, 153
Smith, 10, 46, 80–81
Strawson, 67, 92, 95

terms of cooperation, 124–129
test of time, 36–37, 129–135

us vs. them, 17–20

VUCA situations, 63–68, 174–176

Waldron, 90, 97–98, 101, 208
Walzer, 59
Williams, 29, 40, 43, 169
Winch, 232–233